Mordecai Kaplan's Thought in a Postmodern Age

South Florida-Rochester-Saint Louis
Studies on Religion and the Social Order
EDITED BY

Jacob Neusner   William Scott Green   William M. Shea

MORDECAI KAPLAN'S THOUGHT IN A
POSTMODERN AGE

by
S. Daniel Breslauer

MORDECAI KAPLAN'S THOUGHT IN A POSTMODERN AGE

S. Daniel Breslauer

Scholars Press
Atlanta, Georgia

Mordecai Kaplan's Thought in a Postmodern Age
by
S. Daniel Breslauer

Published by Scholars Press
for the University of South Florida, University of Rochester,
and Saint Louis University

Library of Congress Cataloging in Publication Data
Breslauer, S. Daniel.
  Mordecai Kaplan's thought in a postmodern age / S. David
Breslauer.
      p.   cm. — (South Florida-Rochester-Saint Louis studies on
religion and the social order ; v. 8)
  Includes bibliographical references and index.
  ISBN 1-55540-991-1 (cloth : alk. paper)
  1. Kaplan, Mordecai Menahem, 1881-   . 2. Democracy—Religious
aspects—Judaism. 3. Postmodernism—Religious aspects—Judaism.
4. Judaism—United States. 5. Judaism—20th century.
6. Reconstructionist Judaism. I. Title. II. Series.
BM755.K289B73 1994
296.8'344'092—dc20   94-18513
                                            CIP

Printed in the United States of America
on acid-free paper

In Memory Of Louis Gurian

February 12, 1907--October 11, 1993

Table of Contents

PREFACE

My daughter, a graduate student at the University of Michigan, recently asked, "Why do you call Richard Rorty a postmodernist? I always think of him as a Pragmatist?" Her query is an important one and deserves a detailed answer, although this book is not a place for such a discussion. It is enough to answer that important theorists of postmodernism include Rorty as an exemplar of that approach. That same question, however, usually arises when I call the American Jewish theologian, Mordecai M. Kaplan a postmodernist. The common response is "I always thought that he was a Pragmatist." Perhaps the answer lies in the fact that while Kaplan, like Rorty, uses the language of a Pragmatist, he shares with him a profound skepticism about "truth" or "objective" knowledge. Both thinkers demonstrate their caution by rejecting "scientism," that is an uncritical acceptance of the results of the physical sciences as revealing what is "really" there in the world. While using modernist language and referring to empirical evidence, Kaplan warns against taking science as the key to all reality. He recognizes the relativity even of physical evidence. Rorty sees an evolution in Pragmatism from the early thinkers who, while emphasizing the relative nature of truth, still thought of scientific findings as *the* benchmark of reality, to those who see all distinctions between "appearance" and "reality" as fictional.[1] Kaplan anticipates this later position and so, like Rorty, falls into the category of "postmodern," despite his Pragmatist self-presentation.

That Kaplan, like Rorty, combines the postmodern and the pragmatic explains why a study of his thought belongs in a series devoted to "religion and the social order." Like John Dewey, one of the founding figures in Pragmatism, Kaplan understood the purpose of philosophy in practical and utilitarian terms. A religious philosophy, a philosophy of Judaism, for example, should address modern social life. Kaplan devoted his thinking to what Dewey called "the problems of men." In the pragmatist spirit, he treated those problems to a rational and critical study. His conclusions although couched in the language of scientism often anticipate postmodernism. The motive force of civil concern, however, surges through his writings revealing his principle passions.

Mordecai M. Kaplan (1881-1983) should be studied first, of course, for the significance of his thought in American Jewish religion generally. He influenced every aspect of American Judaism: theology, religious practice, Zionism, and Jewish education. His enduring significance depends both on his accomplishments as a thinker and on his thought as a point of departure for contemporary Jewish reflection. Although Kaplan has often been studied as a Jewish philosopher or as the founder of the Reconstructionist Movement in Judaism, this present research is part of a reappraisal of Kaplan carried on by a small group of contemporary scholars including Richard Libowitz, Mel

---

[1] See Richard Rorty, *Consequences of Pragmatism* (Minneapolis: University of Minnesota Press, 1982).

Scult, Charles Vernoff, and myself. My interest in Kaplan developed from a fierce antipathy in its earliest stages through the positive evaluation expressed in these pages. When I wrote my Ph.D. dissertation on Abraham Joshua Heschel I took Kaplan as a polar opposite against whom I could place Heschel's virtues into sharp relief. In my early writings I continued to use Kaplan as an example of a naive and ill fated attempt to assimilate Jewish religion to the democratic process broadly conceived. I failed to understand the subtle complexity of Kaplan because I concentrated on his public image rather than on his actual writings. Even while recognizing the importance of his intention and goal of revitalizing Jewish religion, I let his modernist self-presentation deceive me. Only gradually have I learned to look behind the facade of modernity to the post-modern impulse that animates his thought.[2]

This study corrects that error. It begins from the assumption that Kaplan's approach to Judaism represents a rather simple program of interpretation. Kaplan understands his task as based on three principles. The first seems clearly postmodern: Truth in general, and the truths of Judaism in particular, cannot be identified with any absolute reality. They depend for their effectiveness and content on the response of those who receive them, interpret them, and give them vitality. Judaism on this reading can mean anything and everything depending on the point of view of the receiver. This first principle, of course, does not by itself help modern Jews decide between

---

[2] See my *The Ecumenical Perspective and the Modernization of Jewish Religion.* Brown Judaica Studies Series 5 (Chico, CA: Scholars Press, 1978). Contrast my articles "The Transnatural Theology of Mordecai Kaplan," in *Understanding God: Jewish Perspectives,* ed. Steven J. Kaplan (Society of Rabbis in Academe, 1993), pp. 15-24; "Mordecai Kaplan, Abraham Heschel, and Martin Buber: Three Approaches to Jewish Revival," *The American Judaism of Mordecai Kaplan* (New York: New York University Press, 1991), pp. 234-253, and "Passion, Social Ethics and Democracy: The Theological Ethics of Mordecai Kaplan," *American Journal of Theology and Philosophy* Vol. 11:1, pp. 35-45.

the "anything and everything" that Judaism might signify. Kaplan seeks to provide a standard or yardstick for judging one interpretation better than another. As a Utilitarian, he chooses survival, of the individual and of the collectivity, as the highest value. Those interpretations which better equip and enable Jews and a community called "Israel" to survive are preferred to those that lessen the chances for survival. This second principle, which Kaplan sees as the principle of salvation, shows the similarity between Kaplan and such modern movements as the pragmatists, an idea has utility only when applied to practical life. Kaplan has learned from utilitarians, however, that a direct attempt to achieve salvation or survival often fails. Human beings frequently misunderstand their own best interests. A survivalist program needs suitable camouflage to be effective. That conviction leads to Kaplan's third principle: since indirect rather than direct utility is desired, any program for survival must be suited for the civil setting in which it will be practiced. This third principle requires Kaplan to restructure the Judaism he conceives of as utilitarian so that it fits the categories of American religiousness generally. Jews must embrace Judaism, he feels, not out of an explicit self-interest, although that is his--Kaplan's--basic motivation, but out of an ostensible concern for the American civil welfare. These three principles show Kaplan reaching what Rorty declares the final stage of "the Pragmatist's Progress," where theories are evaluated "according to their efficacy as instruments for purposes."[3] The question, of course, is whether those purposes are useful

---

[3] Richard Rorty, "The Pragmatist's Progress," in Umberto Eco, with Richard Rorty, Jonathan Culler, Christine Brooke-Rose. *Interpretation and Overinterpretation*, Stephan Collini, ed. (Cambridge: Cambridge University Press, 1992), p. 92.

themselves and whether the evaluation of efficacy is accurate. Many thinkers conclude that Mordecai Kaplan's analysis of Judaism fails to meet this test.

Kaplan's approach to a new American Judaism may have failed to achieve the purposes he had envisaged. His three basic principles, however, seem appropriate ways to understand how American Jews might think about their religion in a postmodern world. This present study investigates how Kaplan's approach to Judaism can enable Jews to understand themselves and reconcile themselves to the postmodern world in which they live. At the same time it articulates the social program, the civil relevance of Kaplan as a force in American Judaism. It combines a sketch of Kaplan's thought, a demonstration of his views of the relevance of Judaism to democracy, a review of his approach to reconstructing Judaism for survival in the modern world, and an evaluation of Kaplan as a postmodernist. The sections of this study focus on these issues.

The first section comprises two introductory chapters--one on Kaplan as a postmodern theologian and one on the crisis of American civil life and thought as a background for understanding Kaplan's approach, noting the crisis of democracy. Kaplan does not appear in that chapter since it sets the stage for the relevance of a reconstructed Judaism not only for Jews but for America as a whole. The next section contains three chapters summarizing Kaplan's development as a thinker and the evolution of his understanding of Judaism in a democratic environment. Of these chapters, Chapter 4 is uncharacteristically short, sketching Kaplan's educational and interpretive philosophy. Chapter 5 is unusually long, illustrating that philosophy is several different endeavors that Kaplan pursued. The second section continues to examine Kaplan's integration of American faith and Jewish religion, but with a greater attention to detail. Its first chapter explores how Kaplan thought the Jewish view of God could enhance life in a democracy. The next chapter shows how Kaplan's interpretive techniques strengthen not only Judaism but American pluralism generally. The following chapter, the last in this section, notes that Kaplan is often dismissed as a naive exponent of "progress." Not only is the charge false, but Kaplan considered religion an antidote to such an overly optimistic view. He reconstructed Judaism not because he trusted democracy and progress but because he feared what it might do without the restraints provided by traditional religion.

The next section focuses on Kaplan's understanding and reconstruction of Judaism, his recognition of how a utilitarian approach to religion would ensure Jewish survival. One chapter sketches his utilitarian approach to prayer and liturgy. His responsive and creative view of Jewish ritual echoes his midrashic understanding of the meaning of revelation. The next chapter explores that midrashic sensitivity, its political implications, and Kaplan's claim for its legitimacy. The third chapter of this section deals with Kaplan's understanding of "salvation" in the context of Jewish communal life, both in the United States and in the State of Israel. Kaplan's realism did not undermine his utopian vision but gave it a critical edge.

The final section of this study shows that Kaplan anticipates a postmodern attitude. He is far from being an uncritical rationalist as his criticism of the medieval Jewish philosophical tradition proves. Chapter eleven investigates that aspect of his thinking. It then explores Kaplan's appreciation of the kabbalah, of Jewish mysticism. While rooted in Kaplan's utilitarian orientation this appreciation also shows Kaplan's sensitivity to postmodernism. Chapter twelve explicitly notes Kaplan's affinities with postmodernism and their relationship to his unusual vision for Jewish nationhood in Israel. Kaplan's understanding of Zionism as a modern expression of Jewish mysticism demonstrates his civil awareness, his recognition, like that of the postmodernists, that theories of interpretation and homiletics also have a political agenda and a civil dimension appropriate for the social order.

My work on this study has been aided by colleagues, students, and family. Professor Jacob Neusner has offered many scholars an impressive model to follow. Not only do his studies of rabbinic materials illuminate a field often obscured, but his wide range of interests is both inspiring and suggestive. His various compendiums gathering previous scholarship in Judaica span the ancient and modern periods. His probing questions focus on contemporary political and social realities no less than on their historical prototypes. He no less clearly than Kaplan stands in Dewey's tradition of studying "the problems of men." I consider it an honor that two of my books now appear in this series which by its very nature recognizes the importance of the civil context in shaping a Judaism. Professor Darrell J. Fasching provided useful advice for improving this manuscript. His cogent criticisms delayed the publication of this book, but suggested to the author many ways to strengthen the argument made. While I owe him gratitude for his insights, I, of course, take responsibility for the errors which inevitably remain.

My wife, Frances, has been a help and support. Discussions with my two children, Don and Tamar, deepened my knowledge of postmodernism. While they cannot be called "my" research assistants since they pursued their own research agendas, this book could not have been written without the prodding they gave me, the bibliographical sources they uncovered, and the stimulation of their thinking. Fellow students of Kaplan such as Charles

Vernoff, Mel Scult, and Emanuel Goldsmith helped me immeasurably. As always the entire library staff at the University of Kansas was helpful and supportive. I am grateful for a Sabbatical leave from the University of Kansas that enabled me to complete this manuscript. Several chapters rework material previously published elsewhere. I acknowledge with gratitude the permission to reprint the following, "Mordecai Kaplan, Abraham Heschel, and Martin Buber: Three Approaches to Jewish Revival," *The American Judaism of Mordecai Kaplan*, pp. 234-53 (New York: New York University Press, 1991). "Mordecai Kaplan's Approach to Jewish Mysticism," *Jewish Thought: An International Journal of History and Philosophy*; "The Theology of Mordecai Kaplan," *Journal of the Society of Rabbis in Academe*; "Passion, Social Ethics and Democracy: The Theological Ethics of Mordecai Kaplan," *American Journal of Theology and Philosophy* Vol. 11:1, 35-45; "Zionism, Judaism, and Civil Religion: Two Paradigms," *Journal of Church and State* 31:2 (Spring 1989): 287-301.

Finally I record a long standing debt -- that to my wife's parents, Louis and Esther Gurian. They have supported my work, stood by in disappointments, rejoiced in my successes, and shared my professional and private life. For the last few years they have resided in Lawrence, Kansas, as a continuing presence among us. Mordecai Kaplan's childhood was marred by a feeling of estrangement from his family. Perhaps, because of this he valued the social setting of family ties and vigorously opposed the idea of the "radical aloneness" advanced by some Jewish existentialists. The Gurians have assuaged such radical aloneness for me. With the death of Louis Gurian in 1993, some of that comfort has been lost. I feel the loss of Louis Gurian as that of a father, and I dedicate this book to his memory.

PART I: INTRODUCTION

Chapter 1:

Mordecai Kaplan as Postmodernist

The Thought of Mordecai M. Kaplan

The thought of Mordecai M. Kaplan (1881-1984) has shown a surprising resilience and ability to survive changes in American cultural life. Steven T. Katz, in a recent essay, links Kaplan with the German theologian Franz Rosenzweig as the only two modern Jewish thinkers who have provided an image of the "whole."[1] Kaplan offers a comprehensive reenvisioning of Jewish religious culture. He reconstructs the basic terms of Jewish theology, transforms the meaning of basic Jewish symbols and concepts, and reinterprets the significance of Jewish images. He places Jewish religion within the context of civilization and its development. This prodigious achievement, however, goes generally neglected by contemporary Jewish thinkers. Kaplan's thought no longer commands the respect and interest it once held. Even the movement he founded, The Reconstructionist Movement in Judaism, has apparently abandoned his principles and theory. The guiding figures at the movement's

---

[1] Steven T. Katz, *Historicism, The Holocaust, and Zionism: Critical Studies in Modern Jewish Thought and History* (New York: New York University Press, 1992), p. 35.

seminary stress mysticism, myth, and existential commitment. They embrace an emotionalism at odds with the rationalism with which Kaplan cloaked his thought. Reconstructionist practice and liturgy has reinstated references to supernaturalism and Jewish uniqueness anathema to Kaplan's style. Even so, the movement retains continuity of thought and practice.[2]

This misunderstanding of Kaplan leads to confusion about his theology and its purpose. Kaplan understood the dynamics of religion in America well. Marc Lee Raphael claims that Kaplan's sociological analysis of the American situation was powerful and accurate. He admits that Kaplan's theological proposals "have never been acclaimed," but praises Kaplan's sensitivity to the predicament of Jews in his generation.[3] Charles Liebman, who entertains serious reservations about Kaplan's plan and program, still admires his ability to address his peculiar audience. He remarks that while some readers find Kaplan's thought trivial, "he really is addressing himself to a certain kind of Jew, and to him he speaks with tremendous power and meaning."[4] Kaplan succeeds in his attempt to create a Judaism that appeals to a particular American constituency and the satisfies the needs of that constituency.

Whether considered successful or a failure, Kaplan's work represents a self-conscious experiment in the creation of an American Judaism. As a reflective response to democratic life and its demands on religion, Kaplan's

---

[2] See for example Arnold M. Eisen, "Jewish Theology in North America: Notes on Two Decades, " in David Singer and Ruth R. Seldin, eds., *American Jewish Year Book* 1991 (Philadelphia: Jewish Publication society, 1991), pp. 25-31.

[3] Marc Lee Raphael, *Profiles in American Judaism: The Reform, Conservative, Orthodox, and Reconstructionist Traditions in Historical Perspective* (San Francisco: Harper and Row, 1984), p. 181.

[4] Charles S. Liebman, "Reconstructionism in American Jewish Life," in his *Aspects of the Religious Behavior of American Jews* (New York: Ktav, 1974,), p. 194.

Reconstructionist Judaism deserves serious study and analysis. Mel Scult provides one source of data necessary for such serious analysis.[5] Scult describes Kaplan's early development and the American influences, both intellectual and environmental that shaped Kaplan's Judaism. He concludes his biography of Kaplan by reflecting on this fact and claims that "Mordecai Kaplan's life embodies the American Jewish experience of the first half of the twentieth century." That experience shaped his sense of destiny and purpose. Out of his process of personal Americanization, Scult suggests, Kaplan discovered his peculiar task: that of finding "ways of making Judaism compatible with the American experience and the modern temper."[6] That task stamped its imprint on everything Kaplan wrote and did and is the key to his importance in contemporary Jewish thinking. That practical approach, however, often disguises Kaplan's theoretical structure. His apparent modernism cloaks a decidedly postmodern sensibility. The purpose of this study is, through the use of biographical allusions, comparison with contemporary writers, and exposition of the historical context in which Kaplan wrote, to strip off that cloak and reveal Kaplan's postmodernism.

Reevaluating Mordecai Kaplan

Scult's biographical discoveries may surprise many who think they understand Kaplan as a thinker and as a human being. His presentation provides a useful counterbalance to the image of Kaplan as rationalist and democrat. His biographical portrait of the master shows Kaplan a complicated human being filled with anger, resentment, idealism, and unrealistic

---

[5] See Mel Scult, *Judaism Faces the Twentieth Century: A Biography of Mordecai M. Kaplan* (Detroit: Wayne State University Press, 1993).

[6] *Ibid.*, p. 363.

expectations of himself and others. One surprising fact about Kaplan which Scult uncovers is that the young rationalist was fascinated by the philosophy of Friedreich Nietzsche. After copying out several citations from Nietzsche's writings, Kaplan once commented, "I do not copy these things because they merely sound pretty and paradoxical, but they are the formulas of my life and thought,"--a striking admission for the Orthodox Rabbi that Kaplan was at the time.[7] Later, in fact, Kaplan would claim that modern Jewish Orthodoxy was, in its origin and expression, merely an application of Nietzsche to contemporary religious life.[8] By that time Kaplan's public approach to the German philosopher was far from positive. He charged Nietzsche with inspiring Nazism and Fascism, with undermining biblical values, and with destroying Western Civilization. Scult's biography, however, shows that despite this apparent change Kaplan remained loyal to his early fervor. This loyalty combined with a sense of mission that left him conflicted and troubled.

That conflict presents itself most powerfully as a political one. Kaplan described Western Civilization as divided between two powerful impulses, those of philosophical rationalism represented by Machiavelli and Nietzsche and those of biblical values and democracy represented by Moses and the prophets. Both traditions, he thinks, admit what Nietzsche called "the will to power;" they differ, however, in their assessment of the meaning of power. The former emphasize individualism, private power, personal success. The latter stress compassion, social virtues, and concern for others. For Kaplan, true power arises from compassion and cooperation not from domination and

---

[7] *Ibid.* pp. 91-92.

[8] Mordecai M. Kaplan, *The Greater Judaism in the Making: A Study of the Modern Evolution of Judaism* (New York: Reconstructionist Press, 1960), p. 324.

control of others.[9] While embracing the democratic ideals of Americanism, however, Kaplan also espoused the independence, the individualism, and creativity of the philosophers. He advised his followers to heed Nietzsche's call to "live dangerously" and to take risks.[10] The contradiction between this rule and his democratic espousal of equality led to inner conflict.

Kaplan's own approach to personal power echoes this intellectual ambivalence. Scult notes that Kaplan's opponents charged him with seeking too much power. They contended that he sought to divide the community, to appropriate for himself some of the meagre resources available to Jewish leaders. As a follower of Nietzsche, Kaplan might have laughed at these petty objections. Instead, as Scult remarks, he was "fundamentally ambivalent about creating a new denomination." He allowed his adversaries to persuade him that divisiveness "fatal to Jewish life." He, therefore, urged his followers to remain in their previous movements. He hesitated to advocate create a competitive movement to Reform or Orthodox Judaism. He was content to allow Reconstructionism to remain a "school of thought" rather than an American denomination of Judaism. The only weapon that his opponents could use against him was precisely the weapon that Kaplan himself gave over to them. They were not slow to use what they had been given. Kaplan's critics prevented the spread of Reconstructionism by warning against its possibly destructive fragmentation of the American Jewish community. Kaplan's agreement with their concern only contributed to the failure of his

---

[9] See Mordecai M. Kaplan, *The Meaning of God in Modern Jewish Religion* (New York: Reconstructionist Press, 1962), p. 211 and his "The Contribution of Jews to World Ethics," in *The Jews*, edited by Louis Finkelstein (Philadelphia: Jewish Publication Society of America, 1949), pp 1025, 1040-1042.

[10] Kaplan, *Meaning of God*, p. 290.

movement.[11] His personality as a philsopher undermined his effectiveness as an organizational leader and builder of communal institutions.

Kaplan's ambivalence toward power reflects a concern that Susan Handelman finds in other Jewish thinkers. She discerns in Walter Benjamin, Gershom Scholem, and Emmanuel Levinas, the desire to find "some interruptive force that can break through the violence and cruelty of immanent history."[12] This struggle within Kaplan suggests the tension between vision and realism, between revelation and naturalism, that I investigated as characteristic of American religion generally, and American Judaism in particular in my previous volume in this series, *Judaism and Civil Religion*. Readers do not need to have studied that former book to understand this one. Indeed, I take pains in the opening section to provide the general background against which Kaplan's thought must be understood. Yet the two books do complement one another. Now and then in the former volume Kaplan appears as an example of the American Jewish approach to civil religion. Here, Kaplan's life and writings become a parade example of how at least one Jewish thinker molded his philosophy to fit what he perceived as the basic dynamics of American civil life. The matching of philosophy and civil reality was not always easy for Kaplan to maintain. This book uses Kaplan's inner conflict as a key to the general American Jewish condition. Thus both books take the shape of American Jewish religion as their subject matter. While my former book, however, looked at the theory of Judaism as a civil religion, this book takes the human predicament of the Jewish thinker as its point of departure.

---

[11] *Ibid*. p. 368.

[12] Susan A. Handelman, *Fragments of Redemption: Jewish Thought and literary Theory in Benjamin, Scholem, and Levinas* (Bloomington: Indiana University Press, 1991), p. 338.

Kaplan struggled not only with an intellectual tension, but also with a pragmatic one. A second conflict raging within him was that between his innate philosophical bent and his recognition of the necessity for practical action. Kaplan was an elitist who often felt that he was expecting too much of ordinary Jews, of what he called *Amcha*, "your people," Moses' disparaging characterization of the sheep God had told him to shepherd. Kaplan concluded that "the bulk of the Jewish people...just didn't measure up to his expectations."[13] While Scult affirms that "Kaplan genuinely believed in the democratic process," the biography shows how Kaplan imposed his will arbitrarily on others, how he often threatened resignation from the synagogue he had founded, and how he considered the administrative, ministerial, and sacerdotal functions of the active rabbinate intruding "into my life directly and indirectly as a nuisance and as a problem."[14] Scult suggests that as a prophetic and "charismatic leader," Kaplan was necessarily lonely. More than that, however, lies at the basis of Kaplan's discomfort. Because Kaplan felt that his rabbinical and institutional activities "only drained him of his strength" it is hardly surprising that his efforts at organizing an alternative Jewish institution never succeeded as he hoped they would.[15] His followers felt chagrined at being restrained in their attempts to foster growth in the movement. His opponents delighted in thwarting Reconstructionism's growth by playing on the ambivalence within that movement's leader.

Yet while this situation should have depressed Kaplan, it did not. He recognized that, by nature, he was a contemplative thinker rather than a

---

[13] Scult, *Judaism Faces the Twentieth Century*, p. 304.

[14] *Ibid.* p. 359.

[15] *Ibid.* p. 360.

political activist. Kaplan knew himself well enough to recognize his compulsive intellectualism. Scult describes Kaplan's literary obsession graphically. The theologian was driven to reformulation after reformulation of his ideas. "For Kaplan," Scult writes, "to exist was to formulate ideas..." The right word would, he thought, produce the right result. "The words themselves," Scult comments, become constitutive, become the totality". Scult also claims that Kaplan understood that he was "caught in the web of his own words" and that "he never built the necessary organizational structures because he didn't want to". Theology for Kaplan, then, was primarily hermeneutical and interpretive rather than substantive. It involved articulating the meanings of Jewish texts, not creating new Jewish institutions or establishing new Jewish structures.[16] Kaplan's political objectives may have failed. He may, however, have provided contemporary Jews with the hermeneutical tools and intellectual perspective needed for coping with a postmodern age.

What Is Postmodernism?

This age may be called "postmodern" in several senses. Seeking to criticize postmodernism, Thomas Pangle confesses that the concept "is nebulous, diverse, and even contradictory in its meanings" and "has different connotations in literature, in architecture and the fine arts, in political theory, and in history..."[17] It sometimes reflects an aesthetic sensibility, a new way of conceiving art and the role of the creative artist. Sometimes it indicates a new political and ethical agenda, a relativism that affirms all values and therefore confirms none. Sometimes it describes an approach to texts and

---

[16] *Ibid.* p. 238.

[17] Thomas L. Pangle, *The Enobling of Democracy: The Challenge of the Postmodern Age* (Baltimore: Johns Hopkins University Press, 1992), p. 19.

textuality, to the role of the reader or the auditor in shaping the reality of meaning.

That last point suggests the way the term is used throughout this study. Postmodern implies a radical critique of meaning, a skepticism about the possibility of discovering the significance intended by a language, a tradition, or a history. Christopher Norris, discussing the "Deconstructive Turn," announces the remarkable postmodern realization that there is no "natural," or inherent, or inevitable connection between that signified and its signifier. This recognition, contradicting the classical philosophical heritage, leaves the postmodernist always wary of claims to significance. "Meaning," he writes, "is always undone by the radical uncertainty which leaves it suspended between statement and suasion, logical form and rhetorical force."[18] To be postmodern means to cope with this radical uncertainty in the varied contexts in which it appears.

History Against The Grain

One obvious context is that of history and political values. Modernity, defined by the two great movements that swept western civilization--the Enlightenment and its political corollary the emancipation of the individual and Romanticism and its political corollary the rise of nationalism--, appears bankrupt to many contemporary thinkers. They reject an appeal to historical fact, to the so-called "progress" that has occurred in the human past. Many who honor the modern inheritance find this avoidance of the past objectionable. Thus Jürgen Habermas compares the Greeks unfavorably with the ancient Hebrews. Because the Hebrew prophets incorporated a historical

---

[18] Christopher Norris, *The Deconstructive Turn: Essays in the Rhetoric of Philosophy* (London: Metheuen, 1984), p.19.

sense into their thinking, they emphasized the ethical. Prophets make a "strategic" use of language because they recognize the power of words to motivate action. Greek philosophers, however, "made the break with the immediacy of the narrative weave of concrete appearances" and thus prepared the way for a crisis in meaning.[19] Habermas advocates an interactive model of communication in which what people do, how they perform, makes a difference in history and reality.

All this takes history seriously as a given which may be decoded and understood. Others who, at least in some measure, anticipate Habermas' views, however, do not share this confidence. One of Habermas' predecessors in the so-called Frankfort School of Marxian thinkers, Walter Benjamin, has often been hailed by postmodernists, precisely for his perception of the problems involved in unmasking history. Benjamin demanded that one brush history "against the grain," that it be rubbed the wrong way so that it can be truly understood. As Robert Alter declares, this task of wresting history from traditionalism typifies many figures now claimed as heralds of postmodernism.[20] Habermas himself hails Benjamin's work and sees it as inherently Jewish. He calls it "among the most moving testimonies of the Jewish spirit."[21] Other students of Benjamin see in his thought a postmodernist call to view history as constantly recreating its meaning, as struggling for significance through the travails of life. Norman Finkelstein understands

---

[19] Jürgen Habermas, *Postmetaphysical Thinking: Philosophical Essays.* Trans. William Mark Hohengarten (Cambridge, MA: MIT Press, 1992), p. 119.

[20] Robert Alter, *Necessary Angels: Tradition and Modernity in Kafka, Benjamin, and Scholem* (Cambridge, MA: Harvard University Press, 1991), p. 83.

[21] Jürgen Habermas, *Philosophical-Political Profiles.* Trans. Frederick G. Lawrence (Cambridge, MA: MIT Press, 1983), p. 34.

Benjamin in this way. He notes the metaphor of history as a woman and comments on the Jewish dimensions of that image. History appears as the abandoned presence of God in the world, the weeping Shekinah, or divine spirit. It suffers the pangs of exile but also finds redemption not through action or performative speech, but through interpretation of texts. Hermeneutics rather than ethics is the basic key to historical salvation.[22]

Communication and Myth Communication

History finds its redemption in hermeneutics. That first principle of the postmodern approach to meaning leads to a second. Interpretation does not uncover the "truth" of an author's intention. Communication is a far more complex and complicated matter than Habermas, for example, recognizes. Postmodernists look to texts not as straightforward declarations of meaning nor even as clearly delineated scripts for performative action. Instead they are mythic maps that need deciphering. In a classic study Paul Ricoeur reflects on how texts mean.[23] Inscription in written form liberates speech from its author's intention. Meaning comes as much from the reader's previous experiences, encounters with other texts, and predispositions. This "disjunction of the meaning and the intention creates an absolutely original situation " and thereby legitimates construing a single text "in various ways."[24]

---

[22] Norman Finkelstein, *The Ritual of New Creation: Jewish Tradition and Contemporary Literature*. SUNY Series in Modern Jewish Literature and Culture, Sarah Blacher Cohen, ed. (Albany, NY: State University of New York Press, 1992), p. 125.

[23] Paul Ricoeur, "The Model of the Text: Meaningful Action Considered as a Text," *Social Research*, Autumn (1971), PP. 529-562.

[24] *Ibid.*, p. 547.

This freedom in approaching texts has stimulated a renewed interest in and respect for myth. The modernist often rejected myth as irrational and mistaken. It was either a false view of reality or a fantastic projection outward of some other truth. In either case it misleads those who believe in it. Despite this rationalist approach, several theorists advanced more positive interpretations. Robert A. Segal traces both this negative view of myth and more recent attempts to refute that view.[25] Postmodernism strengthens the arguments of those who find a contemporary use for myth. As a locus for response it loses no significance because it had once, in the past, been misconceived. Myth, in a postmodern sense, communicates in the same way as all other textual forms--by providing the opportunity for a new situation, an "absolutely original" occasion. Ricoeur admits that structural analysis can determine the "constitutive elements" of myth but, he claims, "meaning is suspended." If it is suspended then those elements can be recombined, united in new ways, used to convey different messages.[26] While rationalists reject myth as untenable, postmodernists embrace it as providing opportunities for creative response, for personal expression, and reaffirmation of identity.

Language and Creativity

The work of Ferdinand de Saussure lies behind much of the modern reflection on myth, both in Paul Ricoeur and in Claude Levi-Strauss who applied Saussure's linguistic theory to mythic narratives. Saussure's contention that the "the bond between the signifier and the signified is arbitrary" led him

---

[25] See Robert A. Segal, "In Defense of Mythology: The History of Modern Theories of Myth," *Annals of Scholarship* (1980) 1:1, pp. 3-49.

[26] Ricoeur, "The Model of the Text," p. 555.

to call writing not the "guise" of speech, but rather its disguise.[27] The task of the student of language is not to decode it as such, not to say what its meaning is or is not, but rather to describe the rules for language, the conditions under which meaning takes shape. Critical analysis does not, then, in the first place, apply to the content of a work, to its message or its signification, but rather to the system it employs.[28]

Such a study means that language consists of codes that are constantly undergoing changes. While the constituent elements of the codes remain in place, their recombined shape communicates a different meaning. The student of language looks at the games people play with their language, at their skill in manipulating signs and symbols, The purpose is "not to discover the meaning of a work, but to reconstitute the rules governing the production of meaning."[29] Language, then, is more than just a naming process. It is a set of guidelines which regulate that process, which provide for spontaneity in that process, which invigorate that process. This view of language offers license for creativity. Certainly nationalism represents one of the most potent playing fields on which the sport of language creation has taken place in modern times. Jews have experienced such a linguistic encounter twice over-- the creation of Yiddish as a literary tongue and the revival of Hebrew as a spoken language grew out of self-conscious manipulation with words and their meanings. Most often such creation has a social purpose. Language creation

---

[27] Ferdinand de Saussure. *Courses in General Linguistics*, Charles Bally and Albert Sechehaye, eds., in collaboration with Albert Riedlinger. Trans. Wade Baskin (New York: The Philosophical Library, 1959), pp. 30, 67.

[28] See Jonathan D. Culler *Structuralist Poetics: Structuralism, Linguistics and the Stuy of Literature* (London: Routledge and Kegan Paul, 1975), p. viii.

[29] Josúe Harari ,"Critical Factions/Critical Fictions," in his *Textual Strategies: Perspectives in Post-Structuralist Criticism* (Ithaca: Cornell University Press, 1979), p. 22.

is frequently an ideological expression of a political agenda.[30] On a less obvious plane, however, philosophers and theologians engaged in the same activities. They too sought to master words rather than let words master them. The postmodern impulse justifies and legitimates this creative struggle with language. The theological agenda of Mordecai Kaplan reflects this impulse. Kaplan is appropriately understood in association with a specific historical location--that of Eastern European Jewish immigrants to the United States and their process of acculturation. This association, however, misjudges his thought if it relegates his entire philosophy to a rationlization of the predicament of these Jews.

Context and Content in Mordecai Kaplan's Theology

A common judgment concerning Mordecai Kaplan identifies his philosophy of Judaism with a particular generation of American Jews. A massive migration of Jews from Eastern Europe to the United States occurred during the period between 1880 and 1921.[31] These Jews, and their children of the second generation, not the most observant or respectful of traditional religious law but, nevertheless, committed to the culture associated with traditional Judaism, sought a new type of accommodation to American life. They desired to retain a cultural and ethnic connection with the Jewish people while transforming themselves into modern American intellectuals. This condition expressed itself as a newly experienced need: that for a "new religious modality that would accept the drive toward secularism at the same

---

[30] For the Jewish cases and the way creation in the two languages often led to bitter struggle see Joshua A. Fishman, *Ideology, Society and Language: The Odyssey of Nathan Birnbaum* (Ann Arbor: Karoma Publishers, 1987).

[31] See Gerald Sorin, *A Time For Building: The Third Migration 1880-1920*. The Jewish People in America (Baltimore: The Johns Hopkins University Press, 1992).

time that it held onto cherished traditional religious symbols."[32] Kaplan's brand of Jewish theology--a naturalism that legitimates Jewish practice on utilitarian grounds--developed in this context and seems well suited for it. The association of Kaplan with the experience of these Americanized and Americanizing Jews often leads to a misunderstanding of the plan and purpose of his naturalistic approach to Jewish religion.

Several contemporary theologians suggest that with the passing of time Kaplan's thought has become outmoded. Eugene Borowitz, for example, argues that with the discrediting of religious naturalism, Kaplan leaves his followers with no choice but a retreat to supernaturalism. Because, he suggests, Kaplan regarded supernaturalism as incompatible with modernity, he forces those who accept his dichotomy to retreat from the modern world. Indeed, Borowitz thinks, many current Reconstructionists affirm a mystical theology of which Kaplan would disapprove.[33] Borowitz's claim seems substantiated by the facts of contemporary Jewish life. Few American Jews or even rabbis identify themselves as Reconstructionists. Originally hoping to provide an alternative that would be acceptable to all factions of American Jewish institutional life, Reconstruction has itself become merely another faction, and a minor one at that. Nevertheless, as Sidney Schwarz counsels, practical success is not the only or even primary measure of the importance of Reconstructionist thought. He argues that "A great disservice is done to Reconstructionism" by judging it only "by its failure to capture a universal following." He advocates a different approach--one that looks at the intellectual achievement Kaplan effected: that of balancing both universal and

---

[32] *Ibid.*, p. 189.

[33] See Eugene B. Borowitz, *Renewing the Covenant: A Theology For the Postmodern Jew* (Philadelphia: Jewish Publication Society, 1991), p. 95.

parochial elements in Judaism to create a Jewish religiousness compatible with the modern temperament and with intellectual honesty.[34]

That intellectual achievement continues to win adherents. William E. Kaufman testifies to the enduring appeal of Kaplan's thought. Kaufman relates the amazement he felt at his first encounter with Mordecai M. Kaplan. Conditioned by an expectation that Kaplan's philosophy was out of date, ideological rather than theological, and arrogant rather than intellectually humble, he expected little from the meeting. To his astonishment he discovered in Kaplan an intellectual modesty, theological rigor, and a "dynamic interpretation of Judaism."[35] Kaufman remarks on Kaplan's insistence on taking the data of human life as his point of departure and grounding his conception of divinity in lived experiences. Kaplan seeks an understanding of Jewish beliefs that "fits the facts of modern Jewish life," a search that impresses Kaufman as uniquely creative. "Of all contemporary Jewish thinkers," he asserts, "Mordecai M. Kaplan has reacted most vigorously and responded most creatively to the unique, unprecedented challenges of the modern age."[36]

From a skeptic, Kaufman clearly became, if not a "believer" then an admirer. Kaplan's impact on American Jewish thought shows the power of intellectual honesty and clarity to win appreciation if not acceptance. Even so stalwart an antagonist as Arthur A. Cohen admits Kaplan's "immense contribution to contemporary Judaism" and only laments that "for too long

---

[34] Sidney H. Schwarz, "Reconstructionism and Conservative Judaism," *Judaism* 33 (1984), p. 172; see the entire essay, pp. 171-178.

[35] William E. Kaufman, *Contemporary Jewish Philosophies* (New York: Reconstructionist Press, and Behrman House, 1976), pp. 175-180.

[36] *Ibid.*, p. 175.

Mordecai Kaplan has been alone and unchallenged."[37] Despite the critics, then, Kaplan's interpretation of Judaism provides a compelling answer to some of the most perplexing problems facing modern Jewish faith. It attracts thinkers from outside the restricted audience of Kaplan's immediate context. One element in this enduring appeal is Kaplan's postmodernism, but that postmodernism arose from the roots of his thinking.

The Roots of Kaplan's Thought

The majority of readers misunderstand Kaplan's philosophical arguments because he couches them in terms appropriate to his selected audience, the second generation of the Eastern European Jewish immigration. His terms and thinking draw, as Steven S. Scwarzschild suggests, from the Germanic tradition of Kant, Hermann Cohen, and John Dewey. His presentation of the transcendent values Judaism offers American society employs a vocabulary familiar in the intellectual context of the early twentieth century.[38] Kaplan's philosophical journey shares many of its details with that followed by many other Jews. Both European and American Jews confronted the challenge of modernity and secularity. They gradually grew to question their tradition, to accept a new social and political status, and to glean the pragmatic teachings scattered by philosophers since the Enlightenment. Kaplan's intellectual

---

[37] Arthur A. Cohen, *The Natural and the Supernatural Jew: An Historical and Theological Introduction*, 2nd, revised ed. (New York: Behrman House, 1979), pp. 218-9; compare also his sections in *If Not Now, When?: Toward a Reconstruction of the Jewish People Conversations Between Mordecai Kaplan and Arthur A. Cohen* (New York: Schocken, 1973).

[38] See Steven S. Scwarzschild, "Modern Jewish Philosophy," in Menachem Marc Kellner, ed., *The Pursuit of the Ideal* (Albany, NY: SUNY Press, 1990), pp. 232-233. Mel Scult, in *Judaism Faces the Twentieth Century*, provides detailed analysis of Kaplan's academic training, his intellectual sources, and his personal contacts. He makes it clear that some of the American "influences" such as John Dewey and some of the Hebraic "sources" such as Ahad HaAm were less determinative than people have previously thought.

biography echoes and anticipates themes in the biography of many modern Jews. His response to those formative experiences, however, made him distinctive. Rather than merely restate the classical dogmas of modernity, Kaplan refashioned Judaism creatively. He adapted it to the language of modernity, but defended it from a postmodern perspective.

Kaplan wrestled with the conflict between tradition and modernity from his youth. His early development consisted of an on-going struggle to come to terms with both Jewish thought and the demands of modern rationalism. These metaphors of physical violence suggest an appropriate passion and engagement. Kaplan did not merely play with ideas, he mobilized all his energies in what he thought of as a vital and urgent battle. The American landscape of the early twentieth century provides the arena for this battle. Tracing the growth of Kaplan's theory of Reconstructionism, Richard Libowitz notes that it is "as much a product of early twentieth century America as of Jewish life." He shows with meticulous detail how Kaplan encountered the challenges arising from his environment and how the thought of American pragmatists, British utilitarians and biblical critics, and Jewish colleagues shaped his philosophy of Judaism.[39]

The details of Kaplan's life and early experiences give Mel Scult sufficient data for psychological analysis. Scult points to Kaplan's relationship with his mother, his training by his father, and his later interaction with colleagues, students, and his own daughter, to demonstrate the resonance of

---

[39] Richard Libowitz, *Mordecai M. Kaplan and the Development of Reconstructionism* (New York: Edwin Mellen Press, 1983), p. x; see the entire book which uses Kaplan's diaries as a primary resource for exploring the internal as well as external struggles that characterized Kaplan's intellectual growth.

psychological categories for understanding the thinker.[40] Born in Lithuania in 1881, Kaplan came to New York in 1889. While his father directed Kaplan's continuing study of Jewish learning, he also permitted him to attend public school. This latter exposure influenced his thinking by making him aware of modern rationalism in its most popular forms. Even his study of traditional Judaism, however, awakened radical ideas. His father encouraged Kaplan's questioning mind. The free thinking but learned Arnold Bogumil Ehrlich was a frequent visitor to the Kaplan household. Ehrlich's scholarly approach to the Bible began to undermine Kaplan's traditional beliefs. Richard Libowitz traces the "long and painful process" of the "erosion of Kaplan's Orthodoxy." He traces the roots of that process back to Ehrlich's tutelage which "aided in the shattering of Kaplan's supernaturalist rthodox faith, but had also pointed to the naturalistic basis" for its reconstruction.[41] Through his youthful encounters, Kaplan confronted the crisis of belief that he came to feel indicative of the modern situation. Tutored in a tradition of intellectual honesty he sought to find a way to present Judaism to modern Jews so as to resolve the inner conflict that he himself had experienced.

Kaplan's Education in American Philosophy

Kaplan's further education provided a more complete recognition of that situation of intellectual and emotional conflict. He earned his undergraduate degree at the City College of New York, participating fully in student activities. He continued graduate work at Columbia University. Here he continued philosophical studies which introduced him to the major modern

---

[40] See Scult, *Judaism Faces the Twentieth Century*, especially pp. 22-29, 67-87, 131, 275, 303-307, 336-337, 353-356.

[41] *Ibid.*, pp. 10-15.

European and American thinkers. Drawing on those studies, he wrote a master's thesis on the nineteenth-century utilitarian philosopher Henry Sidgwick. Traces of Sidgwick's influence appear throughout Kaplan's writings. Utilitarianism, no less, and perhaps even more, than pragmatism provided the touchstone by which Kaplan judged the value of religious ideas. The greatest influence on him at this time, however, was more practical than philosophical. Franklin H. Giddings whose sociological orientation impressed itself on Kaplan's thinking taught the importance of applying ideas to social situations. From Giddings Kaplan derived the quintessentially American lesson that philosophy alone cannot solve social problems. Kaplan gradually combined the pragmatic philosophical tradition he had absorbed with this sociological perspective on group consciousness.

Another of Kaplan's mentors, Felix Adler, pointed Kaplan in an activist direction. Adler, trained as a Reform rabbi, had decided that Judaism lacked the universalism needed in a modern setting. He established a new religious movement, that of Ethical Culture, which sought a rational and moralistic approach to life.[42] While rejecting the personal path that Adler followed, Kaplan accepted many of his teachings. Taking Adler's course on "Political and Social Ethics" given at Columbia, Kaplan agreed on the necessity for a "religion of obligation which is realistically related to the experience of those

---

[42] See Benny Kraut, *From Reform Judaism to Ethical Culture:The Religious Evolution of Felix Adler*. Monographs of the Hebrew Union College # 5 An I. Edward Kiev Library Foundation Book (Cincinnati: HUC Press, 1979).

professing it."[43] This orientation to subjective relevance remains a part of Kaplan's mature thought.

On the basis of his university studies, Kaplan evolved a peculiarly American approach to religion in general and Judaism in particular. American pragmatists such as William James influenced Kaplan's approach to religion and reason. His diaries reflect that influence. So explicit is his debt to James that Richard Libowitz writes that "Kaplan found himself in general agreement with James' theories."[44] James emphasizes the importance of experience and the role of religion in the individual's life. Kaplan accepts the Jamesian perspective but enriches and enlarges it. Rejecting the purely subjective and individualistic aspect of James' thought, Kaplan imagined experience as the combination of the quest for personal salvation with a group consciousness essential for self-understanding.

Kaplan saw a confirmation of this synthesis in the writings of John Dewey.[45] Experience, as constructed by the social context, consists of facts and their interpretation. A belief system gives meaning to facts by providing them with values. Dewey's idea of a "reconstruction of philosophy" which makes the facts of daily life central appealed to Kaplan. He agreed that a purely abstract philosophy or religion could not cope successfully with the demands of modern life. Human beings require a system of thought concrete enough and rooted securely enough in society to enable them to experience

---

[43] See Mel Scult, "Mordecai M. Kaplan: His Life," in Mordecai M. Kaplan, *Dynamic Judaism: The Essential Writings of Mordecai M. Kaplan*, Emanuel S. Goldsmith and Mel Scult, eds. (New York: Fordham University Press and Reconstructionist Press, 1991), pp. 4-5.

[44] Libowitz, *Mordecai M. Kaplan*, p. 27; see the entire section on James, pp. 23-30.

[45] *Ibid.*, pp. 30-41.

their world as meaningful and significant. With Dewey, Kaplan claimed that "the search for truth was to replace traditional claims to Truth."[46] Kaplan recognized the function of religion well enough, however, to disagree with Dewey at a crucial point. Allan Lazaroff notes that Dewey was a thorough relativist who rejected any notion of basic innate human nature or absolute values. Kaplan, however, was an "approximationist" who recognized all actual realizations as "relative" because they were mere approximations of an unattainable truth.[47] If religion is to enable people to take their experience seriously, then it cannot abandon the ideal of truth. It may reject identifying truth with any particular statement or reality. It must at least admit the possibility that truth exists, that it might be reachable, so as to motivate the love of truth and the search for it. Kaplan's study of American philosophers convinced him that religion not only required honest and rational belief. It also demanded a means of interpreting experience in ways that were both persuasive and powerful enough to stimulate a search for truth.

Kaplan's Problematic Membership in American Judaism

At the same time that he attended the secular university, Kaplan continued his studies at the Jewish Theological Seminary, graduating as the last "old class" of the Seminary before its reorganization under Solomon Schechter. Throughout these studies Kaplan complained about the quality of his education. While merely "unimpressed" with his secular studies, he

---

[46] *Ibid.*, p. 38.

[47] See Allan Lazaroff, "Kaplan and John Dewey," in Goldsmith, et. al, *The American Judaism of Mordecai M. Kaplan*, pp. 173-196.

expressed unhappiness with his training in the Seminary.[48] Kaplan felt out of place among the traditional Jews around him and rejected the models of Jewish religion presented by his contemporaries.

Although the Conservative movement with its mixture of innovation and respect for tradition would, seemingly, have been ideal for Kaplan, he still felt uncomfortable in its context. Schechter molded the movement into a bastion of authority and power. He collected in the seminary a galaxy of rabbinic stars. While intellectually more congenial than the rigidly Orthodox, these teachers and colleagues Kaplan discovered at the Seminary offered no real solution to his dilemma. He found Israel Friedlaender (1876-1920) a useful ally. Together they established Young Israel in 1912; together they served on the board of Bureau of Jewish Education sponsored by the New York Kehillah and acted as a counterbalance to Samson Benderly. The names of the two men are linked as part of the group that Baila Round Shargel calls the Conservative Jewish "lieutenants" to Reform Jewish "captains" of American Zionism.[49] He judged the man and his writings a failure. He rejected Friedlaender's model of the medieval symbiosis between Jewish and Muslim culture as inappropriate for American Jewry. American Judaism required a new and uniquely original formulation.[50] Kaplan's equally ambiguous relationships with other intellectual teachers of the time, Cyrus Adler, Steven S. Wise, and even Felix Adler, reinforce the impression that

---

[48] Libowitz, *Mordecai M. Kaplan*, p. 8.

[49] See Baila Round Shargel, *Practical Dreamer: Israel Friedlaender and the Shaping of American Judaism*. Moreshet Series: Studies in Jewish History, Literature and Thought 10 (New York: The Theological Seminary of America, 1985), pp. 12, 129-135, 182.

[50] See Baila Round Shargel, "Kaplan and Israel Friedlaender: Expectation and Failure," in Goldsmith, et al, eds., *The American Judaism of Mordecai M. Kaplan*, pp. 94-121.

he could find no thinker who offered the radically new approach he desired. He needed a hermeneutic to present Judaism not as an antiquated philosophy but as a compelling civilization for modern Jews.

His sense of isolation was exacerbated by personal experience. From 1903 until 1909 he served as "minister" to an Orthodox Jewish congregation, Kehilath Jeshurun (he was only ordained as rabbi during a brief trip to Europe in 1908). During his tenure with that synagogue he underwent considerable internal struggle. While his congregants were "very happy with him, and his salary increased significantly," he was unhappy with himself and sought a way out of rabbinical service.[51] Orthodox Judaism seemed intellectually unacceptable. He did indeed serve as rabbi to Orthodox congregations. This service involved him intimately with the life of American Jews. Nevertheless, his intellectual commitments estranged him from many of his followers. He sought to mediate between the needs of his congregation and his own search for truth. He was caught in a frustrating struggle between intellectual honesty and compassion for the congregants to whom he ministered. He expressed this frustration in a 1906 diary entry: "The lie which I live is so clear and palpable to me, and yet I cannot tear myself loose from it."[52]

This predicament had practical consequences. In 1915 he founded the Jewish Center, an Orthodox synagogue which he hoped to modernize. That hope proved short lived. His radical ways offended some members of the new synagogue. In 1921, after publicizing views that several traditionalists in the Jewish Center considered unacceptable, he created a new type of synagogue, The Society for the Advancement of Judaism (the S.A.J.) which served as the

---

[51] Scult, "Mordecai M. Kaplan," pp. 5-6.

[52] Libowitz, *Mordecai M. Kaplan*, p. 218.

forum for his practical efforts discussed in the next chapter. Indeed he found a congenial home in the S.A.J. and an impetus to experiment with educational and liturgical alternatives. For this chapter, Kaplan's dissatisfaction with Orthodox belief is of primary importance. Despite the island of refuge he found in the S.A.J., Kaplan's intellectual alienation and isolation remained unabated. He often realized that his expectations were unrealistic. He noted that his congregants were,"amcha," an affectionate term for the Jewish masses. This "bulk of the Jewish people" could not satisfy Kaplan's intellectual demands.[53]

Interpreting Judaism as Belonging: The Influence of Zionism

He did find a thinker whose views helped him in his search for a new Judaism, the Zionist ideologue, Ahad HaAm.[54] Ahad HaAm construed Judaism as a cultural heritage and Zionism as a movement of spiritual revival. Kaplan had read Ahad HaAm as an adolescent. While he sometimes admonished others not to identify him with the Hebrew essayist, Kaplan clearly drew inspiration from this Zionist teacher. He turned to Ahad HaAm to discover how the national element in Judaism might create a new basis for Jewish loyalty. Kaplan faced a common American dilemma: that of seeking to affirm loyalty to the Jewish people without appearing disloyal to American democracy. Kaplan claims that modern Jews necessarily have an ambiguous status. They belong to two communities, each of which makes demands upon them. They are members of a secular civil society and accept the political duties associated with that status. As Jews, however, they are also part of

---

[53] See Scult, *Judaism Faces the Twentieth Century*, p. 304.

[54] Libowitz, *Mordecai M. Kaplan*, pp. 43-54; compare Scult, *Judaism Faces the Twentieth Century*, pp. 55, 107, 189, 309-312.

Jewish civilization which obligates them to still other duties. The question then arises as to how these sets of duties are related to one another. Is there an account of Jewish belonging which legitimates both sets of obligations?

Drawing on the teachings of spiritual Zionism, Kaplan proposes a solution to the problem of Jewish belonging. One might belong to a spiritual community without impairing one's political loyalty. This spiritual Judaism uses the resources of the Jewish past to "hold aloft the torch of the ideal and the spiritual." While traditional Judaism emphasized the parochial nature of Jewish nationalism, what Kaplan calls "the new Judaism" makes humanity its center. Judaism becomes an ethical nationhood, a social body whose members inculcate ideals for humanity as a whole.[55] This approach emphasizes the way in which the various aspects of Jewish tradition function to support a social identity. Despite the changing nature of the society with which a Jew identifies, the expressions of Judaism serve to reinforce a single system--that of communal responsibility and social solidarity.

Ahad HaAm, unlike Kaplan, remained a secularist. He emphasized the practical, utilitarian, and cultural aspects of Judaism. His view of Judaic civilization identified its ideals and values with modernity. Kaplan disagreed since, for him, the distinguishing marks of Jewish civilization are "religious," that is they augment secular civilization by providing a different set of values and ideals. Both Ahad HaAm and Kaplan agree that the specific details of Jewish religion are mere expressions of a greater system. They disagree in their evaluation of that overarching system. For Kaplan the system is a religious one, focused on utopian hopes and transcendent ideals. For Ahad HaAm the system is utilitarian and instrumentalist in the rationalistic mode.

---

[55] *Ibid.*, pp. 50-52.

Kaplan, accordingly, rejected the secularist aspects of Ahad HaAm's message. He charged the Zionist author with a lack of appreciation for "the indispensable religious longings and aspirations" of Judaism.[56] Meir Ben-Horin notes the continuing distancing Kaplan employs to distinguish himself from Ahad HaAm. As he remarks, Kaplan "was not an American Ahad Ha-Am...the reevaluation of Kaplan as a Jewish theologian must begin with the revision of an unqualified linkage with Ahad Ha-Am..."[57] Kaplan created a new type of Judaism, a religious national culture in which the dislocated American Jew might find a place to belong. Unlike Ahad HaAm, he takes religious experience seriously as the point of departure for any understanding Jewish culture. This experience, however, is not, he feels, self-explanatory. He thinks that it requires exegesis, interpretation, and a hermeneutics to make it acceptable in the modern context. The search for that hermeneutics led Kaplan down a road that was more postmodern than modern.

Postmodern Elements in Kaplan

Mordecai Kaplan's reconstruction of Judaism anticipates each of the three aspects of the postmodern agenda, if in reverse order. That reconstruction begins by denying that certain words--God, Torah, Israel, Salvation--have fixed and unchangeable meanings. When a thinker can devise some clear, persuasive, and useful idea that might be associated with one of these theological catch-phrases, then Kaplan will appropriate the new idea and garb it in the old word. He realizes that he has transposed the meaning of the word, that it has new connotations and may function in different ways, yet the

---

[56] *Ibid.*, p. 50; compare Schweid, "Reconstruction of Jewish Religion," pp. 42-46.

[57] Meir Ben-Horin, "Ahad Ha-Am in Kaplan: Roads Crossing and Parting," in Goldsmith, et. al, *The American Judaism of Mordecai M. Kaplan*, p. 230; see the entire essay, pp. 221-233.

flexibility of language renders his project justifiable. Kaplan also exemplifies the postmodern attention to texts as opportunities for new situations. His reshaping of Jewish practice and liturgy provides living demonstration of how a heritage becomes the point of departure for new meaning. Finally Kaplan's ethics and social program express a realistic appraisal of progress and history. Kaplan reconceives history to fit a utopian vision, not because he himself is a utopian, but because he locates the significance of the past not in the events described, but in the meanings that may be attributed to those events later. These three points should modify Scult's claim that Kaplan's theology "is the quintessence of modernism."[58] Kaplan, instead, may be thought of as a postmodernist whose ultimate interest lies in textuality and its meanings rather than in things and their structures. Robert Alter laments that three giants produced by the German-Jewish intellectual tradition, Walter Benjamin, Gershom Scholem, and Franz Kafka, have been appropriated by postmodernists. He complains that "later-day intellectuals express a pronounced tendency to convert all three writers into prophets of our own postmodernist dilemmas."[59] As if in response to this criticism, Handelman, discussing Scholem and Benjamin, suggests that they have "deeply influenced the way we think about language, interpretation, history, and sacred texts" and thereby are shapers, if not precursors, of the postmodern age.[60]

Kaplan belongs with these German thinkers. His theological innovation, ahead of his time, was to identify a skepticism of language, a creative appropriation of classical texts and traditions, and a keen ability to rub history

---

[58] *Ibid.* p. 27.

[59] Alter, *Necessary Angels*, p. 89.

[60] Handelman, *Fragments of Redemption*, p. 7.

"against the grain" (in the manner of Benjamin) with "Judaism." Kaplan appeals more to contemporary Jews than to those of two decades ago because his vision, like that of Benjamin, Scholem, and Kafka, required the quiet maturation of time before its relevance became clear.

For Kaplan modern academic rigor is identical with the hermeneutic tradition that he calls Judaism. Hermeneutics might appear as an abstract concern, far from the realm of social involvement, political critique. Post-modernists, however, teach the civil relevance of what may seem esoteric studies. Criticism, as a discipline of the academy, has relevance for political thinking. It teaches a skepticism toward meaning in general and therefore leads to a critical approach to society and social conventions.[61] Certainly the Marxian thinkers of the Frankfort School knew this. Kaplan would understand their approach and would have more in common with the early members of this school like Benjamin and Erich Fromm than with its latter-day rationalists like Habermas. Kaplan would agree that myth and allegory are powerful modes of communication. While recognizing this aspect of his own theology, Kaplan also felt that it was out of step with the mood of modern democracy. He, therefore, tempered it with a utilitarian's sensitivity to society's need for stability. His inner conflict reveals the problems he faced in reconciling his hermeneutics and his philosophy of Conservatism.

The present study takes Kaplan's perspective and inner conflict as signs that he is indeed anticipating the postmodern approach to texts. It looks at the significance of his written corpus for the postmodern age. That significance is three-fold. First, Kaplan's understanding of religion in a democracy addresses questions still essential for American self-understanding. His

---

[61] See Culler, *Structuralist Poetics*, p. 4.

skeptical approach to language actually a offers a prescription for the dilemmas of democratic life. By affirming the human power to create reality by defining it, Kaplan helps resolve some modern American problems with religion. His emphasis on interpretation and creative reappropriatio of traditions helps Americans cope with the necessity for pluralism. His offensive against history moderates and corrects both an overly optimistic assessment of "progress" and an overly pessimistic denial of it. Secondly, Kaplan's reconstruction of Jewish belief, practice, and community looks amazingly postmodern. It begins by affirming the power of language to define, and thus construct, the God-idea. It uses reinterpretation freely and creatively, intuiting the postmodern emphasis on personal response in reinventing tradition. It so construes history that pluralism becomes the content of the Jewish mission.

Finally the significance of seeing Kaplan as a postmodernist overcomes some misperceptions that often obscure the understanding of his thought. One of the most common criticisms of Kaplan claims that he neglects the problems facing human beings both as individuals and as communities. This study shows that Kaplan's optimism is more a dispensable decoration on his thought than it is an essential part of his philosophy. Seeing him as a postmodern illuminates his ambiguous view of progress. His underestimated realism becomes clearer from such a study. Kaplan defines the divine as "that power, not ourselves, which makes for salvation." Although clearly relying on Matthew Arnold's definition of divinity, this view of God requires a detailed study of what Kaplan means by "salvation" and how he thinks the divine helps humanity achieve it. Realizing that Kaplan views the future with some trepidation helps prevent misunderstanding his affirmation of hope for salvation as a naive claim for inevitable progress.

Kaplan also engages in an enthusiastic reconstruction of Jewish religion. He rejected supernaturalism as untenable in the modern world. This approach might appear an arrogant assumption that moderns understand religious truth better than the founders of the faith. Kaplan's rejection of supernaturalism, however, was more tactical than strategic and can be altered without impairing the coherence of his entire system. At one point Kaplan calls his own thinking "the only alternative" to supernaturalism. He opposes Jewish existentialists as guilty of a "failure of nerve" that threatened to reintroduce supernaturalism into Judaism.[62] His characterization implies that Kaplan's contribution to American Jewish thought lies in his radical rationalism, his optimism espousal of democratic ways. Jack J. Cohen, however, understands Kaplan's value differently. Kaplan had the courage to reexamine the fundamental images and concepts of Judaism. He treats them as doors to new perception. Rather than reinstate older perspectives, Kaplan utilizes traditional figures to open "vast resources of wonder." According to Cohen, his "serious and profound attempt to grapple with the meaning of the terms" used in Jewish religion results not in dogmatic assertions but new possibilities of interpretation. Kaplan's approach rejects an "excessive confidence in tradition" so as to free the modern imagination.[63] As Cohen describes Kaplan's philosophical agenda, his concerns and activities seem strikingly postmodern. Kaplan, already in the 1930s, was advancing a postmodern view of Judaism.

Kaplan's effort to redefine Judaism for contemporary Jews comprised a lifetime of reworking Jewish concepts and symbols. That effort arose from

---

[62] See Mordecai M. Kaplan, *Judaism Without Supernaturalism: The Only Alternative to Orthodoxy and Secularism* (New York: The Reconstructionist Press, 1958), pp. 83-88.

[63] Jack J. Cohen, "Toward a Theology of Experience," *Proceedings of the Rabbinical Assembly* 43 (1981), p. 54.

two sources: one practical and the other theoretical. The practical arose from Kaplan's experience in America. Religion in the United States, he discovered, is a tool for transforming civil society, an indispensable adjunct of liberalism. Maintaining domestic tranquillity demands reconstituting religion as a component of social life. The theoretical element in Kaplan is the more obviously postmodern. Kaplan opposes the simplicity of modern scientism, of its apparent self-confidence, its arrogant assumption of total knowledge. He also demands a greater sense of community and social responsibility than that found among most modern thinkers. He turns to the will of the Jewish People rather than to the individual as the source of authority and the elemental constituent of Judaism. In this way he combines "criticisms of the modern search for sources of individual certainty" with a positive emphasis on "the communal, dialogic and textual."[64]   This view has been recognized as distinctively "postmodern" even if some who share it also introduce premodern elements in their thinking. Kaplan's contribution to American religious thought lies in this anticipation of the critical and creative aspects of postmodernism.

Kaplan foreshadows the later postmodern thinkers in at least three ways. Like those thinkers he seeks to provide an exalted ideal which might motivate continued change and self-reconstruction. Like them as well he proffers a dynamic hermeneutics that radically alters ways of reading traditional texts. Finally, like them, he often articulates a skepticism about language and a desire to replace old words with new meanings. Perhaps most significantly of all, Kaplan pursues his goals with a dedication and enthusiasm born of civil commitment. He feels that America demands and requires a reconstructed

---

[64] See Peter Ochs, ed., *The Return to Scripture in Judaism and Christianity: Essays in Postcritical Scriptural Interpretation*. Theological Inquiries. Studies in Contemporary Biblical and Theological Problems, Lawrence Boadt, General editior (New York: Paulist Press, 1993), pp. 1-2.

Judaism for its own social and communal well-being no less that Jews must reconstruct themselves to cope more creatively with the American context. In Kaplan the moral seriousness and ethical consciousness of modernity fuses with the postmodern sensitivity to the insufficiencies of language and the flexibility of interpretation.

Chapter 2:

The Crisis of American Democracy

Religion and Democracy in America

Alexis de Tocqueville defined the "essence" of democracy as the absolute sovereignty of the will of the majority and traced its effects on American culture.[1] While democracy gives legal protection to minorities, he noted, it produces a tendancy toward consensus, a desire of individuals to identify with the dominant group, and a temptation to the despotism of the majority. A process of incremental standardization undermines the promise of liberty within American life. While this process occurs in every aspect of American society, some spheres of activity seem more strangely affected by it. Religious institutions, for example, might well appear to resist the impetus to conformity de Tocqueville sketches. These institutions uphold the uniqueness of their special traditions. They assert a claim to specific identity in a world of anonymity. Religion, one might expect, could remain untouched by democracy's leveling impulse. One of de Tocqueville's analytic

---

[1] Alexis de Tocqueville, *Democracy in America*. Perennial Library edition. Edited by J. P. Mayer and Translated by George Lawrence (New York: Harper and Row, 1988), pp. 246-276.

achievements consists in dispelling this delusion. He penetrated the secrets of religion in America. Indeed, he singles out the religious atmosphere of the country as "the first thing that struck me on arrival in the United States."[2]

Describing American Religion

Studying religion implies that one has at least a working definition of that phenomenon. Students of religion notoriously disagree on precisely what data they will admit as evidence concerning their subject matter. De Tocqueville settles for a descriptive definition. He looks at institutions which, in America, define themselves as "religious." He notes their concerns and activities. On the basis of this professed "religiousness" he judges the utility of their activities. Admitting that he cannot see into people's hearts and minds, he takes a human perspective on religion. He limits his evaluation of religions to a utilitarian analysis seeking "to discover how they can most easily preserve their power in the democratic centuries which lie before us."[3] Following this procedure, he calculates religion's advantages for individuals and societies. He balances the necessity for the forms of religious practice against the dangers associated with a detailed, less flexible, religious tradition. The democratic context, he argues, demands that religion evaluate itself carefully, and he provides pragmatic guidelines for this evaluation. Thus he advises that while "bound to hold firmly" to their defining articles of faith, religions must carefully separate this loyalty to ideals from a self-defeating attachment to secondary concerns. Although their "main business" may be that of restraining an unfettered pursuit of self-interest, de Tocqueville cautions

---

[2] *Ibid.*, pp. 29-30; 442-449.

[3] *Ibid.*, p. 445.

religions against the "attempt to conquer it entirely and abolish it." Such an attempt must fail in any society. In a democracy where "public opinion becomes ever increasingly the first and more irresistible of powers" religion would be foolish to oppose it. A religion, de Tocqueville counsels, "should not needlessly run counter to prevailing ideas."[4] De Tocqueville bases his advice on the general criteria of usefulness and ability to survive in a democracy.

From this perspective he concludes that American religion succeeds in adapting to democratic life. He notes how American clergy "are aware of the intellectual domination of the majority" and acknowledge its power. They do not oppose the majority needlessly. They "freely adopt the general views of their time" and will not combat the majority position "unless the struggle is necessary." Such a strategy fulfills the criteria of utility. He comments that religions have succeeded so well that public opinion supports and protects them.[5] American religions practice a form of utilitarianism that advances their primary goals and aims even while it compromises their secondary concerns.

Evaluating the Utilitarian Approach

Observers of American religion since de Tocqueville agree with his description of the utilitarian aspect of American religiousness, but often disagree with his evaluation. Will Herberg, for example, noted the utilitarian aspects of American religion and the tendency for the various traditions to bend to public opinion in his classic study of *Protestant-Catholic-Jew*. He suggested that American religions tend to resemble one another. Despite

---

[4] *Ibid.*, pp. 447-448.

[5] *Ibid.*, p. 449.

differences in origin, theology, and practice, they take on a characteristically American quality. They are "more like each other than they are like their European counterparts." Compromise with the American Way transforms distinctive religions into clones of one another.[6]

This tactic of compromise appears to many as a cause for lament rather than celebration. Although religions learn to take each other seriously, they also learn to focus on their own self-presentation. As John Murray Cuddihy points out, they master the technique of civility, of getting along: To be complexly aware of our religious appearances *to others* is to practice the religion of civility.[7] Such practice blunts the distinctiveness of each group but also provides the basis for cooperation and coordinated relations with the dominant institutions of American social life.

Those relationships seek to balance the power of one group against the power of another. This struggle of power, according to Cuddihy, had been a class struggle in Europe. In America the same power struggle became institutional competition. Religious institutions must compete against one another and against other, secular, institutions, vying for popular support. In the process, Cuddihy points out, religions compromise their independence and individuality and adapt to the dominant power group in America, that of the middle-class. He draws the inference that becoming American, religion becomes middle-class, modern and civil.[8] Such civility undermines the radical message he feels essential for religious existence.

---

[6] Will Herberg, *Protestant, Catholic, Jew : An Essay in American Religious Sociology.* A new edition, completely revised (Garden City, NY: Doubleday and Company, 1960), p. 82.

[7] John Murray Cuddihy, *No Offence: Civil Religion and Protestant Taste* (New York: Seabury, 1978), p. 2.

[8] *Ibid.*, p. 189.

The American legal system encourages such a development. It privileges cooperation and discourages independence. Under the American constitution religious differences play no statutory role in political procedures. The civil government regards religious diversity as a problem for crisis management. Religious conflict leads to social unrest. Social unrest threatens economic and civil stability. Government aims to avoid confrontations, to prevent divisive rivalries, and to neutralize the potential for a power struggle based on religious competition. To achieve this aim, the government places all religious groups on the same footing. On the one hand, such equalization of groups prevents civil unpleasantness, which might erupt at the favoritism of one group over the other. On the other hand, by weakening each group, it forces religions into a coalition against their secular rivals such as schools and voluntary associations.

Such a coalition tends to deemphasize differences rather than stress them. Many students of American democracy deplore this development. They envision difference as an opportunity for cultural conversation, not a crisis needing management. Some critics disparage the commonality which results from a civil management that encourages the coalition and compromises typical of American democracy. They lament the dilution of the pluralistic inheritance of America's religions. They complain that the "rich treasury" of second languages which Americans possess is reduced to "a vague and generalized benevolence." With that reduction comes an equal dilution of the challenge religion raises to the secular values dominating American life.[9]

---

[9] Robert N. Bellah, Richard Madsen, William M. Sullivan, Ann Widler, and Steven M. Tipton, *Habits of the Heart: Individualism and Commitment in American Life* (San Francisco: Harper and Row, 1986), p. 224.

These criticisms of American religion miss an important aspect of utilitarians which de Tocqueville included in his analysis. He did not deny that religions should struggle against public opinion. He only emphasized that this struggle take place when necessary. Rather than expend its energies in misguided opposition to irrelevant issues, religion should reserve its dissent from democracy for essential matters. His positive description of religion in America arises from his definition of the essential qualities of religion.

De Tocqueville illustrated his view of the difference between the relevant and irrelevant concerns of religion by contrasting Christian and Muslim sacred texts. He uses this contrast to illustrate the genuine subjects of religion. Clearly he offers a decidedly biased picture of both the New Testament and the Quran.[10] While the former, according to de Tocqueville, stresses the general relations between the divine and the human, the latter introduces extraneous matters which will, in his view, mean "that Islam will not be able to hold its power long in ages of enlightenment and democracy."[11] Genuine religion that remains true to its essential nature not only "holds its power long" but will choose the appropriate grounds on which to oppose public opinion. De Tocqueville, therefore, neither advocates that religion capitulate entirely to the tyranny of the majority nor identifies American religion with such capitulation. Religion plays a creative and critical role in maintaining the ideals for which democracy stands. Democracy validates religion not just because religion repeats platitudes but because it recalls citizens to their democratic duties.

---

[10] Baruch Spinoza anticipates this strategy in his own biased contrast between the religion of the Hebrew Bible and the religion of Jesus found throughout his *Theologico-Political Treatise*; see Benedict de Spinoza, *A Theologico-Political Treatise*. Translated by R. H. M. Elwes (New York: Dover, 1951).

[11] De Tocqueville, *Democracy in America*, p. 445.

Religion and the American Utopian Vision

What are the issues over which religion should struggle? De Tocqueville identifies two such issues: those of ultimate values and of a practical opposition to egoism. The first emphasizes a utopian vision that conflicts with America's pragmatic utilitarianism. Religion, he claims, raises human desires beyond those for material goods and "naturally lifts the soul into regions far above the realm of the senses." In this way religion combats an identification of the "good" with any particular material condition.[12] Religion cannot abandon this struggle without denying its very nature. Because of this, de Tocqueville claims that certain philosophies, particularly "seductive" to democratic societies, raise a peculiar threat to religion. Pantheism, for example, identifies the good with the natural world. This unitary view of reality, according to de Tocqueville, undermines the distinction between the visible and the invisible or the material and the spiritual. Without this distinction religion loses its identifying characteristic, and so de Tocqueville advises that "All those who still appreciate the true nature of man's greatness should combine in the struggle against it."[13] The first natural basis of religion, then, lies in its adherence to a strict dualism, positing the opposition of the spiritual and the material.

American society seems in particular need of this reminder. De Tocqueville comments on the lack of philosophic interest typical of Americans.[14] He admits that an overly cerebral approach may destroy a civilization. Ancient Rome, he concedes, failed because it could not respond

---

[12] *Ibid.*, pp. 444-445.

[13] *Ibid.*, p. 452; see the entire discussion on pantheism, pp. 451-452.

[14] *Ibid.*, pp. 429-430; 459-465.

to the practical threat of the barbarian invasions. Nevertheless, he also suggests the reverse process. Too great an emphasis on the practical may threaten a civilization by neglecting the ideals that animate every society. While the Romans illustrate an empire destroyed by its lack of practicality, America, he claims, illustrates the danger of an overemphasis on the pragmatic. Avoiding that danger entails finding a way to change the way people think. Americans should become interested in theory not only practicalities. One need not worry, de Tocqueville comments, that such an interest will overwhelm American pragmatism. Once focused on values and ideals, he comments, people "will look after the practical side of things for themselves."[15] The problem facing America, however, is not that of too great an emphasis on the ideal. Rather the reverse. Every aspect of American life has been tainted by utilitarianism. Even American religion, he comments, has capitulated to this concern. Americans, he comments, not only claim that religion must be justified on the basis of self-interest but also locate that self-interest clearly within daily experience. American religion would seem to be denying its own nature.[16]

Contemporary critics voice a similar lament. Douglas B. Rasmussen, for example, argues that while the intellectuals who formulated the theory of the American revolution assumed the existence of an objective moral order, modern Americans do not. They reduce every quest for truth to a utilitarian effort to achieve some material end. They even interpret the "scientific method" as a technical tool for attaining practical goals, not an instrument for the discovery of truth. The ultimate justification for norms in America,

---

[15] *Ibid.*, p. 464.

[16] *Ibid.*, pp. 528-530.

Rasmussen claims, is utilitarian and pragmatic.[17] He regrets this condition. In his view it weakens the democratic spirit and the ideological foundations of American democracy. Despite this pessimistic judgment, however, a closer analysis shows that American democracy not only relies on religion to offer a set of transcendent values, it provides it with an incentive to challenge utilitarianism on the grounds of a utopian vision.

American thought generally recognizes the difference between the ideals motivating democracy and the realization of those ideals in actuality. Andrew J. Reck refers to this perspective describing what he calls the "Republican ideology" of America's founders.[18] Those founders, he claims, looked to the past for a classical model for their ideal. They presented America as returning to the Greek ideal of a sovereignty of the people. Complementing this orientation to the past, many modern Americans tend to look toward a future perfection that "American society approximates but never perfectly attains." This utopianism "pervades the system" by suggesting that the American system is constantly changing, growing, and "perennially progressive."[19] Whether oriented toward past or future, these ideologies view the present as a pale attempt to realize a more luminous ideal. Americans, in either case, admit that they have not attained utopia and delight in measuring their success or failure by reference to some distant vision. The guardians of this vision, among whom religion is numbered as chief among equals, are honored for

---

[17] Douglas B. Rasmussen, "Ideology, Objectivity, and Political Theory," in John K. Roth, and Robert C. Whittemore, eds., *Ideology and American Experience: Essays on Theory and Practice in the United States* (Washington, DC: The Washington Institute Press, 1986), pp. 75-96.

[18] Andrew J. Reck, "The Republican Ideology," in Roth and Whittemore, eds. *Ideology and American Experience*, pp. 75-96.

[19] *Ibid.*, p. 77.

their fidelity to the ideal by which Americans evaluate the present. Such a view justifies the continuing struggle of religion to criticize satisfaction with any actual material condition. Religions perform an important American function by criticizing the status quo from the perspective of the ideal.

Americans celebrate this aspect of religion by associating it with their communal beginnings, with their Puritan heritage. Whatever its historical effect on American life and mores, the image of this heritage has shaped what Sacvan Bercovitch calls the "ideological symmetries underlying the models of multi-culturalism and consensus."[20] According to this judgment Americans justify the pluralistic competition among religions by reference to Puritan origins. They also legitimate the transformed content these religions preach as echoes of that earlier religious ideology. The Puritans were radicals. They opposed the status quo of their times, or so the myth proclaims. The Puritans symbolize radicalism, cultural pluralism, and consensus, and this symbolism infuses religion with significance as a force for opposition and change. Radicalism understood this way, affirms cultural values precisely by preserving a tradition of dissent. Religions revive the Puritan heritage and remind Americans of the distance between vision and reality. Americans privilege religious complaint, interpreting it as a sign that the community has remained faithful to its originating principle.[21] American democracy itself legitimates the conflict which de Tocqueville considers natural to religion. American religion, on this reading, has explicit permission and sanction to act as gadfly and catalyst to the general society.

---

[20] See Sacvan Bercovitch, *The Rites of Assent: Transformations in the Symbolic Construction of America* (New York: Routledge, 1993), p. 14.

[21] See *Ibid.*, pp. 20-24, 356-367.

Religion and the Challenge of American Individualism

The second natural struggle which de Tocqueville considers necessary for religion involves a contest between egoistic individualism and a social sensitivity to communal needs. American democracy, of course, recognizes this tension. It provides several means of mitigating the effects of individualism.[22] De Tocqueville faithfully reports how Americans respond to the charge of naiveté. They claim that self-interest often dictates an act benefiting others. Every individual depends on the society as a whole. By helping another, one strengthens society. Such a strengthened society will help everyone, both the beneficiary and the benefactor in a particular act. De Tocqueville refrains from judging the truth of that theory, but he muses on its implications. He contrasts its effect on Americans with the characteristic behavior of Europeans: "Every American has the sense to sacrifice some of his private interests to save the rest. We want to keep, and often lose, the lot."[23] In practice, at least, the American theory produces better results than the European theory. American democracy, then, presupposes that self-interest correctly understood leads to a concern for society in general. From self-interest people learn the need to satisfy the interests of society at large.

The problematic nature of that presupposition is unmistakable. Morton Kaplan, for example, admits that the American tradition always recognizes the "inherent tension between individual interests and the common good" but remarks that "the proper mix cannot always be determined by autonomous calculation." This theory does not indicate how individuals learn what is for the common good. It often lacks a positive message. The theory's negative

---

[22] De Tocqueville, *Democracy in America*, pp. 506-527.

[23] *Ibid.*, p. 527.

message is clear: the national society does not provide instruction on the good of the whole. As a political body, the American government does not inform its members of the collective needs. Kaplan wonders how Americans recognize these needs. He shows that early Americans used custom and locality to provide a sense of community even while preserving individual autonomy.[24] Because the general culture abstains from inculcating general values, the task of transmitting sensitivity to the needs of society as a whole falls to private, voluntary, associations. The local community serves as the partner to the general community, mediating between it and individuals.

This appeal to locality helps explain how religion acts to counteract the influence of individualism. De Tocqueville, for example, not only recognizes that the American philosophy of enlightened self-interest may be flawed. He also sees its corrective in religion. De Tocqueville notes that under the American theory of enlightened self-interest, private desire becomes "the chief, if not the only driving force behind all behavior." The question facing American society must be the correct interpretation of "private interest."[25] According to de Tocqueville, religion plays a crucial role in answering that question. Religion, he claims, reminds individuals of their duties to others. It performs this task as much as by what it is, essentially, as by any specific program.

Defining Religion

Americans define religion as another commodity in their market of good, and de Tocqueville uses this definition as the basis for his argument

---

[24] See Morton A. Kaplan, "Is There an American Ideology?," in Roth and Whittemore, eds. *Ideology and American Experience*, p. 220 and the entire essay, pp. 211-228.

[25] *Ibid.*

about religion's utility. He begins by recognizing the importance of the private sphere in American socialization. While he stresses the omnipotence of the majority, he recognizes that democracy preserves individuality by creating a private sphere free from the interference of public institutions. Americans, he remarks, "who mix so easily in the sphere of law and politics are, on the contrary, very careful to break up into small and very distinct groups to taste the pleasures of private life."[26] In a natural reaction to the communal life of democratic politics, people in a democracy retreat into themselves. This egoism, however, may well undermine a sensitivity to the common good. De Tocqueville finds in religion a means by which people regain a sense of connection with the welfare of others. By obligating people to perform tasks *toward* others which must be performed *with* others, de Tocqueville claims, religion neutralizes preoccupation with the self.[27]

This altruistic effect appears to be as natural to religion as its vision of a transcendent good. De Tocqueville remarks that even "the most false and dangerous religions" influence people to think of others besides themselves. While perhaps true, the question remains how religion in American manages to fulfill this task. The answer lies in defining religion as a type of private property, as the locality or sphere of an individual's personal culture. De Tocqueville realizes the many dimensions of property as understood in American thought . It may refer to land, to liquid assets, or less tangible goods such as education.[28] The arguments made for the right to property might, therefore, extend to the right of religion to develop its communal web

---

[26] *Ibid.*, p. 604.

[27] *Ibid.*, pp. 444-445.

[28] *Ibid.*, pp. 52-56.

of interconnected obligations and sentiment. Those arguments focus on the importance of property for the natural development of an individual's true potential.[29] As Tibor Machan explains it, the right to property flows from the very idea of "natural rights." People enjoy such rights as necessary conditions of their existence. The true nature of each individual human being, however, unfolds only as that person works and creates. Human nature cannot express itself without adequate space and equipment for self-development. The right to property assures people the opportunity for attaining their human nature. Thus Machan argues that the expression of human nature requires a "sphere of authority" in which people govern themselves. Lacking such a secure sphere of activity they lose motivation.[30]

The same argument applies to the protection of religion and its right to develop a sphere of social and interpersonal concern. Religion, relegated to the private sphere, is a property like wealth or education. It exists to secure a person's right to natural development. Religions claim that their complex system of obligations and expectations is indispensable for human development. When this argument is accepted, religion establishes itself as the approved mechanism for socializing American individuals. In the name of the right of individuals to develop their unique nature, America grants religion the privilege of creating a sense of community. De Tocqueville concludes that in this way religion in America has vanquished its "most dangerous enemy," --

---

[29] See, for a general treatment, Tibor R. Machan, "Property Rights and the Decent Society," in Roth and Whittemore, eds. *Ideology and American Experience*, pp. 123-143. For a Judaic perspective on the same subject, reaching similar conclusions, see the following articles: Samuel Atlas, "Rights of Private Property and Private Profit." *Central Conference of American Rabbis Yearbook* 54 (1944), pp. 212-256 and Eugene Kohn, "Human Rights vs. Property Rights in Jewish Law." *Reconstructionist* 1, 3 (1935): 7-14.

[30] See the previous references and especially Machan, "Property Rights," pp. 126-128, 138-140.

the spirit of individual independence.[31] Here again the apparent opposition between the spirit of religion and the spirit of democracy resolves itself into a complementary cooperation.

Religion, as de Tocqueville understands it, offers a social antidote to the potential danger posed by individualism. In America, as he recognized, religion provides tutoring in communal values which complements the political freedom granted by the state to each individual. Religious beliefs rather than legal injunctions keep Americans within the bounds of civilized behavior. Thus de Tocqueville comments that "while the law allows the American people to do everything, there are things which religion prevents them from imagining and forbids them to dare."[32] American society requires religion, therefore, since without its struggle and challenge, individualism and egoism would threaten the stability of society. According to this argument, traditional religion offers democratic society a solution to the problem of individualism. It moderates the individualism of secular life with values and concerns that point to social obligations.

The Contemporary Experience

Many modern students of American life recognize the same dangers from individualism that de Tocqueville noted. Kenneth L. Deutsch and Walter Stoffers discern "a crisis of moral foundations" in contemporary America. They argue that by relegating values to the private sphere, democracy encourages moral anomie. Whereas earlier liberal democratic regimes could rely on commitments to established values as the basis for a consensus on

---

[31] *Ibid.*, p. 449.

[32] *Ibid.*, p. 292.

what constitutes the public good, America today, these theorists aver, lacks such a firm foundation.[33] While de Tocqueville counted on religion to rectify this problem, several recent critics claim that democracy dilutes the power of such traditional religions by privatizing faith and compartmentalizing it.[34] These critics question whether the balance that de Tocqueville saw between individualism and communal concern still exists. According to this view, individualism appears to threaten the very society which cultivates it. These critics warn that "this individualism may have grown cancerous" and "may be threatening the survival of freedom itself."[35] The diagnosis portrays an American culture in which one dynamic trend--that toward the liberty and freedom of the individual--has usurped the territory once occupied by its necessary complement--a trend toward social responsibility and communal commitment. These analysts contend that an emphasis on one trend to the exclusion of the other leads, inevitably, to general disaster. Individualism, they suggest, unmoderated by social awareness, promotes a destructive egoism that undermines social responsibility. Pursuing personal pleasure leads to abandoning public duties and shirking the tasks needed to preserve the social good. While they agree that an individualism tempered by concern for the society as a whole is productive, they also charge that an untamed individualism grows like a cancer by destroying the very substance which preserves and legitimates it.

---

[33] Kenneth L. Deutsch and Walter Stoffer, "Introduction," in Kenneth L. Deutsch and Walter Stoffer, eds., *The Crisis of Liberal Democracy: A Straussian Perspective* (Albany, NY: State University of New York, 1987), pp. 1-2.

[34] Bellah, et al. *Habits of the Heart*, pp. 23-224.

[35] *Ibid.*, p. vii.

Alternation and American Religion

John K. Roth offers a contrasting picture, one that agrees more with de Tocqueville. He recognizes that American democracy has always relied on religious ideologies to remind people of their social obligations.[36] Americans do not desire a single, politically enjoined, social philosophy. They reject the idea of an all-embracing ideology. As Roth comments, the imposition of such a universal value system "jars American sensibility."[37] A universal value system would impose a rigid and inflexible ideology less responsive to change than the decentralized approach now employed.

Peter L. Berger and Thomas Luckmann have noted the advantages of a responsive, less comprehensive ideology. Modern nations require a mechanism for what they call "alternation," the successive transformation of an individual and that individual's view of the world.[38] The mobility of modern life forces people to undergo constant change, but such instability often leads to a sense of aimlessness. People fall into a state of anomie when confronted with a lack of security either within themselves or in their lives. Human psychology requires a mechanism for making change appear part of a process of continuity. Berger and Luckmann point to the necessity for "the availability of a legitimating apparatus for the whole sequence of transformation" to facilitate this balancing of change with a sense of tradition.[39] Americans use the apparatus of subcommunities or local cultures

---

[36] John K. Roth, "Ideology and the American Future: Reflections Toward Public Philosophy," in Roth and Whittemore, eds. *Ideology and American Experience*, pp. 229-251.

[37] *Ibid.*, p. 233.

[38] See Peter L. Berger and Thomas Luckmann, *The Social Construction of Reality: A Treatise in the Sociology of Knowledge* (Garden City, NY: Doubleday, 1967), pp. 157-161.

[39] *Ibid.*, p. 159.

as their means of legitimating the process of transformation. Americans may indeed change communities and local loyalties. Since each subcommunity, however, is legitimated as part of the American whole, these changes appear to introduce only minimal discontinuity.

Religions constitute one subset of such localities or customary ideologies. Berger and Luckmann consider religious conversion "the historical prototype of alternation."[40] This example is more than fortuitous. Religion provides an invisible ideology for Americans, a set of values and beliefs that while in theory distinguish one group from another, actually bind all members of American society into a single ideological community. Roth remarks that Americans fail to acknowledge the public ties that they do indeed affirm. They draw on traditional religions for support and guidance. Whether explicitly articulated or not, he claims, American thinkers assume the existence of a reservoir of religious sentiments and teachings which reinforce commitment to the communal good. He uses George Santayna, John Dewey, and Reinhold Niebuhr to show how "relationships of memory and hope are the substance of our lives."[41] Not coincidentally, these thinkers, of whom only Niebuhr was self-consciously articulating the ideology of a particular religious community, influenced apparently unrelated religious groups. Protestants, Catholics, and Jews alike drew upon the thinking of these writers. Their example shows how traditional religion absorbs a general set of American values. By virtue of its ability to affirm transcendent truths, religion in America offers a set of values which justify individualism and communal association at one and the same time. Here again, as with religion's emphasis

---

[40] *Ibid.*, p. 158.

[41] Roth, "Ideology and the American Future," p. 236.

on transcendent values, democratic society itself justifies and legitimates the critical activism with which religion opposes the general culture. The idea of alternation, then, of justifying change and development, must accompany the characteristics of critical utopianism and social awareness as determinative aspects of religion in America.

Postmodernism and the American Crisis

While some critics lament individualism and others decry instability and change, still others point to postmodernism as the evil corroding the fabric of American life and faith. Thomas Pangle recalls de Tocqueville's analysis of America to issue a warning against the "deadening conformism to a bloddless and philistine relativism that saps the will." He joins with critics like Allan Bloom who call for a return to traditional learning and notes that "Tocqueville reapedly recommends that the young be taught to study and enjoy the classics." Without that learning, Pangle suggests America succumbs to its weakness: "For do we not see all around us the postmodern manifestations of the syndromes Tocqueville first described."[42] Pangle's critique of postmodernism draws strength from this charge that it lacks a classical foundation. As a philosophical postmodernism displays many weaknesses. Inspired by Nietzche's insights into culture and human thinking, it often employs rhetorical rather than logical arguments, appears more congenial to literary forms than to philosophical reasoning, and allows a free play of individual response which some philosophers regard as irresponsibility.

Pangle himself, however, notes that postmodernism resembles religion more closely than it resembles classical philosophy. He calls it "paganism,"

---

[42] Pangle, *The Enobling of Democracy*, pp. 213-215.

meaning that as a criticism, yet clearly implying its religious dimensions. The American pluralistic system even paganism; indeed it could be said to defend all paganisms, for one person's true religion may well be another's philistinism or paganism. When understood as religion the supposed defects of postmodernism become advantages, its liabilities are transformed into its strengths. One might well judge postmodernism not by whether it meets De Tocqueville's standards of education but whether it fulfills the functions of religion. Looked at in this way, postmodernism plays an important and positive role in contemporary American life. Ironically, the very things that Pangle finds erroneous in postmodernism the philosophy exemplify the strengths that De Tocqueville identified with specifically American religion!

Pangle rejects what he calls an application of postmodernism to the United States constitution. He characterizes that view as holding constitutionalism as an ideal for the future, not a truth derived from the past. The construction of the sacred as an impossible dream yet to be realized draws his anger. He ridicules a commitment to a "future law" as "rationally ungrounded" and rejects the appeal to "political visions rather than political truths." De Tocqueville saw more clearly when proclaiming that religion had the particular task of envisioning not what was in the present or what had been in the past but what still might be.

Pangle also castigates the postmodernism of Jean-François Lyotard whom he charges with creating a "new paganism" that is actually an "antirational and antiphilosophic feminism."[43] Here he misses an important insight about American individualism. That individualism legitimates and authorizes the private sphere. The field of women's concerns, of irrational

---

[43] *Ibid.*, p. 31.

impulses, of the needs of the dispossessed become in American life the playing ground on which people create their brave new reality. Without allowing this expression of individual needs, Pangle has strangled democracy, providing no outlet for powerful, and legitimized, concerns. The religious imagination as it reinterprets the past in the light of the present can take account of newly expressed desires, can make a place for those traditionally excluded. De Tocqueville recognized this advantage in privatizing religion, but Pangle overlooks it in his critique.

Pangle recoils from the skepticism of postmodernism. He notes in horror that American life has been ""penetrated and shaped by a new, highly problematic and skeptical (not to say nihilistic) cultural dispensation known as "postmodern*ism*."[44] He criticizes the movement for misrepresenting truth, for exalting confusion. What he misses, of course, is that the pluralistic setting of American religion by its very nature makes any claim to absolute truth if not actually dangerous, then potentially disruptive. A democracy cannot afford to allow its citizens to have competing criteria of truth, competing claims to absolute knowledge.ˑ The relativism of American religion generally and of postmodernism in particular is a solution to the American dilemma rather than an additional problem clamoring to be solved.

Pangle overlooks the intrinsically American perspective in this relativism when he critizes Richard Rorty as an example of "American Postmodernism."[45] Rorty, Pangle thinks, misappropriates the pragmatic tradition, especially that of John Dewey. Rorty, Pangle argues, has "eclipsed" the link Dewey establishes "between republican civic virtue and the intellectual

---

[44] *Ibid.*, p. 5.

[45] *Ibid.*, pp. 56-68.

virtues." He has misunderstood the social utility of religion.[46] While Pangle sees this error as the most important failure in Rorty's system, it is not the only one. He also claims that Rorty misrepresents the pragmatic tradition itself. By assimilating postmodern relativism and Pragmatism, Pangle insinuates, Rorty distorts the authentic American tradition Dewey represents. Thus he charges that "Rorty attempts to sidestep the issue by veiling Deweyism's scientistic core."[47] Ignoring scientism, Rorty has recast Dewey as a postmodernist and thus misunderstood him.

That charge of misunderstanding misconstrues how Rorty conceives of Pragmatism. Pragmatism, for him, often swings between two poles. One tries to imitate the rigor of natural science, the other tries to expose the arbitrary nature of that science. Even a single thinker such as William James can vacillate between the two positions. Between these options, Rorty clearly prefers the latter and claims that "this anti-ideological liberalism is, in my view, the most valuble tradition in American intellectual life."[48] To be a Pragmatist, Rorty would argue, does not entail the elevation of scientism to the single standard of reality but rather to provide a means by which even science becomes but one alternative standard avialable for evaluating experience.

This recognition leads to that moral outlook which Pangle recognizes Rorty as possessing but claims that he has insufficient reason for supporting. Rorty proposes a "postmodernist bourgeois liberalism" which replaces the classical view of a "moral self" or agent with a "network of beliefs, desires

---

[46] *Ibid.*, p. 64.

[47] *Ibid.*, p. 62.

[48] See Richard Rorty, *Objectivity, Relativism, and Truth: Philosophical Papers Volume 1* (Cambridge: Cambridge University Press, 1991), pp. 63-64.

and emotions" that is constantly "reweaving itself." Rorty rejects the idea that identifying morality with the oportunity "to work out from the networks we are" as a "relativistic" stance. Instead it takes the network of the moment as a point of departure for further growth. Community, tradition, and social awareness cannot be separated from the networks identified as moral beings. Because Rorty has rejected scientism's identification of one physical representation as *the* standard of truth he can evolve a flexibile liberalism that responds to the most crucial questions raised in democratic society.[49]

Rorty and Pangle agree that Americans face a contemporary crisis. They disagree on the nature of that crisis. Pangle thinks that the lack of absolute standards, the abandonment of a classical education, and paganistic religion have undermined American faith. Rorty calls for a greater skepticism, a more consistent application of the pragmatists's refusal to distinguish between "reality" and "appearance" and a postmodern recognition of the person as a network of forces rather than as a single moral self. Whichever thinker has portrayed American life correctly, others before them have offered similar diagnoses and prescriptions. Among those anticipating Rorty's Pragmatism was Mordecai Kaplan whose view of Jewish religion may be characterized as reflecting a postmodern perspective.

---

[49] *Ibid.*, pp. 175-202.

PART II: MORDECAI KAPLAN AND AMERICAN DEMOCRACY

Chapter 3:

Mordecai Kaplan and American Judaism

Reconstructing Judaism: An Experiment in Freedom

The dynamics of religion in America described in general above applies to the adaptation of American Jews to religious life in a democracy. As C. Bezalel Sherman noted in 1962, Jews confront what de Tocqueville calls "the tyranny of the majority" and turn it to their advantage. Sherman recognizes that whether in spite of or because of their adjustment to American culture, Jews confirm their ethnic and religious distinctiveness with special force. This adaptability shapes every form of American Judaism. Whether identified as traditional or non-traditional, American Jewish institutions judge their success or failure by what Sherman calls the typically American criterion of usefulness. American Jews, he comments, have learned the lesson of American utilitarianism well.[1] Skill in pragmatic adaptation enables American Judaism to succeed as no other Jewish community before it.

---

[1] See C. Bezalel Sherman, *The Jew Within American Society: A Study in Ethnic Individuality* (Detroit: Wayne State University Press, 1964), pp. 195-196.

Jacob Neusner celebrates that success, noting how American Jews have made use of the opportunities democracy provides. He points to American Judaism as an example of how modern men and women can, while living in a secular age, use the mythic resources of an earlier time to create a new type of religiousness. He describes how these Jews "reconstruct out of the remnants of an evocative, but incongruous heritage, the materials of a humanly viable, meaningful community life."[2] Can Jews make use of liberty without abandoning tradition? Can they affirm their tradition without threatening American democracy? Those questions set the agenda for the Jewish experiment with liberal democracy. A study of that experiment demonstrates not only the viability but also the creativity of religion in a democracy. Mordecai Kaplan was one of the most self-conscious participants in this experiment.

The Challenge of Democracy and the Necessity for Religion

While future chapters explore various dimensions of Kaplan's thought-- his theology and his practical religious program, this chapter focuses on his understanding of America's ideological challenge. Like Robert Bellah, Kaplan discovered that American religions often inspire a lack of civility. He would agree with Bellah that, at least Judaism and Christianity, have embraced views that set them inevitably at odds with one another. Bellah's contention that America supports several competing visions of the role of religion would not surprise him.   Like Bellah, Kaplan imagines that Jewish and Christian Americans are advancing "toward a conception of a community of communities that includes us both, even though the boundaries that divide us

---

[2] Jacob Neusner, *Israel In America: a Too-Comfortable Exile?* (Boston: Beacon Press, 1985), p. 129.

are not dissolved."[3] Even more explicitly than Bellah, however, Kaplan seeks to find that new community by reinterpreting old symbols, by reinventing traditions, by reconstructing reality. His early life growing up in America taught him that very skepticism about absolute truths and linguistic certainties that the postmodernist possesses. Kaplan presented religion to America as a solution to its problem of divisiveness, rather than as its cause. This daring move marks a decidedly postmodern vision. Although couched in modernist language Kaplan's gift to religion in America was actually postmodernist in effect. Kaplan built on the scepticism modern linguistic analysts have toward "essential meaning." He offered America reinterpretations of ideas, practices, and values so as to facilitate an environment in which all might flourish.

Kaplan understood his purpose as a double one -- that of legitimating Judaism for Jews alienated from their own tradition and that of conveying the benefits of Jewish religion to a democratic community desperately in need of its aid. That second concern justified and animated his first endeavor. Jews should embrace Judaism not only because it offers them a means to personal salvation. Kaplan claims that they need to understand and accept this path to salvation precisely because their society requires its teachings for its very survival. Kaplan's diagnosis of the American condition and his vision of Judaism's response to it corresponds closely to the analysis begun by de Tocqueville and confirmed by students of contemporary American religion.

Kaplan traces the historic roots of the modern need for religion as he unravels the confusion concerning the meaning of freedom. Democracy, he surmises, actually entails two different types of freedom. Understood as a

---

[3] See Robert N. Bellah, "Conclusion: Competing Visions of the Role of Religion in America," in *Uncivil Religion*, eds., Robert N. Bellah and Frederick Greenspahn (New York: Crossroads Press, 1987), p. 228.

condition of society, freedom depends on the existence of certain political forms. It demands a participatory government representing all members of society. Kaplan applauds the American achievement of freedom viewed as a condition of society. He adds, however, that even political democracy requires more than the social structures of freedom. Democracy's survival depends on a "freedom of the mind" that complements freedom as a social condition. Political freedom, he comments, "must be sustained by an inner freedom, a freedom of the spirit."[4] This is the freedom that cultivates a sense of the spiritual, that combats materialism. Religion may offer secular society a resource for creating that sort of freedom, a freedom that depends feon education of individuals.

Jewish religion, Kaplan argues, offers an example of how to combine the two types of freedom. Jewish history has sensitized Jews to the interdependence of political freedom and freedom of the mind. They have experienced the failure of a liberalism based only on rational philosophy and the bankruptcy of a system relying only on social institutions.[5] Kaplan points to that historical experience to show how Judaism also involves the establishment of separate religious communities seeking utilitarian ends.[6] Jews first embraced freedom as a liberal ideal espoused by the enlightened thinkers and political leaders of the eighteenth and nineteenth centuries. They trusted in the assurances of toleration given by this liberal philosophy. They soon discovered, however, that democracy failed to deliver its promised freedom. Democracy quickly became a tyranny of the majority in which nationalistic

---

[4] Mordecai M. Kaplan, *The Future of the American Jew* (New York: Reconstructionist Press, 1967), p. 283.

[5] *Ibid.*

[6] See Kaplan, *Judaism Without Supernaturalism*, pp. 83-88.

movements defined citizenship in ways that excluded Jews. Jews suffered under nationalistic democracies which legitimated discrimination against minorities in the name of a national consensus. On the basis of this experience, Kaplan explains, Jews understand the two sorts of freedom necessary to democracy and their interconnection.

According to Kaplan, democracy began as what he calls "free enterprise democracy," advocating personal liberty as a philosophical natural right. Jewish experience demonstrates, Kaplan contends, the failure of this theory of personal liberty. The seeds of its decay were planted in its very birth. Kaplan claims that it "no sooner arose than it began to become outdated."[7] It became outdated for at least two reasons. Philosophical arguments proved weak defenses for human rights. Declarations of "the natural rights of citizens" do not ensure the ability for all to exercise those rights. Kaplan avers that it soon became apparent that rights are secured only through laws and constitutions, modes of enforcement, and other political mechanisms.[8] Secondly, "free enterprise democracy" led to social and economic displacement. Poverty, unemployment and personal dislocation alienated citizens from their society. People responded to this problem by advocating what Kaplan calls "mass democracy." This response, as he describes it, proved problematic for modern Jews.

Mass democracy advocates freedom not for the individual but for the group. It sacrifices independence and individuality for communal security. This emphasis on the will of the community leads to dangerous consequences. Kaplan envisages a democracy so concerned with the survival of the social

---

[7] *Ibid.*, p. 88.

[8] *Ibid.*, p. 85.

order that it undermines the possibility for human growth and development. Antisemitic nationalisms advocating exclusion of Jews from the body politic point, Kaplan thinks, to a more general problem. Mass democracy not only legitimates discrimination against Jews. It threatens the well being of every individual and has the potential for denying any citizen the opportunity for personal self-actualization. With this in mind, Kaplan warns that "mass democracy...unless tamed by education in international understanding and by machinery of international government will destroy the human race."[9] Democracy must learn to temper its response to the human need for psychological and economic security without compromising the unique individuality of each person.

Kaplan claims that Judaism, through active programs and policies, can help the American democracy solve these two problems. Judaism can tutor Americans in what he calls the crucial problem of freedom: that of guarding personal independence while remaining sensitive to others.[10] American Judaism performs this function by its example. Kaplan expects Jews to utilize the "rich cultural heritage of the Jewish people" to further such necessary democratic virtues as "self-discipline" and "self-improvement." Jews thereby demonstrate how an ancient tradition can inculcate modern values. Transvaluating specifically Jewish symbols and images into the language of a modern democracy leads to social and communal action. Jewish religious reform provides a positive example for other religious groups in a democracy as well. When Jews revive their own tradition in a democratic key, Kaplan declares,

---

[9] *Ibid.*, p. 88.

[10] *Ibid.*, p. 293.

they "raise the ethical standard of American life generally."[11] Kaplan pushes his argument even further. A careful study of the Jewish tradition, he contends, shows that it advocates social activism. Commitment to the forms, practices, and ideals of Judaism impels a person to make contributions to American society as a whole. Dedication to the God of Jewish tradition, Kaplan argues, not only stimulates a life of Judaic commitment, but also requires Jews "to make of America, too, an instrument for freedom, justice, and love."[12] This presentation of Jewish life transforms tradition into a catalyst for the future. Kaplan shapes Judaism in the image of religion as an activist subcommunity working to improve society and provide the locality within which human beings actualize their humanity. Those who criticize Kaplan for conceding too much to modernity have overlooked his radical vision. He translates traditional religious eschatology into contemporary language. He expresses the ideal hopes of Judaism in rational terms. Nevertheless, his view of religion, like de Tocqueville's, does not allow it to compromise its utopian hope when pursuing its task of creating community.

Judaism in Secular America

Kaplan's thought and writings reflect his accurate perception of the place of religion in America. Even those recent critics who condemn his Reconstructionist movement as too secular, pagan, and naturalistic, fall into the same American mode he uses. Jonathan Sacks, for example, defending the revival of traditional Judaism among American Jews, notes its persistence as a challenging alternative to the problems of modernity. He singles out Kaplan

---

[11] Mordecai M. Kaplan, *Questions Jews Ask: Reconstructionist Answers* (New York: Reconstructionist Press, 1956), p. 37.

[12] *Ibid.*, p. 481.

as an unsuccessful adaptation of Judaism to secularized American life.[13] Nevertheless, Sacks himself resorts to the two arguments for religion that Kaplan employs. Judaism, he claims, provides those enduring ideals which give meaning to facts. Values, Sacks argues, arise from historical events and consist in judging facts in the light of those events. In the case of Judaism that event consists of the covenantal agreement linking the divine and the human originating in the revelation at Mount Sinai. All Jewish values spring from this event. All Jewish practices derive from it. Jews judged their lives and their society using that event as their standard.[14] In this sense the idea of Judaism precedes the experience of American culture and criticizes that culture. Sacks contrasts this way of understanding religion to the approach of secularism. Secularity demands that a religion adapt to the general culture; the use of Sinai as a standard requires that American culture refashion itself in terms of the ideals of Judaism. In this way Sacks demands that Judaism challenge American society and provide an alternative to it. "Does social reality determine our idea of Judaism," he asks "or does Judaism determine our interpretation of society?"[15] From this perspective the role of religion is not that of becoming a mirror to society. Instead religion must examine society, must make demands of it, must require it to justify itself.

While Sacks explicitly rejects Kaplan's teachings, Kaplan would agree with each point that Sacks makes. The two differ concerning the

---

[13] Jonathan Sacks, *Arguments for the Sake of Heaven: Emerging Trends in Traditional Judaism* (Northvale, NJ: Jason Aronson, 1991), pp. 71-72; 111-112; compare his arguments in his *Crisis and Covenant: Jewish Thought After the Holocaust* (Manchester: Manchester University Press, 1992), pp. 100-105.

[14] Sacks, *Crisis and Covenant*, p. 267; compare *Arguments for the Sake of Heaven*, pp. 111-116.

[15] *Ibid.*, p. 105.

implementation of their programs, but both equally reflect the dynamics of American religiousness. The fact that even his opponents echo his ideas reinforces Kaplan's importance as an American Jewish thinker. Whether one agrees or disagrees with his theology or his program of Jewish life, one cannot help but admire how clearly he understands the paradoxical nature of American religion. To be religious in America is to stand for transcendent ideals within a utilitarian community. It is to create an island of communal structures in a sea of individualism. More paradoxically still, American thought itself legitimates this religious opposition. Religion does not oppose America despite American ideology but because of it. Kaplan, creatively, applies this paradoxical approach to religion to the case of Judaism.

Passion, Judaism and Democracy

One way Kaplan mediates between Judaism and democracy is through an appeal to passion. He claims that a passionate dedication to religion leads, inevitably, to a passionate commitment to democracy. This affirmation of emotional engagement may spring from one of two different motives. Proponents of passion often conflict with supporters of reason. Ethical theories divide into two types. One type considers the isolated individual who struggles for the perfection of self the foundation of social improvement. When individuals change, then society changes. The other views centers on activists who shape society. This theory advocates changing society in the belief that society will then shape its members.

Linell Cady suggests such a difference between the philosophy of Soren Kierkegaard and that of Josiah Royce. Kierkegaard's isolated knight of faith wrestles with moral questions in solitude; Johannes de Silentio, rightly named, sketches the internal conflict battling within the knight's soul, hidden from view. Royce rejects this approach. The individual alone, for Royce, cannot derive a moral system. Morality requires at least an imagined community of others. Royce finds the idea that ethics could be "intelligible in terms of the self or, indeed, in terms of the self and other" absurd. Instead he emphasizes a social perspective. Morality, on this understanding, begins in the awareness of a social bond, a tie to others. On the basis of this claim, he argues that: "genuine love is never for the other as an isolated individual but for the other as a fellow member of the universal community."[16]

The difference between Royce and Kierkegaard appears to be based on different ethical systems. Kierkegaard locates morality in the passionate individual while Royce relegates it to a form of social loyalty. The same difference, however, also occurs in the aesthetic sphere. Thomas M. Alexander offers a contrast between the aesthetics of Royce and that of John Dewey that parallels Cady's contrast of Royce and Kierkegaard. Alexander's study of John Dewey shows how a community creates itself through its art, retrieving its world through symbols. Dewey, he explains, finds that "we inhabit the world only with and through each other" by means of shared, participatory endeavor." Cultural expressions, therefore, establish "the possibility for community."[17]

Dewey's emphasis that symbols create the possibility for the the communal contrasts with the philosophy of Royce. For Royce the symbol occurs as a product of the community. Community becomes for him "a process of interpretation, mediating past and future through the symbolic

---

[16] Linell Cady, "Alternative Interpretations of Love in Kierkegaard and Royce," *The Journal of Religious Ethics* 10:2 (1982): 238-263; see p. 258.

[17] See Thomas M. Alexander, *John Dewey's Theory of art, Experience and Nature: The Horizons of Feeling* (Albany, NY: State University of New York Press, 1987), p. 267.

configurations of the present." Royce treasures symbol, mythology and hermeneutics as the way in which individuals make sense of their lives. This view sees culture as a tool for the individual rather than the individual as the creator of culture. While Dewey justifies a pluralistic orientation, Royce focuses on the value of communal configurations for each person.

Alexander's introduction of the aesthetic points in a postmodern direction. Kaplan's ability to conjoin passion, social loyalty, and the idea of a democratic community creating itself through ethics and aesthetics moves toward a postmodern consciousness. Drawing on Royce and emphasizing reason, he invests his ethics with powerful and personal passion. Drawing on the individualists he insists on self-fulfillment and the ideal of salvation as achieving personal self-actualization. This approach to ethics synthesizes passion and reason to produce an extraordinary American social morality.

Kaplan's Exposition of Jewish Ethics

Students of Mordecai Kaplan's interpretation of Judaism note its affirmation of secularity. As Eliezer Schweid remarks, this positive evaluation depends on a moral perspective. Kaplan exalts modernity because it furthers what he sees as the primary ethical task, that of fulfilling human destiny. Kaplan considers science and technology the tools that "made possible democracy--the most ethical form of government..."[18] Understanding Kaplan's view of ethics is indispensable for understanding his view of religion. Kaplan defines God and religion as means that satisfy the real needs of both individuals and the civil body. Ethics, like religion, must be judged in keeping

---

[18] Eliezer Schweid, "The Reconstruction of Jewish Religion Out of Secular Culture," in Emanuel S. Goldsmith, Mel Scult, and Robert M. Seltzer, eds, *The American Judaism of Mordecai M. Kaplan* (New York: New York University Press, 1990), p. 37.

with its pragmatic functions. When Kaplan interprets Jewish ethics, he does so as a functionalist. He shows that Jewish ethics satisfies human needs. He combines this demonstration of the universal value of Jewish ethics, however, with an explication of its emotional appeal and a call that extends beyond reason itself for loyalty to that ethics.

Kaplan's exposition of Jewish ethics appears in an essay explaining "The Contribution of Jews to World Ethics."[19] The very title emphasizes the universal rather than the parochial aspects of Judaism. Kaplan discusses the specific ethical values found in Jewish religion and describes the specific Judaic morality. Nevertheless, he avoids suggesting that only Jews have evolved a moral system. Jews do not differ from others in having established a relationship between morality and religion. All societies create moral rules and invoke divine sanctions to uphold their moral systems. Religious moralities do, of course, differ. Kaplan traces the distinctiveness of different moralities to historical conditions. He attributes divergences to "differences in the opportunities to achieve knowledge and social contact with other groups and ways of life."[20] The superiority of Jewish morality springs from accidents of history, not from inherent genius. Kaplan seeks to avoid any taint of exclusivism or tribal pride that detracts from universalism.

For Kaplan, Israel's singular contribution to human ethics grew out of its historical experience. Victims of imperialism, Jews recognized the failure of power as a solution to social problems. Technological advances do not ensure moral advances. A culture may improve its material condition without creating social improvements. A superior police administration does not

---

[19] Kaplan, "Contribution of Judaism," pp. 680-712.

[20] *Ibid.*, p. 684.

translate into a safer society. Kaplan argues that Jews drew from their experience the conclusion that "the field of human relations is the area most in need of being brought within the dimension of the moral law." That experience taught that the weak need the protection of the strong. That lesson, imprinted indelibly in Jewish tradition, fashioned its peculiar ethical insight, its contribution to world ethics.[21] This view of ethics makes it unalterably social rather than individual. Ethics creates rules to protect the vulnerable from exploitation. Ethics reverses the social tendency to glorify power and substitutes compassion for that power.

Kaplan's own definition of ethics reflects this understanding of the biblical insight. "Ethics," he explains "is the conscious attempt to substitute, in all human relations, the rule of justice and love for that of force and cunning."[22] Kaplan argues that religion, a people's beliefs and values projected outward onto its images of god, vitalizes this social mission. A culture's theology transmits its understanding of that mission. The Jewish moral perspective creates a new view of God, "a conception of God as the champion of the weak against the strong."[23] This theology motivates a specific moral agenda. The desire to imitate God, to be holy as God is holy, reinforces the Hebraic communal ethics. While Jewish ethics requires individuals to curtail their aggressive instincts, its religious basis promises a greater reward in return for such self-restraint. Kaplan considers all instruments of social order--"institutions, laws, and tendencies that help to free men,"--*sancta*, as religious media.[9] For Jews, these instruments become united with an entire

---

[21] *Ibid.*, p. 689.

[22] Kaplan, *Questions Jews Ask*, p. 138.

[23] Kaplan, "Contribution of Judaism," p. 695.

system of social and personal liberation. The set of religious symbols and images of Jewish religion focuses on self-fulfillment. In this way, Kaplan finds that Judaism contributes to humanity a religion of ethics, an ethics rooted in and motivated by religious belief.

Historically, Kaplan judges this ethic an advance in human social organization. Even so, he denies that its attainment represents a certain Jewish genius for ethics. He claims that this ethical religion develops at a particular stage in human social evolution. When religion ceases to be utilitarian and becomes ethical, it advances to a new stage of civilization. When any society reaches that stage, it develops this particular type of religion. This new stage of religious development emphasizes its passionate universalism. Reaching that new stage religion becomes "as inevitable a part of human civilization as is science or art..."[24] The history of Judaism demonstrates to the world the processes of religious evolution. It encapsulates the growth of a religion from supernaturalism to moralism and offers one of the earliest illustrations of how religion serves society by furthering each person's search for salvation. This stage of religion, according to Kaplan, is particularly well suited for American society. Commitment to Jewish religious civilization makes a Jew more loyal to American ideals and values not less so. Religion, understood as ethical sensitivity, contributes an essential ingredient to democratic life.

Loyalty in Kaplan's View of Jewish Ethics

Kaplan argues for the rational and historical veracity of his interpretation of ethics as the content of Jewish religion. The history of religions, however, does not always verify this conclusion. Sometimes religion

---

[24] Kaplan, *Meaning of God*, p. 97.

and morality turn into rivals, each proclaiming its values as supreme and independent of the other. In such cases religion seeks to replace, not reinforce, civil ethics. Reason, as Josiah Royce contends, exacerbates the conflicts between morality and religion rather than reconciling them. It charts the disagreements separating the two camps and only rarely points to agreements between them. Rationality intensifies the antagonism between morality and religion. Royce does suggest that one form of religion may indeed combine elements of both--what he calls the religion of loyalty. He claims that "the spirit of loyalty completely reconciles those bitter and tragic wrangles between the mere moralists and the partisans of divine grace" and teaches the meaning of "our common salvation."[25] Kaplan agrees on the importance of loyalty to a unifying cause and to religion. He claims that an environment of loyalty cultivates opportunities in   which people discover the meaning of life and achieve human salvation. Kaplan explicitly refers to Royce as an authority, claiming that: "The love of God which the Israelite is called upon to foster is the exact equivalent of the loyalty to a cause which Royce so warmly urges as indispensable to salvation."[26]

Kaplan and Royce share many presuppositions about ethics. Royce, like Kaplan, recognizes the communal nature of ethics. He emphasizes that "our moral self-consciousness is a product of our social life." He too sees the function of religion as uniting all humanity. He emphasizes that morality civilizes individuals by subordinating personal good to the good of the

---

[25] Josiah Royce, *The Sources of Religious Insight* (New York: Charles Scribner's Sons, 1912), p. 207; see the entire discussion pp. 165-210.

[26] Kaplan, "Contribution of Judaism," p. 692.

community.[27] Kaplan's view of ethics, then, may correspond to Royce's philosophy of loyalty. When individuals join a cause they find an environment congenial to their self-discovery. Human fulfillment takes place in a social setting. Royce, however, introduces a pessimistic note not found in Kaplan. Royce follows the apostle Paul and anticipates Freud by recognizing the tension inevitably accompanying civilization. He calls the conflict between the good of the individual and that of society "the moral burden" of both the individual and the race. He notes the irony that " The more outer law there is in our cultivation, the more inner rebellion there is in the very individuals whom our cultivation creates."[28] Religion helps individuals wrestle with this problem, helps them overcome the pain of sacrifice that they must bear by providing a unifying vision. For Royce, science, as well as religion, offers an overarching world view that answers the need created by ethics.[29] The two work together to help people reach salvation. He emphasizes the partnership of science and religion correctly understood. A society's morality creates problems, setting in motion an ambivalence to civilization that religion, science, and philosophy must resolve.

Kaplan's theology, in contrast to Royce's, views the interaction of self and society positively. Morality, rather than creating conflict, resolves it. Since Kaplan identifies morality and religion he sees no tension between the two. Royce admits that traditional religion may seek to produce a "unity of the spirit" such as that to which Pauline charity aims; his pessimistic view of human nature and social realities, however, leads him to note the difficulty

---

[27] Josiah Royce, *The Problem of Christianity* (New York: Archon Books, 1967), pp. 139-140; 430-431.

[28] *Ibid.*, pp. 150-151.

[29] *Ibid.* p. 431.

of applying "this account of the loyalty that should reign within a religious family to the problems of a world where faith does not understand faith..."[30] Kaplan disagrees because he feels that religions arise in response to social custom rather than forming it. Religion, almost by definition, acts to reconcile social conflict. Its primary expression, the idea of God, acts, according to Kaplan, as a unifying symbol, bringing together the disparate parts of society. Conflict resolution, he insists, occurs naturally and produces laws, standards, and values. Society, seeking sanction for "these standards, norms, and mores" resorts "to the God idea, for that idea inherently endorses the rightness of that which we regard as right."[31] Religion needs no radical change to reflect new social standards; religions that function healthily respond organically to the evolving mores of society. While Royce and Kaplan agree that religious ethics enjoins upon loyalty, they disagree because Kaplan contends that this loyalty by itself fosters social cohesion and universalism. Such an approach trusts natural processes and includes communal development as part of nature.

"Moral law," Kaplan proclaims, "is an extension of natural law as reflected in man's sense of responsibility and in his empirically validated behavior."[32] Ethics does not impose an external constriction on human beings. Morals arise from experience itself, from natural human life. Unlike Royce, Kaplan denies that the interests of the individual conflict with those of society. Moral influence flows from one to the other creating "a constant and

---

[30] Royce, *Sources of Religious Insight*, pp. 295-296.

[31] Kaplan, *Meaning of God*, p. 19.

[32] Mordecai M. Kaplan, *The Religion of Ethical Nationhood: Judaism's Contribution to World Peace* (New York: Macmillan Company, 1970), p. 60.

beneficent two-way passage between the individual and his organic society."[33] Of course Kaplan realizes that there are those who interpret this interaction as less than beneficent. He views such interpretations as misguided. When people misinterpret the motives impelling ethical action, they will indeed misinterpret the interaction of self and society. "Only nature's God," Kaplan advises, "can validate the ethical traits which help man to control his biological needs and worldly power..."[34] Kaplan draws his conviction that moral restraint represents a positive and satisfying virtue from his theology. God, by definition, strengthens community and self-control by making social virtues personally rewarding. Loyalty to a specific religious tradition encourages and validates loyalty to the greater social group. Kaplan avers that this reciprocal relationship, while natural in a democracy, requires continual reinforcement and may disappear if uncultivated.

Kaplan and the American Aesthetic

Kaplan reflects not only the duality of Royce and Kierkegaard but also the double legacy of Dewey and Royce. Kaplan would agree with Dewey's *A Common Faith*, that "there is a difference between religion, *a* religion, and the religious." Like Dewey he calls for a rethinking of traditional ideas and symbols, for transforming the idea of God into a means of mobilizing human action. Both Kaplan and Dewey recognize in that idea of the divine "all the natural forces and conditions....that promote the growth of the ideal and that further its realization." Kaplan would agree with Dewey's call for a "transfer of idealizing imagination, thought and emotion to natural human relations"

---

[33] *Ibid.* p. 65.

[34] *Ibid.* p. 70.

which would offer the existing churches "the means for a recovery of vitality." Finally he would affirm with Dewey that "The fund of human values" necessary in a democracy "could be celebrated and reinforced, in different ways and with differing symbols, by the churches."[35]

Beyond this, however, Kaplan turns specifically to the Jewish tradition as a resource, not merely for Jews, but for American religion generally. A vital democracy cultivates its own welfare by fostering the public display of religion, insofar as religion exhibits the appropriately democratic values. The supposedly rigid separation of the religious and the secular in American often relegates faith to the private sphere. Kaplan, like Dewey, rejects that separation. Kaplan contends that a society that prohibits the public display of individuality by its citizens has lost its soul.[36]

The demand for public conformity, he thinks, arises from a false notion of religion. The American founders, he notes, did not separate faith and politics. They separated religious institutions from political institutions. They created an American faith built from the civil experience of daily life. In Kaplan's words, they constructed a "spiritual conception of the American people "without benefit of clergy." They knew that a common faith would unite Americans whereas a common religion might destroy them.[37] This common faith grows out of the experiences Americans share. Americans recognize a common fate uniting them. They symbolize that common fate by

---

[35] John Dewey, *A Common Faith* (New Haven, CN: Yale University Press, 1934), pp. 3, 50, 82.

[36] Mordecai M. Kaplan, *Not So Random Thoughts* (New York: Reconstructionist Press, 1966), p. 32.

[37] Mordecai M. Kaplan, *The Purpose and Meaning of Jewish Existence: a People in the Image of God* (Philadelphia: Jewish Publication Society of America, 1964), p. 282.

certain symbols, signs, and political activities. Kaplan considers these the *sancta*, or holy articles, of American life. The recognition of all the ways Americans work to improve themselves, their communal life, and their society creates the basis for the actual religion that animates public life.[38]

With the contents of this common faith, Kaplan argues, the various separate religious traditions of America can agree. While different American groups should not abandon their individual cultures, they should augment them with the common values of American life. Were such groups to "sever the ties" binding them to their respective pasts, they would eventually succumb to "self-hate and anti-social attitudes." Were they to isolate themselves from the general culture, however, they would lose the ability to participate in the general social conversation that makes "fruitful cooperation possible."[39] Sharing the common faith members of different religions can enter into a general dialogue on American culture.

Kaplan gives a theological content to the common faith that he envisions. American faith, he claims, is monotheistic. It sees the world as motivated by order and purpose. That sense of order provides the basis of freedom. For Kaplan, freedom depends on more than the opportunity to make a choice. It means knowing that how or what one chooses makes a difference. He explains that accepting freedom entails taking responsibility for one's actions. Such responsibility depends on the assumption that the same rules apply whenever anyone performs the same actions. Freedom without an assumption that human deeds make a difference in the world is meaningless. Choices becoming meaningful when associated with predictable results.

---

[38] Kaplan, *Questions Jews Ask*, pp. 163, 481, 482.

[39] *Ibid.*, pp. 31-32.

According to Kaplan, democracy needs religion to ensure this basic presupposition. Monotheism defines God as a single, all pervasive being. The unity and comprehensive presence of the deity provide the theoretical grounding for the belief in a single, always applicable set of rules governing human behavior. Democratic religion ascribes to God that single set of rules, that assumed order, without which there is no freedom. Given the monotheistic nature of American religions, Kaplan avers, all ethical religions "can be hyphenated fruitfully" with the common American faith. This view of religion corresponds with de Tocqueville's understanding of American religion. It recognizes the social and pluralistic dimension of religion in America and affirms it. Such a pluralism, however, becomes possible only by combining Royce's view of values as provided by society with Dewey's understanding that a pluralistic imaginative creativity is the precondition for any dialogic community. By beginning with America's values and then constructing a community to recreate those values in a pluralistic way, Kaplan shows himself more flexible than either Royce or Dewey, than either Kierkegaard or Pragmatism. In short, he shows himself as a postmodernist.

Chapter 4:

Interpretation and Pluralism in America

Post Critical Hermeneutics

Peter Ochs has recently suggested an emergent trend among both Christian and Jewish interpreters of the Bible. He calls it "postcritical" and associates it with the understanding of Scripture expressed by Max Kadushin.[1] Kashushin criticized the dichotomy between objective truth and subjective interpretation often made in relationship to rabbinic documents. Seeking an "organic" approach, he emphasized the role texts play within a living and believing community. The "value-concepts" that Kadushin saw as the building blocks of rabbinic Judaism were not merely intellectual nor yet only ethical. As Ochs puts it Kadushin opposed what he saw as reciprocal errors "either imposing an extraneous conceptual scheme on rabbinic Judaism, or else denying that rabbinic Judaism displays any conceptual order."[2] Using Kadushin as an example, Ochs postulates a three-fold argument by

---

[1] See Ochs, ed., *The Return to Scripture in Judaism and Christianity.*

[2] *Ibid.*, p. 10.

postcritical exegetes, who may look "postmodern" in their criticism of modernity but "premodern" in their return to original communities.

These exegetes, Ochs suggests, begin by identifying modern interpretors of the Bible as reductionists who "treat the biblical text as if it had a referent independently of any particular interpretant;" they continue by exposing the dangers in this dichotomization which leads to an ever increasing schematization and polarization of reality; they conclude by offering a more unifying or "triadic" model which takes as its most important point of departure "the biblical text itself, in particular as it is read in the primordial communities" of believers.[3] Not unexpectedly, Kadushin turns out to have been a disciple of Kaplan. Kaplan's postcritical intuition led him to a hermeneutic very close to those of the scholars Ochs celebrates. He too criticized the static dichotomies established by both Jewish reformers and traditionalists. He too emphasized the community as a defining source of meaning. His social perspective, however, led him to see the consequences of both the old and new hermeneutics as educational rather than academic, as practical and pragmatic rather than purely scholarly. Although a postmodernist in inclination and teaching, the force of his elementary experiences shaped Kaplan into more of a modern activist than his theory would have apparently demanded. Thus his hermenuetics draws on his civil awareness even when motivated by anticipations of postcritical thinking.

Alternation and Interpretation

Kaplan's hermeneutical approach to Judaism affirms de Tocqueville's understanding of religion's role in a world of continuing change, its ability to

---

[3] *Ibid.*, pp.13-14.

mediate between the fact of alternation and an individual's desire for stability. Kaplan defines Judaism as a "civilization." By this he means what others might call a "cultural system."[4] A civilization consists of a people's "style of life," of its "aesthetic mood," and "unique content." It is not so much the specific behaviors that a group manifests. It rather signifies the tendencies, values, and structure of a community.[5] Such a system operates instinctively within its membership. Those who participate in a civilization exemplify its inherent impulses through what they do. The specific behaviors they manifest, however, respond to immediate, historically conditioned, and limited stimuli. Changing one or another behavior does not change the civilization. Changing the values, structures, and purpose of the group, however, does alter the civilization even if behaviors in which people engage do not change.

Modern civilization, Kaplan avers, exemplifies a purely utilitarian orientation to human life. Secular society focuses on technology, on the means to achieve an end, but it does not examine which ends are most desirable. The instrumentalist rationalism of modernity seeks the most efficient way of attaining immediate results. It does not question the purpose or ultimate significance of those results. To use the phrase of Max Weber, the modern world is "disenchanted," it assumes that all things can be mastered by scientific knowledge. Scholars debate what Weber actually intended and

---

[4] See the discussion throughout Efraim Shmueli, *Seven Jewish Cultures: A Reinterpretation of Jewish History and Thought*. Trans. Gila Shmueli (Cambridge: Cambridge University Press, 1990); footnote 16, pp. 273-274, discusses Kaplan's system. While agreeing with Kaplan in many respects, Shmueli charges that Kaplan "eliminates from Judaism the pragmatic-technical dimension of ontology." Unlike Kaplan, Shmueli refuses to separate the "religious" and "non-religious" aspects of Judaism.

[5] See for example, the argument throughout Mordecai M. Kaplan, *Judaism as a Civilization: Toward a Reconstruction of American-Jewish Life* (New York: Schocken, 1967).

whether or not his analysis of modernity was accurate.[6] Weber does, in any case, express a common modern sensation. Modern men and women often do feel themselves in an alien world of technological expertise. They feel disenfranchised as human beings in a society where production replaces humanity as the standard of excellence and worth.

Kaplan does not disavow that civilization. He recognizes its advantages. Eliezer Schweid goes so far as to say that for Kaplan, "Science actually took the place of religion in his world-view."[7] Yet even Schweid acknowledges that Kaplan recognizes the failings of modernity. Kaplan feels that technological society cannot cope with its own powers. Secular skills do not contain an inherent ability for self-restraint. Secular philosophy cannot, he thinks, own generate reasons to restrain the scientific ability enabling humanity to pollute the earth. Mechanical creativity cannot provide a self-reflexive code to protect a world from the threat of mass destruction through its ability to create weapons that can annihilate all life. The social and political powers that can organize communal life to its highest efficiency cannot, Kaplan avers, discover a means to restrain their own inner momentum when those social forces promote familial dissolution.[8]

This situation creates two problems. Kaplan feels that religion offers the only possible solution to the inherent contradictions and self-destructiveness within the modern world. At the same time, he contends that modern men and women live in that secular world. A religion which does not take secularity

---

[6] See Gilbert G. Germain, *A Discourse on Disenchantment: Reflections on Politics and Technology* (Albany, NY: State University of New York Press, 1993).

[7] Eliezer Schweid, *Jewish Thought in the 20th Century: An Introduction*. Trans. Amnon Hadary (Atlanta, GA: Scholars Press, 1992), p. 271.

[8] See Schweid, "Reconstruction of Jewish Religion," pp. 37-38.

and modern technology as its point of departure, he claims, undermines its ability to communicate its invaluable message. Kaplan's religious approach to civilization required a transformation of Judaism for two reasons. Society needs religion because secularism cannot solve its own problems. Religion needs a new self-understanding and self-presentation because unless it affirms the benefits of secularism it dooms itself to irrelevance. Schweid notes that Kaplan rejects supernaturalism not just because it is wrong, but because it is counterproductive. Religion, as Schweid notes, has a peculiar functional purpose for Kaplan--it is to make life more sublime. What Schweid calls "Kaplan's most original contribution" follows from this view. In every civilization, not just Jewish civilization, religion acts to correct excesses, to ameliorate social ills, and to regenerate society. That remains the task of religion generally and of Jewish religion in particular.[9]

Schweid understands Kaplan correctly. Kaplan's antidote to modern civilization is Hebraic civilization. Whereas modernity "was all means and no ends," biblical religion was "all ends and no means."[10] Judaic civilization provides the purposes, the values, and the meanings necessary for society today. Since the ends, rather than the specific means, of Jewish religion are primary, Kaplan can transform both the form and substance of traditional Judaism. The specific expressions of the Judaic system can be altered in order to transmit the essence of the civilization more powerfully. Kaplan shows that Judaism helps people confront alternation by showing the compatibility between Judaic and modern civilization. Critics claim that Kaplan's thought makes too many concessions to modernity. This chapter begins by analyzing

---

[9] Schweid, *Jewish Thought*, p. 275.

[10] Kaplan, *Not So Random Thoughts*, p. 13.

that critique and then describes how Kaplan came to his view of Jewish civilization. It continues by outlining the hermeneutical moves by which Kaplan buttresses his claim that Jewish and modern civilizations complement each other. Ironically, while addressing modernity, that hermeneutics exemplifies the postcritical and postmodern approach to exegesis as illustrated in Peter Ochs' anthology.

Kaplan's Hermeneutics of Experience

Kaplan's life-experiences and intellectual development shaped his understanding of religion. His early encounter with the perils of belief taught him to regard the search for rational faith as an essential element in religion. His dialogue with American philosophy made him sensitive to the need for a hermeneutic of experience. His disappointment with the various options available to modern Jews stimulated a desire to create a new alternative, an innovative type of spiritual belonging. These insights come together in his definition of religion. Religion, Kaplan maintains, must function for the benefit of its adherents. The legitimacy of a religious tradition and its view of God depends on their ability to enhance human life. Religion justifies itself by showing people how to "escape frustration and achieve fulfillment." It does so by satisfying three basic spiritual needs: those for belonging, believing, and experiencing; the three "dimensions" of religion as Kaplan defines it.[11] These three needs concern three very different spheres of human action: belonging evolves from human sociability, believing involves the intellect, and experiencing demands sense-awareness and self-consciousness.

---

[11] Kaplan, *Judaism Without Supernaturalism*, p. 3.

The role of religion in each sphere is to provide a sense of the absolute value, a glimpse of the ideal, toward which people strive and in behalf of which they mobilize their resources. Thus Kaplan recognizes the importance of religion as a source of ideals. He uses the term "God" to refer to those transcendent purposes motivating human action. Religion, according to Kaplan, consists in a coherent system of thought which, through its explanation of the term "God" addresses the three basic needs of its followers. A culture uses that term in various ways to express the varying possibilities life offers people; Kaplan considers religion an expression of "the sum of all these ways in which the god idea functions pragmatically in the civilization of a people." Studying the dimensions of religion, then, means investigating how a culture interprets the god-idea.[12] Here de Tocqueville's understanding of how religion helps people cope with change becomes crucial. The idea of God is one way a civilization mediates between ends and means, between enduring purposes and changing technology. By identifying modern Jewish religion with commitment to three central values, Kaplan helps Jews maintain a sense of continuity despite radical changes.

Kaplan and Activist Experience

Kaplan demonstrates that the Jewish presentation of experience energizes people to creative activity. Rather than interpret experience as an end in itself, the term God converts experience into merely one stage in an on-going process. Using religious language interprets every human achievement as but one contribution to the universal, and unending, task of improving the world. When God is interpreted as the power that makes for human self-fulfillment,

---

[12] Kaplan, *Meaning of God*, p. 19.

then any intimation of the divine, that is any human experience, points beyond itself to future fulfillment. Religion teaches people an activist approach to life and change. Kaplan's hermeneutics transforms a commitment to Jewish tradition from a passive acceptance of the past into a willingness to experiment, into a creative discontent with any one stage of development, and into an impulse to move dynamically from one stage to another.

Kaplan interprets this activism as the central value of belief in God. An acceptable idea of God must unite the disparate values of humanity. His definition of divinity combines a practical emphasis on the highest human ideals with an instrumentalist use of reason to achieve human progress. An authentic Judaism, he claims, must have certain pragmatic results so that we "leave the world the better and the happier for our having lived" and must also be "compatible with reason which is the last court of appeal."[13] In this statement Kaplan once again construes Judaism as an authentic American religion. It enables Jews not only to cope with change but stimulates them to produce a tradition of development and human improvement. This process of amelioration implies an acceptance of that instrumental rationalism characteristic of modernity.

The Rationality of Judaism and American Religion

Kaplan insists that Judaism affirms this modern utilitarian rationalism. Judaism, he argues, does not deny the validity of reason, in fact rational criticism is one of its constituent elements. Kaplan reinterprets the Jewish tradition in ways that, he thinks, will appeal to modern Jews. He considers three requirements essential for the believability of any modern Jewish

---

[13] Kaplan, *Purpose and Meaning of Jewish Existence*, pp. 298-300.

theology: an emphasis on immanence, freedom, and universalism. These three arise from three verities Kaplan associates with modern science: rejection of supernaturalism, the priority of process over conclusions, and the need to search for truth. A religion forfeits credibility by describing reality in categories alien to common experience. In modern times, Kaplan suggests, scientific categories mediate common experience. Scientific rationalism, Kaplan contends, enables people to develop themselves more fully, to discover their belonging in the world through the force of experience.[14] Since people affirm their place in the world through science, religion cannot ask them to sacrifice scientific thinking. Because supernaturalism makes such a demand, Kaplan advocates rejecting it. Once rejected, religion, Kaplan claims, will gain the authenticity "we associate with scientific fact" by integrating its claims as part of normal experience.[15] As its name implies, supernaturalism posits God outside of nature, transcendent and above normal experience. Kaplan insists that a modern religion must abandon this view and discover God within natural experience, as immanent in the human world. By interpreting the tradition in terms of immanence, Kaplan has given empirical change a sacred status. While some religions turn to the past to find intimations of the divine, Kaplan's Judaism turns toward nature and science and thereby accommodates the rapid changes associated with modernity.

This emphasis on immanence, however, does not entail a capitulation to materialism. Kaplan's stress on the idea of progress renews the theme of religious utopianism associated with religion as an interpreter of experience. Religion posits a divine reality, Kaplan explains, that surpasses all human

---

[14] Kaplan, *Future of the American Jew*, p. 308.

[15] Kaplan, *Purpose and Meaning of Jewish Existence*, pp. 306-307.

achievements. Since no present knowledge is sufficient, religion must affirm an infinite process of experimentation and search. A rationally compelling religion cannot offer dogmatic assertions about reality. He argues that "Freedom of inquiry is incompatible with the belief in the eternal validity of some specific revealed doctrine as a source of truth."[16] Modern scientific method refuses to be bound by such dogma. The very nature of divinity, as Kaplan describes it, affirms that scientific premise. Religious individuals, he notes, "feel the need to be free" because God requires human freedom. If God represents those forces that enable personal fulfillment, then God ensures the freedom within which such fulfillment occurs. Religion serves self-fulfillment precisely by its definition of divinity as the guarantor of free inquiry.[17] Kaplan's view of God not only identifies the divine with verifiable forces in nature. It also affirms the very basis of science. Because divinity provides the environment for human salvation and because that salvation depends upon the freedom to experiment, the God-idea itself affirms human liberty. Again, Kaplan has taken a potentially conservative theological value, that of salvation, and shown it to be an impetus to change and development. He has transformed the hope for divine salvation into a reason to accept and welcome personal growth and self-improvement. Free inquiry leads to reconsideration of ideas and values, to constant reevaluation of one's beliefs; it therefore legitimates those intellectual changes so characteristic of the dramatic shifts in modern thinking.

This dedication to inquiry also means that a rational religion will inevitably follow that path of cooperation and compromise which students of

[16] Kaplan, *Questions Jews Ask*, p. 162.

[17] Kaplan, *Future of the American Jew*, p. 283.

American religion find so fascinating. Kaplan espouses a view of truth that includes an affirmation of pluralism. He claims that a religion which restricts rather than expands its adherents' potential for development testifies to its estrangement from God.[18] When testifying to true divinity, however, religions are "as inevitable a part of human civilization as is science or art." They are needed because, when recognizing the immanence of God and the necessity of freedom, they stimulate a quest for truth.[19] Since God is immanent in the world, human beings only glimpse those divine forces with which they come into contact. Their vision of divinity depends upon the nature of their experience. Experience, however, is limited and particular. Jewish religion, for example, demonstrates a particularity born of its unique history. Jewish revelation differs from Christian or Muslim revelation because of different experiential foundations for the recognition and identification of empirical forces as divine.[20] Pluralism provides one of the most important sources of the "other," of those possible alternative visions of reality essential in an age of change. Religious tolerance, therefore, represents still another way in which Judaism, as constructed by Kaplan, affirms that alternation so crucial to modern American religious experience.

This view of religion as a pillar of rationality upholding the right for a pluralistic search for truth in a spirit of free inquiry fulfills the criteria necessary for an American religion. It exalts a rational ideal of pluralism and self-development within community. This similarity with American values explains why Kaplan does not reject religious relativism entirely. He wryly

---

[18] *Ibid.*, p. 382.

[19] Kaplan, *Meaning of God*, p. 197.

[20] Mordecai M. Kaplan, *The Greater Judaism in the Making* (New York: Reconstructionist Press, 1960), p. 470; compare *Religion of Ethical Nationhood*, p. 103.

remarks that it is flawed but nevertheless "the closest approximation to absolute truth" among modern philosophies.[21] Taken as a whole, Kaplan's theology recapitulates the American approach to religion. As William A. Clebsch suggests, Kaplan represents one adaptation of the view of religion which was the touchstone of philosophy in the thinking of William James. While many American theologians "temporalized the absolutes of the old religion without really relativizing them" others, like Kaplan and James, go beyond this approach to claim that both "religion and its deity existed for the sake of mankind." Such a view, by placing human needs before divine principles, implies a flexible religious tradition. Ideals may remain constant, but because needs change with changing societies, religions must respond to the new environment without, at the same time, compromising its ideals.[22] Kaplan's hermeneutic of reason led him to recast Jewish religion and its texts in a new light. Future chapters explore how Kaplan reconstructed the building blocks of Judaism into a religion to meet the social realities of America.

Such a commitment to modernism and reason seems to run counter to the postmodernist impulses in Kaplan's hermeneutical approach. Kaplan's affirmation of rationality, however, disguises a deep distrust of all claims to final truth. This chapter began by announcing Kaplan's hermeneutic as one designed to legitimate pluralism. To achieve that legitimation he makes three basic moves: first, he upholds alternation, continual change, as the basic fact of life; secondly he applies this fact to his educational process--no philosophy or philosopher emerges untransformed from Kaplan's grasp; finally, Kaplan makes all meaning contingent on context--since the modern context exalts

---

[21] Kaplan, *Questions Jews Ask*, pp. 150-151.

[22] William A. Clebsch, *American Religious Thought : A History* (Chicago: University of Chicago Press, 1973), pp. 123-124.

reason, Kaplan provides a rationalist version of Judaism. Each of these three moves expresses Kaplan's basic assumption that "truth" has been replaced by "the search for truth," certainly a modern insight, traceable to Gotthold Ephraim Lessing, 1729-1781. Nevertheless, the kind of use Kaplan makes of this idea appears peculiarly postmodern. Jean-François Lyotard characterizes the "postmodern" by its suspicion of great narrative myths, of heroes and eternal truths. The postmodern identifies itself by its "incredulity" and unwillingness to accept absolute values unmediated by context. The great advantage of postmodernism, according to this definition, is that it "reinforces our ability to tolerate the incommensurable."[23] Kaplan's superficially modernist rationalism actually performs this function and continually reminds people of the incommensurability of reality to human categories. His hermeneutic only bears the external trappings of modern rationalism; when analyzed from within it reveals itself as postmodern.

---

[23] See the introduction to Jean-François Lyotard, *The Postmodern Condition: A Report on Knowledge*. Trans. Georff Bennington and Brian Massumi. Foreword Fredric Jameson. Theory and History of Literature 10 (Minneapolis, MN: University of Minnesota Press, 1984), p.xxv.

Chapter 5:

Kaplan's Realistic Utopianism

Education For the Trace: Kaplan as a Deconstructionist

Mordecai Kaplan called his movement "reconstructionism," emphasizing that it was rebuilding, and reconceiving of Judaism. A more postmodern, and in fact more accurate, description would be "deconstructionism." The term is more accurate because Kaplan never assumed that his movement would offer one and only one "reconstruction" of Judaism. He recognized and legitimated a plurality of Reconstructionist theologies, liturgies, and approaches to Judaism. The same openness and encouragement of experimentment appears throughout his thinking and publications. Kaplan refuses to think of education as a process for the accumulation of facts. Instead, he insists that education presents opportunities, that it transforms facts, ideas, and symbols into motive forces which inspire action. Geoffrey Hartman describes Jacques Derrida's idea of the "trace" as just such a motive force. Hartman suggests the yearning for totality which turns modern thinkers away from books or philosophies and "into life" (as Franz Rosenzweig put it). In that turning away, books and ideas become mere tools for something greater than themselves. They are signals of a reality which, if understood, lived, and known, would undermine all self-conceptions, all presuppositions, all security. When learning becomes a searching for an overflow of meaning, for a trace of that which makes the defined reality inadequate, then education is a continual process of unmasking texts or theories. Education, understood this way, continually calls for rethinking fundamental ideas, for reimagining meaning, for recreating reality. Kaplan's educational experiments always reveal this radical intentionality which Hartman celebrates. Hartman might well understand Kaplan's determination to write new prayer books that bring the unwary worshipper to sharp attention. Hartman could applaud Kaplan's curriculum for Jewish education which never leaves an issue fully resolved but always awaiting interpretation. In this way, Kaplan achieves what Hartman suggests as the postmodern effect: "the mind is always being trashed: nothing is resolved enough to be dissolved."[1]

God and Community in Kaplan's Theology

Kaplan united civic patriotism and loyalty to Judaism. To achieve this combination he reshaped Jewish theology. He devoted himself to transforming the meaning of Judaism because he saw in the idea of God a tool for actively improving American communal life. This activity self-consciously altered traditional ways of understanding Judaism. Kaplan justified the innovations he introduced by suggesting that Jewish thought has always adapted to the cultures and civilizations among which Jews have lived. The Hebrew Bible, for example, uses various names for the deity, many derived from earlier religious traditions. Kaplan explains that these names reflect the evolution of

---

[1] Geoffrey H. Hartman, *Saving the Text: Literature/ Derrida /Philosophy* (Baltimore: The Johns Hopkins University Press, 1981), p. 15.

the idea of God from that of a deity restricted to a particular tribe into a universal divinity. As the view of God undergoes development, he conjectures, the text refers to the deity by a different name. This view finds confirmation in contemporary studies of the Bible. Modern biblical scholarship has traced "the early history of God."[2] What might be called "the repertoire of descriptions of God" in the Bible draw on several ancient sources-Canaanite, Mesopotamian, and Egyptian.

Kaplan draws an important conclusion from this fact of theological change and development in the Bible. He recognizes that as human beings change, their view of divinity changes as well. This understanding of the development of the idea of God provides the basis for Kaplan's advocacy for a new way of interpreting that idea. God's development and change becomes for Kaplan a model for human self-transformation. He announces that "We have nothing to fear from metamorphosis. That, indeed, is how we began our career as a people."[3] This dynamic view, however, raises an important question. Might not a stage of human culture, then, require abandoning the idea of God altogether? Perhaps modern Jews would do better to reject using the term "God" as inappropriate in a secular democracy. Kaplan refuses to accept this reasoning. The very dynamics of Jewish thought in the past testifies to an on-going attachment to the god-idea among Jews. The term carries with it an emotional content not exhausted by rational categories. To reject using religious language because it conflicts with secularism means to capitulate to just those forces which religion counterbalances. Refusing to change religious language means evading the responsibility of offering

---

[2] See Mark Smith, *The Early History of God: Yahweh and the Other Deities in Ancient Israel* (San Francisco: Harper, 1990).

[3] Kaplan, *Future of the American Jew*, p. 539.

modernity a potent alternative to secularity. Refusing to use religious language means abandoning the very purpose of minority traditions in a democracy. Kaplan, therefore, concludes that "It is just as wrong not to use God's name when it can help to give a lift to the human spirit as to use God's name in vain."[4] Contemporary Judaism must continue the process of adapting theology to changing needs not only because this process characterizes the Jewish approach exemplified in the past but because it is also a necessary contribution Jews can make to American society and the democratic process. Kaplan creates just such a contemporary theology by reconstructing Jewish belief out of the building blocks of biblical thought.

Kaplan's understanding of biblical theology stresses three important ideas. The first concept is that of change, of dynamic evolution. The Bible, Kaplan argues, represents a growing and developmental tradition. Biblical theology, as he understands it, cannot be summarized in any single system of thought. Views of the divinity, of humanity, or of the world found in the Bible differ from passage to passage in response to the changing needs and realities of the particular culture represented by the author of any specific biblical text. Secondly, Kaplan realizes that by combining these diverse passages the biblical editors created a unity out of diversity. The Bible, by its very method, he assets, establishes a "tradition." It maintains continuity through history by using terms hallowed by past usage but reinvigorates them by giving them new meanings. Key concepts such as covenant, holiness, and the divine reappear in biblical passages. Their persistence creates the impression of a single tradition. While reading those passages carefully shows that the interpretations of the terms differ, Kaplan affirms the necessity for

---

[4] Kaplan, *Not So Random Thoughts*, p. 147.

viewing the Bible, and later Judaism, as a single whole. Finally, Kaplan regards the Bible as essentially pragmatic. He claims that it tests the validity of its reinterpretations by discovering how they motivate people to perform their civic duties. Religious change as described in the Bible, whether the changes from the early religion of Abraham to the succeeding faiths of Moses or David or later changes introduced by Israel's prophets, justifies itself by its pragmatic effects. When change mobilizes resources and inspires personal responsibility, Kaplan interprets the biblical record as insisting, then it is a positive part of society. When it capitulates to convenience, he concludes from studying the critical narratives and prophetic castigations of the Bible, then it has forfeited its reason for existence. Kaplan's biblical theology offers Americans a paradigm of salvation.

The Realistic Basis of Kaplan's Thought

Kaplan's reworking of biblical theology for the modern time exemplifies that combination of acceptance of the dominant culture and fidelity to ideals that de Tocqueville urges on religion. He accepts American utilitarian values because they do not compromise his Jewish utopianism. He seeks to educate American Jews in democracy so that Judaism can educate democracy in social consciousness. Kaplan's theology embraces a naturalistic view of reality. God as an idea represents those aspects of the world that make for human development. Kaplan's social vision leads him to consider belief in God one of the central contributions religion makes to American democracy. He realistically asserts that only vibrant particularistic religious traditions can supply democracy with its most vital needs.

Several critics claim, on the contrary, that Kaplan espouses a naive view of democracy, that he capitulates to a patriotic identification of the will of the people with the will of God. Thus Norbert Samuelson, in a valuable study questioning "Can Democracy and Capitalism be Jewish Values," criticizes the basic principles of Kaplan's view of democracy.[5] Samuelson claims that Kaplan naively thinks that a democracy inevitably seeks the good of the governed, acting for the best interests of the majority and is thus constrained in its actions. He criticizes this idea since a democratic government need not act for the *perceived* interests of its constituency but for their *actual* best interests. This latitude in action means that the theoretical restraints on government activity often fall short. But, Amuelson instists, governments justify any action, however deleterious it might appear, even though the majority opposes it, since politicians feel bound only by *their own* construction of the best needs of that majority. Kaplan, then according to Samuelson, fails to understand the ways in which a democratic government can legitimize its own self-serving activities.

Samuelson also criticizes Kaplan for thinking that since religious individuals constitute a democracy's constituency, its government naturally supports religion. Samuelson notes that the idea of Jewish chosenness suggests that Jews should serve the interests of the divine. God's interests, however, need not be those of any particular human collectivity.[6] A democracy, he argues, can easily satisfy a religious constituency without satisfying the demands of religion. The needs that animate a religious tradition, Samuelson avers, are those of God, not of humanity. A humanistic democracy may serve the civil needs of its people and still ignore the needs of the divinity as

---

[5] Norbert M. Samuelson, "Can Democracy and Capitalism be Jewish Values? Mordecai Kaplan's Political Philosophy," *Modern Judaism* 3:2 (May 1983), pp. 189-215; see especially pp. 197-207.

[6] *Ibid.*, pp. 206-207.

perceived by the religious traditions to which these citizens belong. Such traditions, Samuelson comments, will find the democratic process inadequate. "God," he notes," is not a constituent of any nation and at least in theory, the interests of God and the interests of any human collective need not be the same."[7] Samuelson seems to imply that Kaplan has naively posited a harmony between democracy and religion unsubstantiated by the facts.

It is just that point, however, that Kaplan rejects. His definition of God identifies the divine precisely with the best interests of every individual. A nation that neglects the interests of God also neglects the interests of its constituency. Nations and individual both, of course, as Kaplan admits, may misjudge their own best interests. They may misunderstand the meaning of God; they may misconstrue the human condition. Kaplan, no less than Samuelson, recognizes that a democracy serves the *real* rather than the *perceived* interests of its members. It looks to its citizens for guidance especially because of its skepticism about any perception of truth. The wise no less than the foolish may deceive themselves or be deceived. The reason democracy relies on the majority, he declares, is not a naive faith in the wisdom of the collective mind. The system of majority rule arises as a safeguard against revolution and chaos. Even the wisest minority cannot rule without the support of the majority. If the majority contests the value of policies which, in fact, are beneficial, the benefit is lost in the ensuing social unrest. Kaplan remarks that "The only reason democracy favors majority rule is a pragmatic one." The majority will create a safer government than will the minority, it will not create a "better one." Safety demands the sacrifice of the

---

[7] *Ibid.*, p. 207.

promise of absolute wisdom for the security found in majority consensus.[8] A society depends on stability for its efficient working. Such stability depends on heeding the needs of all constituents. Majority rule assures that this need for stability prevents social excesses.

Democracies lie open to the temptation toward oligarchy. The self-confidence of a wise minority may undermine the consensus essential for social survival. Majority rules is a problem only if the majority does not remain flexible and attentive to minorities. The solution to the problem of the majority lies not in replacing it with a wise minority. Rather it consists in educating the majority as to its own best interests. Minorities, of which religious communities are primary examples, offer that guidance which can lead a democracy to self-improvement. Their existence and the necessity for accommodating their needs acts as an antidote to the temptation toward oligarchy. Kaplan argues for the minority religions precisely because they act as a corrective to oligarchic tendencies.

Religions, however, must guard themselves against temptations of their own. Religions must engage themselves with civilization no less than society must be open to religious teachings. Religions face a temptation of withdrawal into themselves. Isolationism in the name of some ideal often leads religion to abandon its social mission. Religions distance themselves from the market-place of social interaction. Such self-involvement prevents a religion from carrying out its function in a democracy, that of challenging secularism. Kaplan recognizes this temptation toward disengagement. He counteracts it with a call for involvement. Democracy must welcome its religious minorities; religions must welcome their tasks within democracy. This realistic approach

---

[8] Kaplan, *Not So Random Thoughts*, p. 31.

leads Kaplan to state that "As soon as a religion becomes disengaged from its civilization, both become subject to corruption." Kaplan seeks to transform parochial Jewish religion not to merge it with democratic civilization, but to improve both.[9] Kaplan espouses religion for realistic reasons. Democracy needs to learn practical lessons from its minority religions: lessons on how to develop a social conscience, how to mobilize its citizens for the good of the entire society, and how to unite a potentially contentious communal body.

Kaplan's Education in Democracy

Kaplan demonstrates these practical lessons in his own activities. His practicality first took shape as an educational program.[10] This interest and continuing concern mark Kaplan's distinctiveness. Theologians theorize; they rarely implement their own theories. Those who dedicate themselves to institutional projects and educational programs do not usually write theological systems. William Cutter remarks on this extraordinary aspect of Kaplan's activity and remarks that "the group of educators with which he was identified were, in effect, a hothouse for the nurturing of ideas that captured the imaginations of a larger public..."[11] As a practical course of action Kaplan's pedagogical program illustrates his impulse toward interpretation. Education recasts traditional religion to fit modern need. At the same time, from a theoretical perspective, Kaplan's impetus toward education reflects his concern with human salvation as a social reality, that is, salvation understood in accordance with democratic values. Not surprisingly, Kaplan's involvement in

---

[9] *Ibid.*, p. 137

[10] See William Cutter, "Kaplan and Jewish Education: Reflections on His Influence," in Goldsmith, et. al, eds., *The American Judaism of Mordecai M. Kaplan*, pp. 370-384.

[11] *Ibid.* p. 376.

the aims and purposes of education led him beyond pedagogy to social services. His influence on Jewish communal agencies reflects his realistic approach to salvation in a democracy. As Harriet A. Feiner notes, his ideas in this sphere "reflected his total approach to Jewish religion and community...(and) were set in the context of religious naturalism, humanism, and evolving civilization."[12] His efforts on behalf of the Jewish express his concern for strengthening America. Only by offering a secure economic and physical life can a democracy win the support of its members. Kaplan uses Jewish communal values to animate reform in institutions which supply citizens with this basic needs. Kaplan applied this approach not only Jewish agencies, but to the American economic system. Influenced by the Marxist critique of capitalism, he nevertheless articulated a form of democratic liberalism. He trusted less in the "revolution of the proletariat" than in educational reform. "Society could be reconstructed," Rebecca Trachtenberg Alpert says of his thinking, "through educational processes that would help people understand how social forces work, and through political action..."[13]

Such an activist approach to religion might appear overly pragmatic and materialistic. Kaplan denies that his practical concerns dilute the spiritual message of Judaism. Religion, according to some theorists, represents a person's ultimate goals and highest expectations. Kaplan, in many ways, agrees. He organized his life to further what he considered the most important purpose of religion--that of transforming society. Emmanuel Goldsmith correctly understands this aspect of Kaplan's approach to Judaism. Goldsmith

---

[12] Harriet A. Feiner, "Kaplan's Influence on Jewish Social Work," in Goldsmith, et. al, eds., *The American Judaism of Mordecai M. Kaplan*, p. 362; see the entire essay, pp. 357-369.

[13] Rebecca Tractenberg Alpert, "The Quest for Economic Justice: Kaplan's Response to the Challenge of Communism, 1929-1940," in Goldsmith, et. al, eds., *The American Judaism of Mordecai M. Kaplan*, p. 390; see the entire essay, pp. 385-400.

remarks on what Kaplan considered the "highest conceivable purpose of human existence" -- that of creating a society in which people lived lives "motivated by what he called a sense of active moral responsibility."[14] That desire to use religion to instill a sense of community and interhuman concern parallels the second aspect of religion in America noted by de Tocqueville. Kaplan's reconstruction of Jewish life sought to use religion to educate American Jews in the social awareness democracy espouses but requires voluntary bodies such a religions to inculcate and transmit to individuals. This view stresses what might be called "soteriology," or "knowledge of salvation," a concern at the heart of Kaplan's approach to religion in a democracy.

Meir Ben-Horin suggests the dialectical aspect of salvation in Kaplan's thought.[15] Salvation balances the needs of the individual against the requirements of society. It appeals to faith (*emunah* in Hebrew) and dictates actions (*musar* in Hebrew). Kaplan advocates what philosophers since Aristotle called the "Golden Mean." Salvation occurs when society fulfills its task by enabling individuals to achieve their personal goals and when individuals perceive the fruit of their self-fulfillment to be contributions to the social whole. Kaplan claims that secular life cannot, on its own attain this salvation. Secularism tends to stress the individual, to make the good of the unique person more important than that of the society. Only religions can animate the social sensitivity necessary to balance personal and communal concerns.

---

[14] Emanuel Goldsmith, "Mordecai M. Kaplan: His Interpretation of Judaism," in Kaplan, *Dynamic Judaism*, p. 22.

[15] See Meir Ben-Horin, "Mordecai Kaplan's Soterics: Individuality and the Social Order," *Journal of Reform Judaism* 27:2 (1980), pp. 12-29; while the discussion here draws on this article, readers should see its companion essays "Salvation in Mordecai M. Kaplan's Theology," *Journal of Reform Judaism* 26:1 (1979), pp. 1-16 and "Mordecai Kaplan's Soterics: The Jewish People," *Journal of Reform Judaism* 27:4 (1980), pp. 75-82.

American institutions, dedicated to secularity and the separate realms of the civil and the religious, cannot mediate between private and public needs, individual and social desires.

No where does Kaplan find the need for religion as an important voluntary organization in America more essential than in the realm of education. He claims that American life suffers because it has created from a false dichotomy--that between secular and spiritual values. Americans, by erecting a wall of separation between church and state, have also denied their political system the religious nourishment necessary for survival. State education, exclusively secular, fails to transmit the universal, humanitarian, and idealistic values which animate political life. This lack of education in values, Kaplan concludes, leads to widening "the gap between the secular and the spiritual interests of the American people."[16] He feels that Jewish religion can overcome the problems caused by this gap.

Kaplan's Educational Experiments

Kaplan's involvement in Jewish education demonstrates his commitment to using religion as a tool for awakening a sense of communal loyalty. In 1909, he became principal (later called dean) of the Jewish Theological Seminary's newly created Teachers Institute, a position he held until the 1940s. Mel Scult notes that the early years withthe Teachers' Institute and the New York Board of Jewish Education "constitute a series of beginnings and a series of conflicts." Kaplan was caught between the demands of his superior at the Jewish Institute of Religion, Solomon Schechter, and the leading Jewish educator, Samson Benderly. From this struggle, Scult contends, Kaplan

---

[16] Kaplan, *Religion of Ethical Nationhood*, p. 156.

derived his own sense of the type of institution needed by American Jews. Within Jewish education, he made his own distinctive contributions. Scult maintains that through these contributions "Kaplan helped to create the profession of Jewish education."[17] Among his contributions, Kaplan transformed Jewish education. He demanded higher standards in both secular and Hebraic knowledge. The curriculum was taught in Hebrew by outstanding Hebraists. He brought into Jewish education "many people who later became leaders and shapers" and his support for such educational experiments as the School for Jewish Communal Work and the Central Jewish Institute helped reconfigure Jewish teaching and learning in America.[18]

Kaplan's work in as a trustee of the Bureau of Jewish Education for the New York Kehillah brought him into close contact with Samson Benderly, the director of the bureau and perhaps the single most influential force on American Jewish education in the history of American Jewry. Kaplan's efforts at transforming American Judaism, therefore, took a clearly pedagogical shape. In 1918, when he formed the Jewish Center, Kaplan began creating a practical program aimed at modernizing Jewish Orthodoxy. His innovations led to arguments and debates with leaders of his congregation. During his tumultuous leadership with the Jewish Center's Orthodox members, Kaplan found support in Benderly, who mediated several of these disputes. Benderly's practical approach to Jewish education influenced Kaplan's own program.[19]

Both Kaplan and Benderly agreed that the survival of Judaism in the modern world required a new type of religious life. The modern Jewish

---

[17] Scult, *Judaism Faces the Twentieth Century*, p. 126; see the entire discussion from pp. 101-126.

[18] See Scult, "Mordecai M. Kaplan," p. 6

[19] *Ibid.*

problem, Kaplan and Benderly argued, lay in the need for a "social adjustment" which would reconstruct Jewry from "a nation in exile" into a universal civilization. Benderly tried to realize this ideal by creating a new Jewish communal order, the New York Kehillah. The failure of the Kehillah appeared to Kaplan as a sign of the "general state of demoralization in Jewish life," so he redoubled his efforts to transform Jewish self-consciousness.[20]

From 1919-1931 Kaplan labored to realize his new conception of Judaism. His actions often caused conflict both within the general community and within his own family. He criticized Orthodox for being out of step with modernity. He called for a transformation of Jewish life so as to foster Jewish social solidarity, reformulation of Jewish practice to reenforce this solidarity, and the creation of a new code of Jewish law to reconstruct Jewish self-understanding. One outstanding innovation occurred in 1922--the introduction of a ceremony marking a girl's maturation into womanhood, the *Bat Mitzvah*, corresponding to the male ceremony of *Bar Mitzvah*. As Mel Scult puts it, Kaplan had four reasons for creating this rite--his four daughters. The ritual apparently appealed to Kaplan's congregants. While "There is no record of any opposition within the congregation," Kaplan met "considerable resistance from his mother and mother-in-law." In the face of merely familial dissent, Kaplan remained strong. After the Bat Mitzvah, however, some congregational dissatisfaction arose. Kaplan's daughter had said the blessings over the reading of the Torah and had even read from the scroll itself. Congregants found this advance toward equality too radical. In future ceremonies, the girl undergoing Bat Mitzvah would not engage in such activities. Mel Scult wryly comments that Kaplan's congregation was in the strange situation of "having many bas mitzvas but no women who were ever again called up to the Torah." He notes that "Kaplan chose to follow his flock rather than to act on his conscience."[21] Despite his theoretical principles, Kaplan recognized the pragmatic power of the popular will. Ultimately realistic considerations rather than theology would determine what Judaism could survive in America.

Kaplan often took such a compromise approach. One of his most controversial changes was the removal of the popular prayer Kol Nidre from worship on the eve of the Day of Atonement. The prayer, while important in popular culture, has a long legacy of rabbinic opposition to it. Kaplan retained its famous melody but substituted Psalm 130 for the familiar prayer and thus eliminated the supernaturalist overtone. Kaplan attempted to weather the storm of protests he received. When, however, his son-in-law, Ira Einstein, suggested a revised version of the original *Kol Nidre*, Kaplan accepted his suggestion and reintroduced the prayer with, what he considered the proper revisions.[22] Through such compromises Kaplan used liturgy as a means of educating Jews for American democracy. This pedagogical approach to prayer illustrates his commitment to shaping American spiritual life through a self-consciousness representation of official religious traditions.

Ira Eisenstein comments on this aspect of Kaplan's work.[23] He notes that the urge to transform the liturgy had personal roots. Kaplan became more and more aware of his inability to affirm the liturgy. As he recognized the gulf between his beliefs and the content of Jewish prayer, he sought ways of

---

[21] Scult, *Judaism Faces the Twentieth Century*, pp. 300-301.

[22] Scult, *Judaism Faces the Twentieth Century*, pp. 286-290.

[23] Ira Eisenstein, "Kaplan as Liturgist," in Goldsmith, et al, pp. 319-331.

overcoming this discrepancy. His response to this problem developed dynamically rather than dogmatically. He experimented with forms of prayer to see what techniques conveyed his ideas most clearly. Pedagogical consideration guided this evolution of liturgical innovations. Eisenstein shows how Kaplan altered his original opposition to the *Kol Nidre* prayer and included the liturgical piece with "clarifying phrases" and insertions to make his new interpretation clear. Eisenstein comments that "To drive the lesson home, Kaplan strengthens the conclusion of the traditional formulation..." That phrase reveals the pedagogical impulse in this effort.[24] The most radical changes that Kaplan introduced in his new liturgical works come in his *Haggadah* for Passover. Eisenstein explains this radicalism because of its pedagogical intention. Since the work was "designed for edification of the young" Kaplan introduced innovations to clarify the ethical and moral lessons of the Passover ritual.[25] Liturgy offered a practical vehicle for educating a new generation of Jews. It transmitted the ideas of Judaism in ways that could reinforce rather than contradict the basic values of democratic life. One guiding principle in Kaplan's reconstruction of the liturgy was ethical: "affirmations unethical by modern standards...were elided as unacceptable on principle." Jewish worship, for Kaplan, functions to teach ethical ideals.[26]

Judaism as a Civilization in Kaplan's Pedagogical Perspective

By 1928 Kaplan had conceived of writing a book to explain both the philosophy and basic principles involved in his new program of Judaism as

---

[24] *Ibid.*, p. 322.

[25] *Ibid.*, p. 324.

[26] *Ibid.*, p. 330.

a civilization. At the heart of this philosophy was the belief that only "the most thorough overhauling of Jewish ideas and Jewish life" could enable Judaism to survive in the modern world.[27] This approach really combined two ideas: in the first place it assumed that Judaism could function as a social and communal laboratory in which American Jews might learn the skills needed for sensitive living in a democracy. On the other hand, Kaplan's espousal of this function was couched in terms meant to appeal to Jewish self-understanding. He did not defend his reinterpretation of Judaism merely on the grounds that America needed it. Instead, he claimed that only his program for a reconstructed Judaism could save Jewish religion in the modern period. He saw his own work as a response to the crisis that affected Judaism from within. Other American Jews not only recognized the crisis of belief and loyalty that threatened to overwhelm American Judaism, but also acknowledged Kaplan's creativity in responding to that crisis. In 1931 Kaplan applied for and received the Rosenwald Prize for the best manuscript on "the inner problem of Judaism," a subject which Kaplan had considered at length. He saw the basic challenge to American Jewry as that of redefining the status of the Jew and the meaning of Judaism. His manuscript explored a new way of conceiving Judaism and a new interpretation of the religious culture which constitutes Jewish civilization. The book Kaplan produced, his acknowledged masterpiece and programmatic manifesto, *Judaism as a Civilization*, called for an elaborate rethinking of Jewish religion. Survival in modern times, Kaplan argued, required that Jews reinterpret their tradition in terms of democratic values, that they restructure their practices to foster the democratic way of

---

[27] Libowitz, *Mordecai M. Kaplan*, p. 123; see pp. 93-133.

life, and that they reconceive of religion so that it creates an awareness of social responsibility binding its members together in group loyalty.[28]

One of the most extraordinary aspects of Kaplan's proposal in *Judaism as a Civilization* is its pedagogical emphasis, particularly in the realm of public worship. He draws attention to the original function of Jewish poetry-that of conveying religious values. Jewish liturgy, he notes, offered traditional Jews an outlet for artistic creativity denied in other realms. Hebraic poetry legitimated itself as expressions of prayer. Prayer, as poetry, provided an avenue for artistic self-expression, a means for communicating private concerns in a public setting. Kaplan uses the example of poetic prayer to show how even in its beginnings Judaism transcends an authoritarian demand that Jews sacrifice their individuality to the group as a whole. He urges Jews to see Jewish practices as poetry in action, as symbolic expressions of ideas. He points to the use of music and poetry as means of communicating social ideals and urges Jews today to emulate earlier ages by a similar usage.[29] This program flows directly from his pedagogical view of Jewish liturgy. Since the purpose of a liturgical service is to shape the way people understand life, prayer must use every means possible to evoke new visions of the world. The creative arts provide the most effective tools for such evocation. They are primary instruments in helping people confront reality as it is and imagine it as it should be. Kaplan's technique for achieving this end is essentially postmodern. He unmasks the contexts of the past, showing the historical contingencies behind supposedly "eternal" verities. This ability to reduce past truths to contextual suppositions resembles the uncovering of that "trace"

---

[28] See Libowitz, *Mordecai M. Kaplan*, pp. 133-189 and Kaplan, *Judaism as a Civilization*.

[29] Kaplan, *Judaism as a Civilization*, pp. 434, 457-458.

which reveals the contingency of our models of existence. Secondly, Kaplan uses this "trashing" of the mind's view of history as a call for the interpreter to take responsibility for the interpretations given. Kaplan trains those who follow his method to see themselves as creative participants in the process of constructing and giving meaning to reality.

There are at least two ways in which religion fashions a perception of reality: deciding which aspects of human experience are most valuable and rooting all experience in social life. These two are precisely those that a democracy needs. The first provides a means of counteracting the neutrality of technology, the lack of any internal system for judging which ends modern tools should serve. The second supplements the corrosive aspects of American individualism with a bracing social sensitivity.[30] Kaplan explicitly accepts this task. He claims that the imaginative arts generally counteract life's ugliness; they show that humanity can improve the world by reconstructing it aesthetically. Religion performs a similar task for secular individualism. As he puts it "If the imaginative arts redeem life from ugliness, it is religion that redeems life from secularity."[31] Liturgical education brings Americans salvation from the potentially dangerous individualism of democracy. Jewish worship correctly understood teaches an important lesson not only for Jews but for the entire country.

Kaplan's Expression of Practical Jewish Civilization

The programmatic plan of Kaplan's masterwork soon found expression in actual fact. The practical efforts that led to the burning of Kaplan's prayer

---

[30] *Ibid.*, p. 347.

[31] *Ibid.*, p. 443.

book followed quickly after the publication of his major work. He created a bi-weekly magazine, wrote a book on "the meaning of God," and published several liturgically innovative works. He introduced a new ritual for Passover, a revolutionary *Haggada of Passover*, which by both its inclusions and exclusions indicated a new approach to Judaism. While not encountering the same outcry as the, later, prayer book, this work did arouse opposition. Several of Kaplan's colleagues in the Jewish Theological Seminary wrote a protest against this work.[32]

These practical activities were inevitable consequences of the philosophy explained in Kaplan's prize winning book. That book itself inspired both admiration and vicious hostility. As Richard Libowitz notes, "Reactions to *Judaism As A Civilization* confirmed Kaplan's status as the most controversial Jewish thinker in America."[33] The debate that followed focused on the specific proposals Kaplan made and his rationalistic emphasis. Kaplan's explicit arguments suggested that only a rationalistic and scientific Judaism could survive in America. What few realized was that these arguments really served a different purpose. Kaplan's explanation of Judaism as rationalistic and democratic was couched in the language of survivalism. In fact, the utility of religion for democracy, rather than that of democracy for religion, lies at the heart of his theory.

Kaplan's vision of a new Judaism articulating American utilitarianism, but supplementing it with a religious sensibility undergirs his practical activities. That vision conceives of human knowledge as composed of three dimensions: wisdom, reason, and intelligence. He associates the first with

---

[32] Scult, "Mordecai M. Kaplan," p. 11.

[33] Libowitz, *Mordecai M. Kaplan*, p. 192.

human needs as mediated through religion, the second with facts as understood by rational categories, the third with strategic use of material resources based on humanity's place in the world. He suggests that his "transnatural" religion confronts each of these in ways modern Jews can accept.[34] His vision for American Jewry integrates a "modernist" conception of reality with a postcritical recognition of the limits of that conception. He proceeds more self-consciously than most modern thinkers, aware that he is providing a radical reinterpretation of reality for the sake of reinforcing the images and symbols of a particular tradition.

The three dimensions he notes correspond to three ways in which his view of Judaism differs from that found in Orthodox Jewish writings. Drawing on the idea of wisdom, or universal knowledge, he denies that Jews have an exclusive claim to truth. He opposes the concept of the Jews as a "chosen people," preferring to refer to the "vocation" or spiritual calling of the people of Israel. He also emphasizes the importance of a religion of reason, a rationalism that replaces supernaturalism with a realistic theology. Finally, he advocates the use of intelligence in reconstructing Judaism. While authoritarian religion, he claims, demands the abdication of intelligence in the name of loyalty to tradition, true religion demands an intelligent reconstructing of the past. Only such intelligent use of Judaism can make it a useful tool for the improvement of American democracy.

Democratic Religion and The Chosen People

American Jewish thinkers have struggled with the meaning of the concept of "the chosen people" and evolved several strategies for coping with

---

[34] Kaplan, *If Not Now*, pp. 38-39; 96.

its apparent contradiction to egalitarianism. The idea that God has selected one group among all humanity and given it a special, and more exalted, position, conflicts with America's professed sense of human equality. Some Jewish thinkers explain the idea of chosenness as an expression of the "Jewish mission" and not of any sense of superiority. Others claim that it represents acceptance of special obligations, not special privileges. Kaplan emphasizes its incompatibility with the civil status accorded the American Jew.[35] Kaplan believes that religion's most important task involves projecting a view of reality, establishing a sense of the order of the world in which human beings live. Religion, he explains, enables a person to move beyond the struggle to survive as an end in itself to an understanding of life in the service of values and ideals that transcend life. From a practical perspective this means that Judaism should understand its history as an exercise in communal sympathy, as a preparation for ethical nationhood. Religion becomes ethical, Kaplan avers, when it provides a sense of universal meaning that lifts its members beyond their parochial boundaries. He uses an organic metaphor for the achievement of this sense of universal meaning. Human beings, he thinks, intimate significance in reality only by discovering the way every human life is interwoven with "ever-increasing webs of relationship with the rest of reality."[36] To meet Kaplan's criteria of effective religion, a religion must continually evaluate its philosophy of life, its understanding of the purpose of human existence and its conception of the patterns governing that existence. Kaplan constructs what he thinks of as an acceptable, believable, and ethical

---

[35] See the entire discussion throughout Arnold M. Eisen, *The Chosen People in America: A Study of Jewish Religious Ideology* (Bloomington: Indiana University Press, 1983); see on Kaplan, pp. 73-98.

[36] Kaplan, *Greater Judaism* , p. 468.

religion out of the elements of Judaism. His commitment to a responsive religious life in which context determines meaning would lead him to affirm the necessity of challenging even that construct. No single envisioning of Judaism can survive; only a process of on-going and self-perpetuating revisionings can assure a tradition's survival.

In the case of religion for modern Jews, Kaplan constructs a faith which, he believes, corrects the problems inherent in the traditional of the Hebrew Bible. Whereas the biblical text finds meaning in a nationalistic and parochial social web, modern Jews, Kaplan believes, find meaning only in that web of interconnectedness that extends beyond the self and immediate society to include all humanbeings.[37] Biblical religion as Kaplan describes it emphasized the exclusive history of the Jewish people and explained the importance of Judaism in terms of that history. This approach produces what Kaplan finds a peculiarly pernicious idea in biblical religion - that of the chosen people. Biblical religion considers Jewish history the unfolding of a divine plan. God seeks to use humanity to create an ideal world. After experimenting with others, God decides that the Jews alone are capable of fulfilling the divine purpose. Kaplan claims that this religion fostered "an ethnic consciousness, which for intensity and far-reaching consequences in their lives, was without a parallel in the life of any other people."[38] In biblical times Jews needed an incentive for survival. During periods of persecution the Jewish conviction of chosenness inspired heroic loyalty to Judaism. In the modern context, however, the idea only exacerbates intercultural hostility, warfare, and competition. With this in mind, Kaplan rejects the biblical idea.

---

[37] Kaplan, *If Not Now*, p. 111.

[38] Kaplan, *Greater Judaism*, pp. 34-36.

He legitimates only that idea of God which brings unity and harmony out of the divisiveness of contemporary life. He urges modern religion to devise a philosophy of history that "imposes on its adherents loyalty to a universally valid code of ethics."[39] Kaplan views biblical theology as based on the parochial history of a clanish trabe. Its web of meaning feels alien and irrational to contemporary universalists, he claims, and therefore he charges that contradicts the ethical impulse of modern religion. A Judaism based on such an unacceptable presupposition, he argues, cannot hope to survive in the modern world. Jews, quite rightly he affirms, reject a biblically based Judaism as irrelevant and inappropriate for a democratic society.

Jews, Kaplan claims, will accept Jewish religion only when it shows how Jewish history, destiny, and civilization help them achieve personal goals while maintaining their ties with a wider society.[40] A modernist, following the absolutism of either the Enlightenment or the Romantics would object to diluting the "true" meaning of Jewish religion in this way. Kaplan, like the postmodernists, doubts the possibility of discovering such a "true" meaning. Meaning emerges from the interpreter's context. For American Jews, he feels, only that meaning emerging from the American Way will be persuasive, credible, and therefore "true." Accepting the American criteria of utility as his highest value, Kaplan judges Jewish practice by its ability to evoke democratic action. As a shrewd observer of American life, however, he realizes that this evocation must be couched in traditional language. He argues that only a traditionalism shorn of its supernaturalism and reshaped to fit a democratic environment can achieve this goal. This goal represents a realistic,

---

[39] Kaplan, *Future of the American Jew*, p. 220.

[40] Kaplan, *If Not Now*. pp. 67-68, 79.

but religiously inspired, view of salvation. The variety of pedagogical technique that Kaplan uses--educational reform, liturgical innovation, and biblical exegesis serve a single function: to link the components of Jewish images and practices to the web of interconnection that alone gives a coherence to a Jew's existeence in America. Discovering that coherence, learning that the disparate parts of life are elements in a single pattern, provides what Kaplan will call "salvation," the sense of the worth and value of life. Although traditional Jewish Orthodoxy would not accept Kaplan's view of salvation, his ideas resonate with many Americans.

Kaplan's Contribution in Perspective

Kaplan's theology succeeds on many levels. He offers American Jews a persuasive articulation of their religious experience. American Jews do indeed seek ways of feeling at home in a world increasingly alienated from them. They do require rationality in their beliefs. His rational, pragmatic view of salvation echoes the actual yearnings of American Jews. Some analysts find this realism the greatest failing of Kaplan's philosophy. American Jews, these thinkers argue, welcome a liberal style of life but prefer a more conservative ideology. They fall into a "folk" way of religion but insist that their leaders articulate an "elite" formulation of their faith. Reconstructionism seems an insignificant option because theology plays so small a role in religious life.[41]

Norbert Samuelson adds another criticism that seems to aim at this aspect of Kaplan's plan. Kaplan's use of the democratic idiom makes it difficult for him to criticize democracy. Samuelson contends against Kaplan that "the system of traditional Jewish practice, while not perfect by modern

---

[41] See Liebman, "Reconstructionism in American Jewish Life," pp. 256-262.

standards" does indeed offer a "viable program of life" that need not be sacrificed to that of Americanism.[42] Rather than idealize democracy or capitalism, the modern American Jew should reaffirm the inherent values found in Jewish tradition itself. Kaplan would not disagree with this sentiment. He would, however, distinguish between the activist aspect of Jewish theology, which presupposes an existing Jewish community and the more utilitarian aspect of Jewish practices which create that community. Samuelson may be right, the language of pragmatism and democracy may no longer be the best ways to reconstruct a modern Jewish life. Kaplan's program, however, may also be right--the aim of such reconstruction must be the creation of a viable community that balances respect for the past with sensitivity to the present, and which inculcates concern for the national and international community.

Whether either Kaplan or Samuelson correctly analyzes the language necessary for communication in a democracy, Kaplan at least exhibits a healthy skepticism of any language whatsoever. His guarded use of the symbolism of progress reveals his perceptive ambivalence. That many have misunderstood his views only shows that he succeeded perhaps too well in dressing his message in an attractive guise. He trusted, however, that those who needed to could pierce the outer shell hiding the kernal of his thought. He at least possessed this ability when analyzing previous Jewish thinkers. This penetrating recognition that words and concepts inevitably fail to perform their required tasks led him to press them into service for him in extraordinary ways. The next section shows how Kaplan's pragmatic recognition of what American civil society requires expresses itself in a

---

[42] Samuelson, "Democracy and Capitalism, p. 215.

reconceiving of Jewish religion. That reconception often makes use of apparently historical argumentation. When analyzed, however, that argument unravels. Kaplan succeeds not because he is a profound historian, but because he uncovers the limits of all historicism. He reconstructs Jewish belief, exegesis, and salvation history, not by returning them to some pristine original condition but by proving that they are effective only when modified. Only when the symbols of Judaism, the traces or overflow from Jewish life, point beyond themselves and reality to that which cannot be either conceived or expressed. To make Judaism effective, it must be turned into a system that includes its own destruction within it. Kaplan's technique exposes how when one understands Judaism one passes on from it to something else, to life. Yet the passage to life is never complete and so the process of moving through Judaism and beyond it never ends. The next section shows how Kaplan uses a postmodern approach in his reconstruction of Judaism that is skeptical of language, that affirms the interpreter as the key to the interpretation, and that transforms facts into a plethora of traces. Kaplan's postmodernism becomes clear in action rather than theory as he struggles to create a Judaism that reflects the modern American environment while remaining true to his utilitarian training and his instinctual recognition of the limits of knowledge.

This postmodernism also underscores Kaplan's peculiar impotence in attempting to mobilize a political movement within Judaism. Kaplan understood the problematic nature of dogmatic proclamations about Judaism too well to compete with others who could use that rhetoric. His social perspective denied absolute reality to the structures that institution builders had erected. He trusted to the insight of individuals. Jonathan Culler makes two observations in regard to postmodern criticism that fit Kaplan's predicament. On the one hand, Culler hails the excess of wonder that "inclines critics to puzzle over elements in a text." That puzzlement is productive and creative even if "excessive." Kaplan trusts that individuals will, with his guideance and tutorship, see through the disguises taken on by texts and practices to discover their own powers of creation; that they will penetrate structures which are merely apparent and learn to create their own realities.

Culler also remarks on the danger of an approach which privileges all interpretations and offers no grounds for judging one framework of interpretation superior to another. He contends that too great an emphasis on the relativity of textual meaning and its construction by those who receive the texts confirms a structure in place by denying that there is a structure."[43] This perspective clearly blunted Kaplan's edge within the American Jewish institutional community. He lacked a theoretical forum from which to criticize the present and therefore lacked a basis for power. His very postmodernism tends to weaken Kaplan's potential as an critic of the status quo and as an institution builder. He doubts his own truths and undermines the credibility of his theory by "deconstructing" it before the very eyes of his most ardent followers. For an institution-builder such deconstructive insight proves fatal. Kaplan the community leader fails because Kaplan the philosopher sees so clearly. Despite that limitation which hedged in Kaplan the human being, his thought offers those who follow both a Judaism with potential for criticizing America and an American religiousness from which to re-vision Jewish faith.

---

[43] See Jonathan Culler, "In Defence of Overinterpretation," in Eco, et. al, *Interpretation and Overinterpretation*, pp. 122-123, 119.

PART III: JUDAISM'S CONTRIBUTION TO DEMOCRACY

Chapter 6:

Belief in God and American Democracy

Modernity and Belief in God

Kaplan's understanding of Judaism's role in American life gains credibility when placed in the context of general theories of religion and its place in democratic life. A democratic society, such as that of the United States, seeks to moderate ideological conflicts and divisions among its citizens. Religions often stimulate such conflict, but may play a stabilizing role as well. A democracy within which religions war against each other confronts a clear danger. A democracy in which secularity alone prevails, however, may lack a source of mediating ideals. Indeed, irreligion may prove as disruptive as overly zealous religiosity. This duality pervades every aspect of democracy's interaction with the realm of values and ideals. In a rapidly changing world ideological controversy may sometimes stimulate heightened creativity, but it may also exacerbate social problems. Robert A. Nisbet, for example, notes that "Out of such conflicts, to be sure, have come some of the great intellectual and moral achievements of American civilization, but out of them have also come some of our bitterest social and moral problems."[1]

Seymour Martin Lipset reviews the dynamic interaction between religious groups and American politics. The political agenda of any religious sect in America, according to his findings, may well disturb the civil status quo. It often seeks to use civil forces for its own purposes. Mobilizing the institutions of society to serve a parochial set of concerns, Lipset recognizes, threatens the well-being of the entire state. He discovers a "tendency to enforce virtue by law" and "an identity between religious commitment and intolerance of ambiguity."[2] Despite the misgivings these discoveries arouse in him, Lipset also recognizes the positive effect of having a variety of religious traditions working at cross purposes from one another. These special interests tend to defuse potential political explosions. He notes that "American Protestant sects have more often served to draw off antagonism from the social arena to the religious order." This deflection of potential strife aids social stability. Religious conflict may, ironically, provide greater political consensus.[3] Pluralism strengthens society more than a unity artificially imposed by establishing a single religious tradition. America's approach to religion disproves the myth that unanimity is more productive than diversity.

The ideology of American pluralism, from Lipset's perspective, makes sense. That ideology supports only those religions which reject both

---

[1] Robert A. Nisbet, "The Impact of Technology on Ethical Decision-Making," in Robert Lee and Martin E. Marty, eds., *Religion and Social Conflict* (New York: Oxford University Press, 1964), p. 13.

[2] Seymour Martin Lipset, "Religion and Politics in the American Past and Present," in Lee and Marty, eds., *Religion and Social Conflict*, p. 117; see the entire essay, pp. 69-126.

[3] *Ibid.*, p. 116.

superstition and atheism. According to this ideology, superstition brings rigidity, fundamentalism, and a type of religious imperialism out of place in a pluralistic democracy. Atheism, following similar lines of thought, stimulates despair, aimlessness, and selfishness. Under a religion of superstition a nation would feel the tyranny of claims to absolute truth. Under atheism a nation would dissolve into the competing whims of individuals. A religion that recognizes its role in supporting government, that sees its function as reinforcing communal values, moderates between these two extremes, keeping the good of the nation always in mind.

The United States maintains a pluralistic environment by affirming the right of the individual established religions to compete in the marketplace of ideas. In order to succeed in this competition, each religion must present itself as both compatible with modernity and as peculiarly advantageous for its members. American religions must prove their credentials as "modern." They must avoid superstition and show their acceptance of practical reason. They must also avoid atheism and show their spiritual contribution to a secular society.. Mordecai Kaplan's understanding of God as "that power not ourselves which makes for salvation" addresses the various concerns of that agenda. This chapter sketches his understanding of theology as a religious contribution to American secular democracy, showing that Kaplan actually approaches Judaism as a postmodern prism which reveals the delicate illusions on which American faith bases itself.

Democratic Religion Against Supernaturalism

No matter how valid a religion may be in theory, Kaplan claims that it fails in its task if that theory belies human experience. Religion cannot simply develop a philosophy of life. It must also enable its adherents to experience that philosophy as part of their daily existence. In the case of a democracy, a religion must provide just those exercises in freedom necessary for good citizenship. Kaplan seeks a set of practices that combine respect for tradition with the inculcation of sentiments appropriate for a democracy. Supernatural religion fails in precisely this test.[4] Such religion "speaks in terms that are alien to the personal experience" of its modern adherents. This failure, according to Kaplan, lies less in the religious tradition itself than in its intellectual leaders. These leaders could easily translate supernaturalism into "naturalist religious experience." By neglecting this task, these leaders render the religion meaningless. A beautiful philosophy has no significance if it appears to lack substance and reality. Only when a religion can "transform the vicarious experience of the reality of God into a personal experience" does it succeed in fulfilling its obligations.

Kaplan suggests that Jewish leaders fail in this effort because they remain wedded to a supernaturalist biblical theology. Biblical religion expresses the conviction that human beings can succeed only by using magical or theurgic practices to influence God. Sacrificial procedures seek to achieve divine favor. Ancient Israel sought to ensure the natural cycle of rain and agricultural growth through a system of ritual practices. When religion seeks to propitiate the deity, to compel the divinity magically by obedience to irrational commands, it falls into theurgic supernaturalism. The Bible promises that punctilious observance of traditional practices assures success and therefore represents a magical view of reality.[5]

---

[4] Kaplan, *Purpose and Meaning of Jewish Existence*, pp. 306-307.

[5] Kaplan, *Judaism Without Supernaturalism*, pp. 37-47.

Kaplan claims that modern Jews cannot accept such a view of religion. Their personal experience leads them to a more positive and optimistic view of themselves. They find success within reach of their own capabilities. They do not need magic to understand natural patterns of weather or seasonal cycles. Biblical religion taught that rain was a reward for obedience. In a less sophisticated scientific environment, that teaching induced people to follow Jewish law. A modern, technological perspective, Kaplan explains, rejects supernatural causation as an explanation of events. The claim that atmospheric conditions depend on human moral behavior, for example-a biblical comonplace-only makes Jewish belief appear absurd. Such a claim, Kaplan argues, built upon an inappropriate assessment of personal needs, undermines the potential value of Jewish religion.[6] Not only will the claim fail to motivate Jewish practice, it will alienate modern Jews from the entire Judaic tradition. Associating Jewish practice with an inadequate view of human experience deprives that practice of meaning and value. Not only Jews, Kaplan feels, but America as a whole is deprived of an important resource for democracy when Jewish leaders fail in their task of presenting Judaism in its most positive and modern light.

Democratic Religion and Authoritarianism

For Kaplan traditional theology not only denies the personal value Jews may expect to find in Jewish practice. It also distorts the social meaning of that practice. Jewish leaders fail not only because they obscure the personal advantages of belief in God. They also fail because they ignore the social dimension of religious belief. Religion should generalize from individual

---

[6] Kaplan, *Not So Random Thoughts*, p. 164.

experience to show the common experience that binds members of a social group together. A theocentric religion neglects to emphasize the value of religion for the society no less than its value to individuals. Kaplan suggests that the supernaturalist view of God demands a "uniform regimen" of observance. He claims that traditional religious leaders exacerbate this requirement for uniformity. Biblical heroes emphasized religious conformity and created a philosophy to "convince those who disagreed of the truth" of a particular creed or version of religion. The internal conflicts described in the Bible, according to Kaplan's exegesis, arise from a contentious claim that God demands one and only one type of worship.[7] If religious practice seeks to satisfy a demand of the deity, then divergence from that practice leads to divine displeasure. On these grounds Kaplan rejects traditional religion. Such religion decries deviation from the divine norm as a threat to personal and social well-being. It fears an irrational retribution for changes in traditional thought and behavior. Because it has no rational basis for its acceptance of tradition, Kaplan avers, it invokes what modern people can only interpret as an irrational authoritarianism which excludes all who deviate from the community whatever their motives.

Kaplan understands that Americans, whether Jewish or non-Jewish, reject any semblance of tyrannical authority. Such an approach symbolizes the evil that Americans fought a revolution to overcome. If Judaism aligns itself with totalitarian irrationalism it risks self-destruction. Paranoid leads will reject changes essential to the religion's continuation and survival. Although Kaplan does not begin with theology but practical reality, his pragmatism leads him eventually to a revision of Jewish religious thought. His analysis takes the

---

[7] Kaplan, *If Not Now*, p. 111.

failure of modern Jewish leaders as its starting point. Jewish leaders today, he claims, have so misunderstood their roles that they themselves pose the greatest current threat to Jewish existence. Modern Jews, he argues, no longer follow any single order of observance. They follow an American pattern of diversity and individualism. Pluralism of practice has replaced uniformity as the preferred form of Jewish expression in modernity according to Kaplan's analysis of the situation. He therefore feels that insisting on uniformity destroys communal solidarity rather than strengthening it.[8] The biblical approach, in his view, can only lead to Jewish conflict and hostility as one group of Jews regard another as unauthentic. A modern religion, succeeds only by showing how diversity strengthens group identity rather than weakens it. Jewish leaders, however, ignore this truth. He thinks that this fateful failure arises from the antiquated theology these leaders espouse. Because they hold to an outdated view of the divine, Kaplan affirms, these leaders blind themselves to God's actual will in the modern age. He characterizes the traditionalist view of God as an authoritarian tyrant demanding one and only one way of response. The leaders emulate their ideal model. They insist on a hierarchical and absolutist social structure because their mythic theology convinces them that this is the pattern of reality. Kaplan reverses the procedure. He does not begin with a theological example and then apply it to reality. He starts first with an analysis of the human situation and then asks what idea of God fits that situation. In the modern condition, he thinks, authoritarianism conflicts with the basic values of democracy and therefore alienates most modern Jews.

---

[8] Kaplan, *Judaism As A Civilization*, p. 215.

Kaplan's Modern Theology

Kaplan notes that any modern theology must begin by taking account of the success human beings have had in manipulating their environment. He considers as one of the touchstones of modernity the view that human survival depends on how people affect the world around them. Kaplan claims that the centrality of human power to mold the world marks modern experience as different from pre-modern. He notes that biblical Judaism emphasized human creativity, the mutuality between God and the Jewish people.[9] In the course of Jewish history, as Kaplan describes it, that principle of mutuality became obscured as social, political, and economic necessity shaped Judaism into an increasingly authoritarian mold. In the middle ages, human initiative took the form of rabbinic decrees, *takkanot*; the threat of modernity, Kaplan laments, limited even that expression of independence. The Jew, as Kaplan reads modern history, became in traditional Jewish thought more and more of a passive servant to the divine. Modern American Jews, Kaplan avers, reject this model and so have questioned traditional faith. The crisis of Judaism as a religion, he feels, arises not because Jews disbelieve in God, but because Jewish thinkers no longer show God's relevance for individuals seeking personal self-expression.

Kaplan's Reconstructionist interpretation of Judaism offers a theology uniquely tailored to his view of the modernity generally and the American experience in particular. Because its theology rejects supernaturalism in favor of humanism, it reverses the traditional scale of Jewish values and replaces the theocentric approach of the Hebrew Bible with a religion focused on human beings and their needs. As Kaplan formulates it: "Biblical philosophy

---

[9] Kaplan, *Greater Judaism*, p. 509.

of history assumes man's relevance or importance to God. Modern man must experience God's relevance to man."[10] Kaplan phrases this as if it distinguishes the modern from the premodern. Actually his emphasis on the human construction of the divine is a postmodern element. Kaplan like the postmodernists and unlike the modernists recognizes that meaning resides not in things themselves but in what people attribute to them. Kaplan claims that a responsive and spontaneous Judaism arises when traditional texts interact with modern American Jews; the reader forms the text by bringing to it American presuppositions. Out of the interplay of text and reader Kaplan expects a new Judaism to emerge, a Judaism tied to tradition but one that is also a distinctly American religion. This new Jewish religion illustrates what he calls a "transnatural theology" and which he claims will solve the problems inherent in biblical religion.

Kaplan's theological innovation ascribes a unique power to individual readers who, as it were, invent God and their own tradition out of the needs they bring with them when they approach that tradition. Kaplan hopes to teach people to find God by analyzing their own deepest desires, their own aspirations for personal development. The idea of God remains a religious ideal because, for Kaplan, most people are ignorant of their real needs and require some external instrument to bring the true necessities of life to their attention. A view of God, in his view, should help believers realize the necessity for honesty, responsibility, loyalty. Identifying God in such a way, Kaplan suggests, teaches people to discover the importance of the God-idea

---

[10] Kaplan, *Religion of Ethical Nationhood*, p. 47.

for their personal development. Human beings need such a view of God as the basis for their ethical and moral maturation.[11]

Kaplan sets as his agenda the defining of God in terms of human experiences of self-transcendence. He discovers an idea of God relevant for modern Jews by studying how people grow towards their fullest potential, the fulfillment of which he designates as "salvation." God for Kaplan, as for traditional Judaism, denotes that compelling force in the universe enabling salvation. Kaplan and traditional Judaism part company not with identifying God as the source of salvation but in their distinctive definitions of salvation. Salvation, for Kaplan, but not for traditional Judaism, refers to a this-worldly personal self-actualization. His theology, accordingly, analyzes analysis of moments of human self-expression. In such moments, he argues, human beings recognize that they are aided by a more than human set of forces. They discern, according to Kaplan, that nature and circumstances combine to enable self-realization. By calling this combination of forces, this "transnatural" impetus aid to human actualization, God, Kaplan claims to have identified a deity confirmed by human experience, whose reality will "influence the conduct of people" because it verifies human ideals.[12] The meaning of God in this view depends upon human intellectual effort in constructing a viable God-idea. The relationship of this meaning to the American context lies in its ideological and practical implications. Ideologically, such a view of God reinforces democracy's concern with the individual and the rights of the individual. Practically, it stimulates creativity

---

[11] See *Greater Judaism*, pp. 67. 68, 86, 120 and *Judaism Without Supernaturalism*, p. 110; *Questions Jews Ask*, pp. 84, 87, 94, 103; *Meaning of God*, pp. 26-30, 82-83.

[12] Kaplan, *Greater Judaism*, pp. 457-459, 473, 490-491.

and initiative, inspiring people to take responsibility for their actions, for the consequences of how they affect the world around them.

God: The Force Not Ourselves That Makes For Salvation

Kaplan's reflections on the meaning and definition of God developed during the 1920s and 1930s. He thought of God as "the Living Universe," or as "the life of the universe." He tests the "God-idea" by its ability to contribute to "self-fulfillment or salvation."[13] Kaplan draws on the pragmatic tradition of Dewey and James to argue that a view of God must translate into an experience of reality. Because he follows these teachers, he argues that the problem facing modern religion does not consist in "a lost faith in God" but rather in an inability to recognize an experience of divinity.[14] Since experience, Kaplan thinks, not philosophy, prevents Jews from affirming their faith, he derives his new definition of divinity from experiential data. Modern Jews, in Kaplan's estimation, turn to religion for help in achieving their highest aims. They seek aid in attaining self-fulfillment, he affirms, denying that they require the articulation of a doctrine derived from traditional sources. Religious humanism, rather than philosophical rigor, in his view, animates their concern. Kaplan recognizes the validity and power of this new orientation to religion. He therefore argues for a functional rather than essential definition of divinity. The word "god" in his vocabulary denotes a function rather than a static entity in the world. He calls this function the promotion of human self-fulfillment or salvation: "God denotes the power or process, both in the cosmos and in man, that makes for human fulfillment,

---

[13] See Libowitz, *Mordecai M. Kaplan*, pp. 112, 161-175.

[14] Kaplan, *If Not Now*, p. 67; compare his *Questions Jewish Ask*, p. 98 and *Future of the American Jew*, p. 259.

both individual and collective, or for normative man."[15] This definition emphasizes the function that the divine plays in human life rather than the human obligation to the divinity.

Kaplan's mature thought frequently refers to God in this way as the Power, not ourselves, that makes for salvation, clearly indicating that by "salvation" he means human self-fulfillment, whether for the individual or the group.[16] Understood in Kaplan's definition, salvation refers to a this-worldly achievemtn. For him, people reach salvation when they realize their potential, when they actualize the possibilities inherent in their personal, social, and human status in the world. Actualizing that status, Kaplan claims, depends upon achieving selfhood within a self-reflective community. This affirmation arises from his experience of the inadequacy of Jewish social self-conceptions. He cannot conceive of a Jewish view of human self-fulfillment that does not include a communal dimension. This social aspect to his thought shows that by defining God in terms of human salvation he envisions religion as a comprehensive system applicable to every part of human life.

Kaplan's wording of his definition for God clearly owes much to Matthew Arnold's formulation that the biblical view of divinity is of "a Power that makes for righteousness--not ourselves." When, in 1905, he first read Matthew Arnold's work, Kaplan found it convincing. Kaplan himself declared that his discovery of Arnold aroused an immediate feeling of affinity and

---

[15] Mordecai m. Kaplan, "Between Two Worlds," in Ira Eisenstein, editor, *Varieties of Jewish Belief* (New York: Reconstructionist Press, 1966), p. 141; compare *If Not Now*, p. 86; *Judaism Without Supernaturalism*, p. 150; the discussion in *Questions Jews Ask*, pp. 77-144 and p. 481; *Future of the American Jew*, pp. 45, 182; *Religion of Ethical Nationhood*, pp. 48-49 and his *Greater Judaism*, pp. 471-473; 490-491.

[16] See Kaplan, *Judaism Without Supernaturalism*, pp. 21-23, 52-53, 119; *Meaning of God*, pp. 53-54.

sense of admiration. Arnold's characterization of the Bible as more concerned with God as a force for righteousness than as an exercise in metaphysics gave Kaplan a basis for reevaluating traditional sources. Arnold's description of God combined a realistic approach that eschewed imagination with a recognition of a transnatural power of more than merely human dimensions. As Richard Libowitz puts it, Arnold "enabled Kaplan again to believe in a God through which the community sought salvation," thus solving the problem initiated by Ehrlich's critique of orthodoxy.[17]

Despite his debt to Arnold, Kaplan was not a blind disciple. He offers a nuanced explanation of his definition of God not found in Arnold. Arnold, clearly following Spinoza's lead in identifying the Bible as a book of legislation and ethics rather than a revealed work of inspired philosophy, emphasizes God as a power for righteousness. Kaplan focuses on a more general aspect of the divine: it represents those powers working for salvation. The difference between Kaplan and Arnold suggests the extent and comprehensiveness of Kaplan's definition. Kaplan would certainly agree that "righteousness" represents one element in human salvation. Human beings do seek to create a just social order and to exhibit justice in their own lives. Unlike Arnold, Kaplan refuses to limit human self-fulfillment to such an aim. He seeks to include every aspect of human activity under the aegis of those forces that can be called divine.

Again unlike Arnold, Kaplan refuses to offer an unambiguous definition of the divine. His term "self-fulfillment" or salvation takes on many different meanings. He vacillates between several different implications in his definition. Sometimes the "Power" he envisages "makes for" meaning. This

---

[17] Libowitz, *Mordecai M. Kaplan*, pp. 41-43.

suggests that God consists of those aspects in the world that impel people to surpass themselves, that make their life-experiences stages in development. This emphasis is individualistic. Kaplan, however, also stresses the social. Even when basically concerned with interpreting facts, Kaplan introduces a social element in his definition. The divine element within human experience, he thinks, links one event with another "into ever-increasing webs of relationship." Those relationships create a social world, a community's construction of reality. A theology or definition of divinity represents an intellectual image of that social world, of that view of reality.

Defining God that way implies that society projects its beliefs and values as transcendent truths which unify all human experience. This understanding of the God idea focuses on its intellectual meaning. At other times Kaplan focuses on the activism implied in generating a view of a divinity. He often identifies salvation as achieving a social goal. He considers this goal part of the purpose for which human beings strive in their daily activity. Thus he explains that the social aspect of salvation entails "the ultimate achievement of a social order in which all men shall collaborate in the pursuit of common ends." Understood this way the idea a society has of "God" represents its ideals of action, its social goals not its social self-image.

Still a third view identifies "God" with motive forces activating human behavior. The power that makes for salvation, according to Kaplan, has a dynamic effect on people. It forces them to transcend themselves; it "impels us to grow and improve physically, mentally, morally, and spiritually."[18] This last point synthesizes the others. While sometimes inner forces motivate self-transcendence, at other times a person needs the inspiration and support of

---

[18] Kaplan, *Greater Judaism*, p. 468; *Meaning of God*, pp. 53-54; *Judaism Without Supernaturalism*, p. 110.

other people and social structures. Looked at this way, the variety of meanings implied in the term "salvation" indicates Kaplan's sense that people look to the divine to aid in attaining several ends. Self-fulfillment involves every aspect of human existence and the divine resources on which human beings draw to achieve that fulfillment span all the different aspects.

The difference between the way Kaplan and Arnold define divinity points to Kaplan's understanding of religion as a means by which people feel at home in the world, in their society, with themselves. Arnold pictures an "ethical" home for humanity in the world. Kaplan's choice of the word "salvation" suggests a broader conception. Human beings are "at home" in the world only if that world satisfies every need -- social, intellectual, moral, physical, and emotional. In Kaplan's system, the idea of God expresses a human conviction that the human cosmos can satisfy all these needs.

Kaplan holds that satisfaction of needs produces a sense of belonging in the widest meaning of the term. Such "belonging" demands self-understanding as well as acceptance by others. It demands a context in which an individual feels an organic connection with other people, with the natural world, and with the universal principles of the cosmos. Religion, in Kaplan's sense, acts as an agent for belonging. It not only provides an environment for sociability but also for the self-knowledge needed for any social life. Kaplan defines God, in the first instance, as those forces aiding people shape themselves, their society, and their cosmos as contexts for belonging. Belief in God, at its root, expresses the conviction that people belong in the world and society and that through their actions they make their place in the universe, in community, and in life more secure, comfortable, and productive.

This emphasis on belonging as the widest meaning of salvation differentiates Kaplan's definition of the God-idea from Arnold's more narrowly ethical perspective. Nevertheless, the implications of his theology do include an emphasis on righteousness. The test of a God-idea, Kaplan insists, lies in its ability to motivate moral action. "Godhood," he claims, "can have no meaning for us apart from human ideals of truth, goodness, and beauty, interwoven in a pattern of holiness."[19] Whether an idea of the divine truly corresponds to the reality it names, Kaplan explains, depends upon its approximation of those ideals that animate human actions at their best. Kaplan includes aesthetic, ethical, and intellectual ideals alike, but stipulates that they must be "woven in a pattern of holiness." He does not construe the various aspects of reality that lead to human self-fulfillment as independent. Kaplan stipulates that religion must recognize not merely the existence of such elements in the world but also their unity. They all derive from a "transnatural" Power, a single source beyond nature.

Believing: The Rational Dimension in Kaplan's Thought

Kaplan appeals to reason as the basis for his belief in a transnatural monotheism. While Kaplan's definition of God begins with the reality of human redemption, its rationalism marks its distinctiveness. Kaplan gives primacy to "belonging" over "believing" for practical, not ideological reasons. His personal struggle to find a philosophically honest interpretation of Judaism marks his approach to theology. Nevertheless, he realizes that satisfying the need for rational belief must come after fulfilling the needs for belonging and experience. We feed hungry people, he notes, before attempting to teach them poetry. In the same way, he continues, the relevance of a God-idea depends first upon its pragmatic worth, but then, secondly, on the elegance of its

---

[19] Kaplan, *Meaning of God*, p. 26.

intellectual formulation.[20] A religion must not only offer its adherents a framework in which to comprehend the cohesion and significance of their lives or a social vision that affirms their position in a community. He maintains that religion earns the right to fulfill these needs by its uncompromising rationality. While religion inspires people to act on their spiritual needs, Kaplan refuses to justify religion on the basis of needs alone. Religious beliefs and ideas, he contends, must be consistent with scientific truth. Here Kaplan follows in the footsteps of his American exemplars. William James, for example, who defined religion as an "enthusiastic temper," demonstrated pragmatically in exemplary lives, admits that religious experience often remains unaroused "until certain particular intellectual beliefs or ideas" come into play.[21] Renouncing intellectual probity, American philosophers argue, a religion relinquishes its claim to philosophical rigor. Appeals to the suprarational, as James demonstrates in his study of such phenomenon themselves have a foundation in logic, science, and experience. Lacking this basis, American pragmatism judges, religions fail to persuade believers.

Kaplan agrees. He announces that any religion demands that its members "accept, in general, its outlook on the world." Religion, on this understanding functions by creating rituals and symbols to affirm that acceptance. In this way, Kaplan assumes, Judaism requires Jews to observe certain formal practices that inculcate a specific view of reality.[22] He draws a practical conclusion from this theory. When the world view becomes unconvincing, he thinks, the practices no longer have a rationale. The

---

[20] Kaplan, *Religion of Ethical Nationhood*, p. 5.

[21] William James, *The Varieties of Religious Experience*. Edited by Martin E. Marty (New York: Penguin, 1982), pp. 514-515.

[22] Kaplan, *Judaism Without Supernaturalism*, p. 116.

effectiveness of religious practice depends on the credibility of its God-idea, on the coherence and persuasiveness of the beliefs about reality it expresses. Kaplan argues that modern Jews must understand the divine in rational terms. An idea of God, he claims, can influence people only if "based upon a verifiable conception of the human spirit." A valid definition of divinity, accordingly, must personify those beliefs about reality and human potential verified in everyday experience.[23]

Kaplan admits that modernity makes such verification difficult. His long process of disillusionment with Orthodoxy convinced him that the contemporary spirit necessitates a naturalistic, not a supernaturalist defence of religion. Kaplan begins by assuming a modern mentality that rejects supernaturalism, magic, and god-centered thinking. Such a mentality, in his mind, requires a reimagining of traditional theological concepts. For Kaplan, an idea of divinity justifies itself by its honest representation of human experience, by its ability to motivate human beings to improve themselves and their communities, and by its refusal to "hide behind the cloud of mystifying paradoxes."[24] Kaplan pursues this ideal in his analysis of Jewish religion. Whether explaining the modern meaning of Jewish rituals, suggesting the significance of Jewish beliefs, or rejecting the idea of Jewish chosenness, Kaplan considers metaphysics "virtually obsolete" in a world permeated by "functionalism or scientific methodology." He therefore uses a "religious humanism which is modern, scientifically-minded" to reinterpret Judaism. This is a tactical move intended to make the Judaism he constructs acceptable to

---

[23] Kaplan, *Greater Judaism*, pp. 490-491.

[24] Kaplan, *Religion of Ethical Nationhood*, pp. 5-7.

the particular audience he addresses.[25] He will accept only that set of doctrines which fits a modern Jew's preconceptions about the world, not because those preconceptions are true by a logical or empirical standard, but because any theory contradicting them would have no utilitarian value.

Kaplan's Rationalistic Approach

Kaplan realizes that his view of the divine changes the emphasis given in the Hebrew Bible. He denies, however, that he has introduced an essential change in Jewish religious thought. He sees no dichotomy between his rational approach to the meaning of God and that taken by the tradition. While he agrees that his approach differs from that of the Bible when read literally, he affirms that the tradition, correctly understood, confirms his views. Kaplan assures modern Jews that "Jewish tradition can without difficulty be translated into naturalistic religious experience."[26] Such a claim seems extraordinary in the light of modernity's assault on traditional religion in general and on Judaism in particular. From its inception, the modern temperament directed its most pointed criticism to religious belief. Religious leaders defended their beliefs by pointing to the miracles supporting it, to the revelation given it by God, and to the supernatural benefits accruing to those who appealed to their deity. Naturalistic experience contradicts each part of this defense. Miracles, by definition, deny that natural law inevitably rules experience. Modernity, in opposition to the belief in revelation, asserts that any person can discover the truth without recourse to a supernatural revealer. Naturalism condemns the appeal for supernatural aid as an unwarranted superstition. Kaplan articulates

---

[25] Kaplan, "Between Two Worlds," p. 139.

[26] Kaplan, *Purpose and Meaning of Jewish Existence*, p. 307.

his transnatural theology to show how the rationalistic interpretation of the deity, its practical effects, and its relationship to tradition combine in a persuasive paradigm for modern believers. Again, while disguised as modernism, Kaplan's thought undermines the rationalist's self-confidence and deconstructs theology in ways anticipating the postmodern.

A Functional View of Divinity

This "transnatural" theology includes what Kaplan identifies as the three major elements corresponding to the three challenges of modernity, functionalism, empiricism, and personalism: the term "God" refers not to an entity but to a function, divine manifestations appear in nature, and belief in God goes beyond the proof of natural facts.[27] For Kaplan, God exists not as an object in the world but as a function that objects exemplify. As noted above. Kaplan identifies this function as "making for salvation." The functional aspect of this definition arises from the way in which Kaplan describes discovery of the divine. For him, discovering God does not entail isolating a particular object within empirical experience. Instead, he claims that every time human beings discover purpose and significance they find evidence of God. People would find life valueless without such a sense of meaning, he avers. That people do in fact attribute value to life seems to him confirmation of the existence of divinity. In that sense, for Kaplan, human existence depends upon belief in God. Whether they use the name "God" or not, Kaplan feels, people cannot live without some conception of general purpose or significance. To live, he assumes, people must posit something that functions to give life meaning; they assume God, even if they deny God.

---

[27] Kaplan, *Questions Jews Ask*, pp. 94, 103, 125.

Atheism may be possible as a theoretical statement; it is impossible as a premise for living a human existence. Kaplan sees the theologian's task as presenting theism in such a way that people acknowledge what they had been unconsciously practicing all along.

Kaplan's View of Evil

This task requires Kaplan to develop a persuasive theory of reality. His reinterpretation of the divine as a functional process draws on natural evidence, the evidence of human experience. A serious critic of Kaplan contends that "No reconstructionist ever encountered the cosmic powers which make for life's worthwhileness." The critic continues by suggesting that Kaplan's position is self-contradictory. Kaplan begins by taking experience as the basis for all theories. He ends, however, by denying the power of experience when it seems to contradict the "divine forces" that cultivate human freedom, self-development, and progress.[28] The criticism appears for focus on the problem of evil. Kaplan's denies that the challenges of life's imperfections refute his belief in God. He clearly recognizes evils in the world. Humanity, he admits, faces several challenges from the world at large and from other human beings in particular. In fact, religion, Kaplan avers, functions to make people aware of the reality of evil. It teaches people to live "with clear recognition of the reality of evil" and "will combat pessimism" not by providing palliatives and illusions but by cultivating "creative faith in the possibility of the good".[29] Kaplan realizes that many theologians disagree with this activist interpretation. Jewish philosophers, for example, sought to

---

[28] Eliezer Berkovits, "Reconstructionist Theology: A Critical Evaluation," in his *Major Themes in Modern Philosophies of Judaism* (New York: Ktav, 1974), pp. 169-171.

[29] Kaplan, *Meaning of God*, p. 63

rationalize life and deny the reality of evil--for them "evil was merely non-existence." Jewish mystics, however, "not only recognized the reality of evil but was preoccupied with the problem of combatting it in *this* world."[30] Kaplan prefers the mystics to the philosophers since he feels that a God-idea succeeds only by mobilizing human resources. He advocates only that view of divinity which enables people to overcome the challenges of evil by stimulating action and self-confidence. Kaplan claims that his view of the divine follows the mystics and motivates action against evil more efficiently than a speculative or supernaturalistic theology.

Kaplan explains how, in his view, Jewish theology responds to the problem of evil: by identifying that against which humanity must struggle. Kaplan opposes two ways of understanding evil. Some systems equate it with the physical, the natural, that which is unchanged by human culture. These systems construe the sexual urge as one of humanity's chief stumbling blocks. In contrast, that which Kaplan calls the Jewish approach to ethics, identifies evil as perversions in the sphere of human relations. In particular, he thinks Judaism identifies such evil in the spheres of power: evil is the "lust to dominate." Judaism's view of divinity warns people against this lust and teaches them to restrain it.[31] Kaplan illustrates how the stories, associated with Jewish supernaturalism reveal a divinity concerned about protecting each individual's rights, championing the poor and defenseless. He claims that although modern Jews cannot accept the supernaturalism of these stories they can learn from it the purpose of religious law--harmonizing power and goodness. Defining God as those forces enabling individuals to exercise their

---

[30] Kaplan, *Greater Judaism*, p. 127.

[31] See the discussion throughout Kaplan, "Jewish Contribution to World Ethics."

own talents and develop their special skills, he argues, conveys the requirement to tame the will-to-power. All this transposes into naturalistic language the ideas expressed in the supernatural language of the Bible and makes the biblical approach to evil accessible to modern Jews.[32]

Kaplan uses biblical examples to prove his point. Kaplan's extended treatment of the story of Abraham, the Bible's paradigmatic Jew, illustrates his view of evil.[33] The Bible presents Abraham as a counterpoint to Adam. Whereas Adam evades his responsibility, Abraham accepts his. Whereas Adam brings sin and suffering on the world, Abraham brings success to his descendants. One of the most problematic aspects of that success, Kaplan admits, is that Abraham's heirs displace the original inhabitants of the land of Canaan and appropriate it for themselves. Read naturalistically, this story says that the original inhabitants through "wickedness" lost the land. Abraham is told to wait until they have, as it were, destroyed themselves. Kaplan interprets this history as proof that evil inevitably gives way before moral goodness. He claims that while such a view might have dangerous consequences from a modern standpoint, nevertheless, "it undoubtedly expresses a new kind of group sensitivity to ethical values."[34] The problem of evil, then, becomes a means by which the Jewish group stimulates its members to strive to become more moral. The teaching that one's fate in life depends upon one's morality, he argues, inspires people to live more responsible lives. A religion motivates ethical behavior by teaching the social consequences of any individual deed.

---

[32] *Ibid.*, pp. 1029, 1049.

[33] *Ibid.*, pp. 1023-1024.

[34] *Ibid.*, p. 1024.

Thus, Kaplan does not naively contend that people inevitably succeed in attaining their desires. Instead, he justifies apparent failure as a type of success. Being human does not entail achieving goals, but rather struggling to achieve them. When people rise to meet a challenge, even if they do not fully resolve it, they display their humanity. In this way evil calls forth the most human aspects of a person's character. Defenders of Kaplan argue against his detractors on just these grounds: Kaplan does not deny evil, instead he recognizes it as a test waiting for human response.[35] Evil, however, is only one aspect of the problem the critic points out. The more basic question is whether Kaplan indeed has the empirical proof he needs to make his claims about God's existence.

Nature and Kaplan's View of God

Kaplan's functional definition of God begins with the facts of nature. He discovers a search for meaning inherent in human nature. He points to evidence that confirms such meaning: those natural "forces and relationships" that nurture and support human ideals. In this way his functional view of the divine leads into a consideration of cosmology. His thought takes cosmology as seriously as does that of the medieval Jewish philosophers.[36] In his view God's manifestations appear in the empirical world of nature. Belief in God, for Kaplan, goes beyond the facts supported by these manifestations themselves. The facts merely show that various natural phenomena do support the human search for meaning. A belief in God combines these forces into

---

[35] See Lawrence Troster, "The Definition of Evil in Post-Holocaust Theology," *Conservative Judaism* 39:1 (1986), pp. 85-86, 88-89 and the response by Emmanuel Goldsmith, in *Conservative Judaism* 39:3 (1986), p. 89.

[36] See Richard Hirsch, "Mordecai Kaplan's Understanding of Religion and the Issue of Cosmology," in *Jewish Civilization: Essays and Studies* 1, edited by Ronald A. Brauner (Philadelphia: Reconstructionist Rabbinical College, 1979), pp. 205-219.

separate but related exemplifications of a general principle: the universe itself confirms humanity's highest visions. Kaplan admits that natural evidence alone cannot provide proof of such a principle: "We cannot infer the existence and nature of God from our sensory experience of the outer world." In that sense, belief in God is transnatural: an ideal abstracted from, but transcendent to, human experience of nature. In Kaplan's thinking, God does not interrupt the process of nature. Nevertheless, he claims that such a view, while rejecting the interventionist doctrine of miracles, still affirms a doctrine of divine purpose. Nature, for Kaplan, does indeed demonstrate purpose and plan, it does progress towards an ultimate goal. This plan and progress, according to Kaplan, need not imply a supernatural deity who imposes the divine will on the world. God's reality as the *principle* of daily renewal need not, Kaplan insists, entail either that God acts according to an arbitrary will or that God exist as an independent being.[37] Instead of supernaturalism, the modern Jew can affirm the principle of change as the basis for evolution and progress. Understanding God's creativity, for Kaplan, means recognizing the existence of "change that is not entropy." The Jew who accepts the functional reality of such change, he asserts, affirms the divine as the principle of creation without attributing either arbitrary desire to God or imagining God as one being among all others.[38]

Kaplan traces the roots of this belief to human experience: people experience success in their struggle to satisfy their needs. He suggests that when people accomplish their goals they gain self-confidence. Reflecting on this experience, he muses, they generalize about the nature of life itself.

---

[37] Kaplan, *Purpose and Meaning of Jewish Existence*, p. 97.

[38] *Ibid.*, p. 79.

Kaplan's transnatural religion interprets that generalization as recognition of a cosmic principle reinforcing modern optimism. While not drawn directly from sense experience, then, his rational religion does use empirical data--the data of the human response to the natural world.[39]

The Personal In Kaplan's View of the Divine

While Kaplan emphasizes the compatibility of his God-idea with rationality and empirical evidence, his definition of divinity begins with subjective human experience. He admits that God cannot be inferred from "sensory experience of the outer world." The facticity of divinity in his system grows out of human introspection, not out of analysis of the external world.[40] The word "God" as Kaplan uses it refers less to external realities than to the human perception of those realities. The divine manifests itself in the human will. Human beings in his opinion attain salvation only by exercising choice and decision. The experience of such willed salvation provides, for Kaplan, the basis for divinity. People, he posits, experience the divine whenever they "escape from the sense of frustration" and gain "a feeling of permanence in the midst of universal flux." In his philosophy all human acts of personal transcendence through an effort of the will verify religion's claims.[41] The human response to nature, rather than nature itself, constitutes Kaplan's proof for the usefulness of the idea of God.

Kaplan's cosmology combines with his functionalism to offer a social program that stimulates communal awareness. He believes that human beings

---

[39] Kaplan, *Future of the American Jew*, p. 259; *Questions Jews Ask*, p. 128.

[40] Kaplan, *Questions Jews Ask*, p. 128.

[41] Kaplan, *Greater Judaism*, p. 78.

create their world by making an ordered meaning out of the random sense data they receive. Creation, as he understands it, refers the synthetic formation of significance occurring when facts and meaning combine. In so far as Kaplan defines God as the source of meaning, God is creator, since without these signifiers of purpose, creation could not occur. God, defined by Kaplan as the sum of those positive forces aiding human self-development, "creates" the world by providing a transcendent purpose that unifies a human life. To call God creator in Kaplan's sense means to affirm that human beings are enabled to make sense out of the chaos of experience because they intuit a meaning that unifies that experience. People recognize God as creator, for Kaplan, when they experience the "meaning of the world" through self-reflection. According to him they exhibit God's reality whenever they experience the world as valuable and meaningful. Without this sense of meaning, Kaplan avers, human life would lack direction and coherence. In this sense he calls God "creator" of existence.[42] Thus, salvation or self-fulfillment in Kaplan's theory depends on an intuition of purpose and meaning of personal existence. God, according to this view, represents those personal aspects of human life that inspire and call forth the highest human ideals. To call God "personal" for Kaplan means that no human fulfillment is possible except through actualizing one's personhood. God, understood in this way, also comprises the moral, a point on which Kaplan is insistent. That God represents a principle by which persons actualize their potential also emphasizes the ethical demand "to choose between right and wrong, good and evil."[43] God's function in human salvation in Kaplan's view is to ensure the

---

[42] Kaplan, *Questions Jews Ask*, pp. 90-94.

[43] Kaplan, *Questions Jews Ask*, p. 110; *Judaism Without Supernaturalism* p. 27.

motivation and idealism needed for personal growth and development and to confront each person with the freedom to choose. Kaplan finds in this theology a means to inspire personal devotion precisely by requiring people to make choices and to live as humanly as possible.

The significance of this emphasis becomes clear when related to the philosophy of Nietzsche. Nietzsche remarked on the claim that "self-preservation" was the ultimate goal of all organic life. He saw that desire as a result, not as the foundational impulse. Nietzsche identified the primal concern as a "will to power." Individuals desire autonomy, self-development, self-creation.[44] Kaplan has made the idea of God the key to such auto-creativity. Ironically, he seems to take Nietzsche at his word when he says, "If there were gods, how could I bear not to be one?" Kaplan assures this forerunner of postmodernism that the theology of divinity works precisely to make him into one of the gods.

---

[44] See Friedrich Nietzsche, *Basic Writings of Nietzsche* Trans, ed, and with Commentaries by Walter Kaufmann (New York: Modern Library, 1992), p. 211.

Chapter 7:

Education and American Religion

Religions of Revelation and the Spirit of Democracy

While belief in God provides the underpinning for democratic liberty, the price of that liberty is interpretive vigilance. Perhaps the greatest threat to a democracy lies in the temptation to tyranny that arises from a life of freedom. In the wake of World War Two, members of the displaced Frankfort School in the Institute for Social Research focused on the meaning of authority, the threat of totalitarianism, and the inner drive that paradoxically makes the first free choice a decision for bondage.[1] In this spirit, Erich Fromm describes the development of democratic liberty and the terrifying aspects of individualism it creates.[2] Protestantism, he claims, began a process of individuation, cutting people loose from the ties that had bound them to the outside world. Capitalism continued that process and added new economic freedom for the individual. While offering more opportunities that new liberty isolated people even more dramatically, leaving them at the mercy of great

---

[1] See Martin Jay , *The Dialectical Imagination: A History of the Frankfurt School and the Institute of Social Research 1923-1950* (Boston: Little, Brown and Company, 1973), pp. 113-142.

[2] Erich Fromm, *Escape From Freedom* (New York: Holt, Rinehart and Winston, 1941).

impersonal forces sweeping around them. A democracy institutionalizes that experience of liberty. It provides structures that divide human activity into independent and isolated spheres which leave individuals free from external authorities. Yet, Fromm points out, such spheres of liberty by themselves do not ensure a free and productive life. He claims that progress occurs only when democracy offers the opportunity to develop personal initiative and spontaneity "not only in certain private and spiritual matters, but above all in the activity fundamental to every man's existence, his work."[3] A democracy unable to provide its citizens with such an integrated freedom according to Fromm faces grave danger.

The experience of living in an impersonal world, Fromm suggests, overwhelms many modern people. They rebel against the isolation and powerlessness they feel. Modernity, Fromm remarks, imbues people "with a feeling of insignificance and powerlessness." [4]In the face of this feeling citizens in a democracy often cope with their freedom, he warns, by sacrificing it. At its best democracy stimulates spontaneity and a positive use of freedom. In other cases, he advises, democracy arouses in its members a fear of freedom. Citizens, he warns, seek refuge from their isolation by rejecting liberty for promises of a renewed sense of security and belonging. Fromm points to the temptation to "eliminate the gap that has arisen" between the "individual self and the world."[5] He shows how that gap emerges in three realms--that of religion, that of the economy, and that of democracy. These three can be related to three modern concerns of religion: the meaning of

---

[3] *Ibid.*, p. 299.

[4] *Ibid.*, p. 128.

[5] *Ibid.*, p. 163.

revelation, the nature of ethics, and the structure of education. Each of these three can be understood as what Fromm calls authoritarian, as a refuge from that individual freedom democracy promises. A revelation can provide an immutable blueprint of truth; it can establish an absolute set of values and rules that must be followed without question; it can offer a pedagogical indoctrination into a tradition. Fromm understands these temptations and addresses each of them in his work. While offering a psychology of religion, he also provides a model of the interpretive process. He demonstrates how to decode traditional materials so they stimulate thought, choice and humanism rather than authoritarianism. Although clearly "modern" rather than "postmodern," Fromm points the way to that interpretive stance which finds an infinitude of meanings in a text whose literal meaning seems untenable. Kaplan follows this approach, and so a study of Fromm's hermeneutics may illuminate the orientation that Kaplan chooses.

Humanistic Religion and Interpreting Revelation

Several of Fromm's books contrast humanistic and authoritarian religion.[6] Religions, he claims, fall into one of two types. Any of the particular traditions, Judaism or Christianity or even atheism, for example, may exemplify either of these categories. Paradoxically Fromm maintains, the atheist may, in truth, espouse humanistic religion and the "believer" actually practice a type of idolatry best described as authoritarian religion. The difference between the two types of religion according to Fromm lies in their respective openness to human innovation, initiative, and creativity. The crucial

---

[6] See Erich Fromm, *Psychoanalysis and Religion* (New York: Yale University Press, 1950); *You Shall Be As Gods: A Radical Interpretation of the Old Testament and its Tradition* (New York: Holt, Rinehart and Winston, 1966).

test he employs is whether the religion in question is one furthering human development and stimulating the "unfolding" of "specifically human powers or whether it is "one paralyzing them."[7] A humanistic religion for Fromm enables its adherents to achieve self-fulfillment and provides a mechanism by which they can attain that goal.

An authoritarian religion, as Fromm understands it, often offers its followers an "escape from freedom" through the authority of revealed scriptures. Fromm claims that taking scriptures as a powerful "other," individuals surrender their independent thinking to the revealed will. Such an approach represents what Fromm calls "the tendency to give up the independence of one's own individual self and to fuse one's self with somebody or something outside of oneself in order to acquire the strength which the individual self is lacking."[8] Humanistic religion, by contrast, according to Fromm, uses a revealed scripture to stimulate a creative humanistic response. Fromm often uses a famous talmudic example to illustrate humanistic religion. According to that story several rabbis were debating whether a particular type of stove was ritually pure or impure. The majority of rabbis, following Rabbi Joshua, concluded that the stove was impure. Rabbi Eliezer the Great, however, held out against the majority. To prove that the stove was pure he resorted to several miracles. Finally, when the other rabbis continued to ignore his arguments, Rabbi Eliezer appealed for a divine judgment. A heavenly voice called out "Why do you argue against my son Rabbi Eliezer? Everything he states is true!" Rabbi Joshua, however, cited Deuteronomy 30:12, stating that the Torah "is not in heaven." God has

---

[7] *Ibid.*, p. 26.

[8] Fromm, *Escape From Freedom*, p. 163.

given humanity the task of interpreting Torah and must accept the verdict given by pure human logic.[9] A humanistic religion refuses to allow the divine to veto human ingenuity.

Fromm explores the freedom associated with such creative interpretation of revelation. He claims that the rabbinic understanding of the Bible taught people to look at a revealed text as a point of departure, as an inspiration for independent thinking. He argues that this approach to an authoritative scripture, an approach that refuses to retreat into the text as an escape from decision making, forces people to choose positive freedom. Revelation, he cautions, cannot substitute for a responsible use of liberty. Accepting the authority of a scripture does not, Fromm holds, mean abdicating reason, but rather discovering a new arena in which it must be employed. Fromm considers such an approach to the Bible an essential step in the preparation for "the concept of complete freedom."[10]

Fromm recognizes that texts other than those of a religious tradition offer exercises in such freedom. He shows how analysis of dreams, fairy tales, and rituals provides equal access to such freedom. Through such a creative approach to texts, Fromm suggests, people confront their inner layers of personality. Learning to decode the recondite language of these works affords an insight into the possibilities of human freedom. Fromm argues that this "forgotten language" of myth and symbolism "brings us in touch with one of the most significant sources of wisdom."[11] Humanistic religions may not be the exclusive means by which people learn to decode this language.

---

[9] *Ibid.*, pp. 45-46; *You Shall Be As Gods*, pp. 62-64.

[10] Fromm, *You Shall Be As Gods*, p. 23.

[11] Erich Fromm, *The Forgotten Language: An Introduction to the Understanding of Dreams, Fairy Tales and Myths* (New York: Grove, 1951), p. 10.

Nevertheless, a humanistic approach to revelation may indeed transform a revealed scripture from an authoritarian refuge from freedom into a gateway to positive freedom. Fromm, as in the story of Rabbi Eliezer, often explicitly refers to Judaism as an example of a humanistic religion and applies his interpretive technique to that tradition.

Revelation and Humanistic Ethics

The distinction between authoritarian and humanistic religion finds its complement for Fromm in a distinction between authoritarian and productive ethics.[12] As with authoritarian religion, so authoritarian ethics in his typology demands submission and a surrender of the will. It offers an escape from freedom by supplying absolute standards and rules by which to determine every human act. The criteria for a good action, according to authoritarian ethics according to Fromm, lie outside of the human being. He describes this ethics as one which holds people to an external standard, one which demands that they measure up to ideals that stand over against them. By acting against their inclinations, by submitting to a heteronomous authority, the authoritarian ethics Fromm depicts promises its followers moral worth. In such a view, an outside source informs humanity about "what is good" and thereupon "lays down the laws and norms of conduct."[13] Fromm contends that in such a system the human individual escapes the necessity for decision making by resorting to these heteronomous laws and this external authority to determine what is good and right.

---

[12] See Erich Fromm, *Man For Himself: An Inquiry into the Psychology of Ethics* (New York; Holt, Rinehart, and Winston, 1947).

[13] *Ibid.*, p. 18.

A productive ethics, according to Fromm, makes human happiness the standard of ethical action. While, as an emotion, this goal seems subjective, Fromm claims that, in fact, it stems from certain objective conditions. Fromm describes how human beings feel deprived and unhappy when their inherent powers are crippled. He suggests, in contrast, that they feel joy and satisfaction when they successfully complete a task. The first criteria he sets for a productive ethics is the ability to affirm and confirm this experience of human success. A productive ethic, as he portrays it, stimulates those actions, the completion of which provide people with a sense of satisfaction in personal achievement. Fromm calls the objective conditions necessary for this experience "productivity."[14] For an ethic to be humanistic rather than authoritarian it must focus on creating the essential environment for human success: it must encourage human productivity.

A second ingredient that Fromm associates with an experience of success is more intangible. Productivity, to be satisfying, he feels, must engage the full range of human possibilities. Mere mechanical production, according to Fromm, leaves a person unsatisfied. Were people only to interact with the world as a set of "dead," impersonal, or isolated things, they would get no joy from their productivity. Fromm insists that an ethics must awaken people to an awareness of the living, passionate, aspects of the world. An ethics should stimulate engagement with the world, interest in others, an intimate relationship between an individual self and all other selves.[15] Froom argues that an authoritarian ethics locks the individual within an isolated and

---

[14] *Ibid.*, p. 177.

[15] *Ibid.*, p. 109.

self-contained system. By contrast, he claims, productive ethics discloses the ever new possibilities of interaction with those outside the self.

Fromm does not discuss the religious dimensions of ethics or a specifically religious ethics. Nevertheless, one may assume that an authoritarian religion would espouse an authoritarian ethics. A humanistic religion would advocate a productive ethics. Since Judaism considers its revealed texts no less an ethical system than a system of ideas and values, the question of whether it is or is not a productive ethics is crucial. Again, Fromm's analysis raises but does not answer the problem. Can a modern view of revelation enable Jewish ethics to be responsive, creative, and productive? Jewish law, halakha, sometimes seems to use a humanistic approach that stimulates productivity. At other times, however, it employs an authoritarianism at odds with Fromm's ideals. Only a consistent mode of interpretation that deliberately focuses the halakhic process on human self-development can ensure continuing the humanistic impulse in Jewish ethics.

Spontaneity and Religious Education

Fromm recognizes that the beginnings of modern freedom stem from the Protestant Reformation. Luther, he suggests, removed the authority of the Church in religious matters and thereby passed all responsibility to the individual. In this way, Fromm claims, Luther's ideas became "one source of the development of political and spiritual freedom in modern society." At the same time, Fromm laments that the Reformation left human beings more powerless and isolated than ever before. He depicts the newly liberated Protestant individual as plagued by a sense of "the existence of an innate evilness," unrelieved by the promise of forgiveness through church indulgences. This condition, Fromm concludes, "makes it impossible for any man to perform any good deed on the basis of his nature."[16] Luther, Fromm concludes, left the individual with an unproductive freedom, a nominal freedom within which a person could not enjoy spontaneity of response.

Fromm contrasts the freedom of spontaneity with the pessimistic freedom that leads to isolation and despair. The way to overcome the dichotomy established by the Reformation is through character formation in the social process. Ideas, Fromm argues, "have an emotional matrix."[17] He looks to education to provide that matrix. Education, according to Fromm, shapes the way these ideas develop in a society and become dynamic forces. Fromm defines "the social function of education" as that of preparing each person to play a particular social role. He feels that the economic and political needs of a society determine the aims and purposes of its education. Because he recognizes that education socializes each individual to specific concerns and skills necessary in the society, Fromm analyzes its effect on creating character. He discovers that the techniques of pedagogy rather than any particular curriculum or content area are most formative. He remarks that the "methods of education" rather than the goal or aim of education exhibit the character of a culture. The experiences a student undergoes rather than the facts a student learns, he comments, "constitute one of the mechanisms by which character is formed."[18] He traces the dichotomy between the authoritarian and humanistic through pedagogical forms. He calls an educational system that treats its students as hostile creatures to be tamed and mastered authoritarian. He charges that such a model of learning stifles

---

[16] Fromm, *Escape From Freedom*, p. 93.

[17] *Ibid.*, p. 307.

[18] *Ibid.*, pp. 313-314.

individual spontaneity. In contrast, he calls an educational system that creates opportunities for creativity humanistic. He holds that such an orientation reinforces personal initiative and treats students as sources of wisdom, not merely recipients of it. This type of education, he thinks, enhances the probability of spontaneity.

Fromm diagnoses the problem of American education as one that imagines students as passive recipients of information "mainly useful for the purposes of the market." Fromm declares that what he calls the "marketing orientation" works against creativity, productivity, and spontaneity.[19] He finds American schools guilty of this sort of pedagogical model. The purpose of American education, he muses, seems to be that of "breaking the will" of the child. So-called "liberal" forms of education, he insists, actually aim at the same ends. They merely disguise authority from its "overt" expression in several covert ways, establishing an "anonymous authority" which the students must internalize.[20]

This type of learning according to Fromm assumes that human nature is evil and negative. It begins with a lack of faith in human ability. He describes a humanistic education, in contrast, as beginning with faith in human potential. The purpose of such an education, he avers, is not to impose a curriculum on a recalcitrant subject, but to provide an environment for the realization of individual capabilities. An education based on faith in each person's worth and value Fromm posits as the very opposite of a manipulative education which imposes an external will on the child.

---

[19] Fromm, *Man For Himself*, pp. 83-84.

[20] *Ibid.*, p. 160.

Fromm acknowledges that religions also exhibit these two views of humanity. Some lack faith in human beings. Others inculcate faith in human potential. A democracy, he argues, requires faith in the individual and an educational system reflecting that faith.[21] In these reflections Fromm does not explicitly analyze religious education. A defense of Judaism within a democracy, however, would offer just such an analysis. It would seek to discern how a Jewish education might be an education in humanistic faith, an education that unlocks personal potential rather than imposing an authoritarian structure on it.

Revelation and Democratic Faith

Mordecai Kaplan's view of revelation in the Jewish tradition parallels Fromm's concerns at almost every point. Kaplan recognizes that an authoritarian revelation needs an exegetical method for making it an inspiration to independence. He also proposes a view of revealed ethics that stimulates rather than stifles human choosing. Finally, he imagines a religious educational system that provides a laboratory for democratic experience. Kaplan contends that an American religion verifies its claim for a divine revelation on the basis of its affirmation of human freedom. He considers a religious text such as the Jewish *Torah* a divine revelation only when it promotes human self-fulfillment. A religion whose view of revelation restricts rather than expands its adherents' potential for development, he holds, testifies to its estrangement from God.[22] Certainly, Jewish views of the divine differ from those of non-Jews. This difference, however, Kaplan claims, stems from

---

[21] *Ibid.*, pp. 209-211.

[22] Kaplan, *Future of the American Jew*, p. 382.

a difference in historical experience. Jewish revelation as he describes it differs from Christian or Muslim revelation because of different experiential foundations for the recognition and identification of empirical forces as divine.[23] Kaplan's test of a true religion does not examine its traditional origins but rather its effect on those who believe in it.

From Kaplan's perspective belief in the validity of a religious revelation depends neither on its supernaturalism nor on its dogmatic assertion of truth. Instead, modern adherents to a tradition can, he believes, recognize its validity as one component in an organically related complex of truths. Such a view of revelation entails, he feels, an affirmation of diverse religious traditions rather than the claim that any one tradition alone represents the entire truth humanity needs. For Kaplan, each particular revelation needs the complementary content of every other tradition. Thus, he argues, Jews should revere *Torah* as revelation insofar as it exemplifies the experience that have taught them the importance of freedom and the presence of natural forces supporting human self-fulfillment. They cannot, however, deny the revelatory force of other traditions. Kaplan identifies "all institutions, laws, and tendencies" that lead to salvation as divine revelations.[24] All these traditions are needed to protect democratic society from the idolatrous absolutes pursuing them. Democracies often succumb to the temptation to absolutize one or another truth. The variety of revealed religions, however, guards against such temptation.

Some critics argue that Kaplan's interpretation of revelation is flawed. These critics, like the Reformation theologians Fromm discusses, posit an

---

[23] Kaplan, *Greater Judaism*, p. 470; compare *Religion of Ethical Nationhood*, p. 103.

[24] Kaplan, *Future of the American Jew*, p. 130.

inherent weakness in human beings. Fromm and Kaplan, they would argue, place too much confidence in human ability. Human beings cannot, they claim, predict in advance the form that the divine address takes. Human finitude precludes a definitive statement about God's nature. Kaplan rejects this view and charges existentialist theology with advancing "Kierkegaard's and Freud's gloomy notions" about humanity. He recommends instead philosophical naturalism's "revolt against the pessimism of traditional religion."[25] The brooding death-fascinated aspects of existentialism could support such a charge. At the heart of Jewish theological existentialism, however, lies a willingness for surprise that Kaplan does not recognize. Existentialists often begin with empirical evidence no less than Kaplan and demand rationalist rigor. Rationalism, however, leads beyond itself to recognize its limits. Thus, Franz Rosenzweig admits that reason must judge the biblical story of Balaam's talking ass as a myth or fairy tale. Nevertheless, he insists that when he hears it read in synagogue "it speaks to me out of the open Torah" it takes on another meaning. He is ready to be surprised by that meaning without laying down conditions as to what can and cannot be accepted as true.[26] Some Jews find Kaplan's rationalistic strictures adequate only as a point of departure. They discover just that meaning which Kaplan defines as religion only beyond the limits of rational inquiry and scientific method. Only a transcendent faith can supply the sense of purpose modernity requires.

Kaplan recognizes the force of such an argument but relegates it to an exclusive elite. He claims that this esoteric approach satisfies only "Jewish

---

[25] Kaplan, *Judaism Without Supernaturalism*, pp. 9-10.

[26] Nahum N. Glatzer, *Franz Rosenzweig: His Life and Thought* (New York: Schocken, 1961), pp. 245-246.

intellectuals who look to religion to open up to them areas of experience that transcend both science and philosophy." He thinks the appeal of such an esoteric view too restricted to be useful for modern Jews.[27] He has patience only for a popular ideology accessible to the general public. Kaplan's response to his critics, then, relies on his argument that the Jewish approach to revealed texts should teach a lesson to Americans generally. The optimistic and humanistic emphasis on exegesis corresponds well with the American need to provide an alternative to a flight from freedom. The existentialist criticism of Kaplan misses the problem of democracy to which he addresses his interpretations of Torah.

Kaplan and Idolatrous Religion

Kaplan, like Fromm, perceives the dangers lurking behind democratic freedom. He claims that the institutional protection of spontaneity cannot succeed without being infused with the passion which theology brings. He charges that naturalistic philosophy alone is "unable by itself to motivate what we generally understand as the good life." While he avers that his reconstruction of Judaism succeeds where philosophy fails, he might also agree that in changed conditions a changed theology is needed. Perhaps a theology combining his realistic appraisal of life's potential with an existentialist recognition of the surprise ensured by God's ultimate freedom to perform the unexpected can achieve what neither theology accomplishes alone.

Kaplan's opposition to any idolatry or fixation on one unchanging truth suggests that he would welcome innovations such as the integration of his realism with existentialism. Understanding his view of idolatry as neurotic

---

[27] Kaplan, *Purpose and Meaning of Jewish Existence*, pp. 285-286.

fixation requires reviewing his functional definition of the divine. Although sketched generally in the previous chapter, the review here focuses on the dynamic effect of belief. Theology works, according to Kaplan, only when it stimulates active change. As people grow and develop their symbolic system of self-representation, he feels, should also change.

Kaplan's view of God, his theology oriented towards people's needs, opposes false notions of the divine. Kaplan describes such a theology as a tapestry in which the "human ideals of truth, good, and beauty [are] interwoven in a pattern of holiness." He regards that tapestry as a changing one in which colors and textures take on new forms in response to new challenges. He suggests that the penalty for refusal to change, for a theology that remains stagnant, "is the failure to reach the conviction of life's true worth."[28] He argues that "any form of worship directed to a God who is conceived in terms that no longer satisfy the deepest spiritual insights of the age" represents idolatry. An ethically sensitive religion continually fights the temptation to idolatry.[29] A theology that remains fixated at an early stage of development becomes what Kaplan would term idolatrous.

Kaplan understands idolatry as multivalent. All idols, however, share a common element--they fall short of evoking the fullest possible "opportunities for self-development." Kaplan affirms that "for all times and for all causes the criterion that distinguishes falsity from truth [is] *not enough*."[30] Various useful aspects of human life--nationalism, any "partisan loyalty," and even science itself may become an idol. Kaplan argues that historical change may create

---

[28] Kaplan, *Greater Judaism*, pp. 197, 26, 31.

[29] Kaplan, *Meaning of God*, p. 6.

[30] *Ibid.*, pp. 146-147.

idolatry as "the truths of one age commonly become the idolatries of the next." An inherited God idea, accepted without critical thinking, becomes an idol, requiring a "holy iconoclasm...to destroy such unholy idolatry."[31] Jews, Kaplan urges, must struggle against such idolatry, revolting against the attempt to impose traditional views on a new generation.

Kaplan's theology provides a standard-nature's God-that not only identifies idolatry but also the faith which renders false religion idolatrous. Complacent religion, he charges, contradicts a natural principle--growth and development. Kaplan considers that contradiction alone reason enough for rejecting such religion. Kaplan recognizes another form of idolatry--routine. He cautions that routine worship may become idolatrous, that communities may "identify God with that which is ungodly." He warns that dogma and withdrawal from the world are "not the way to deal with the danger of idolatry."[32] Instead he advocates an active reformulation of the religious tradition, continual reassessment of a religion's message. One form of his activism is that of interpretation. By reinterpreting tradition he moves from complacency to a participation in the creative process itself.

Democracy and Jewish Education

This approach to idolatry also applies to an idolatry of writing, of learning, and of education. Geoffrey Hartman contends that Judaism channelled the energies that other religions put into making artistic images, into the craft of writing. "The prohibition against images," he suggests,

---

[31] *Ibid.*, pp. 172-173.

[32] *Ibid.*, p. 257.

"obliged a channeling into the written word of imaginal energies."[33] Kaplan recognizes this maneuver, but thinks that it does not go far enough. Students must be taught an iconoclasm of writing and interpretation no less than of artistic images. As a postmodern, Kaplan educates students for response, not for recapitulation of truths. He demands a "democratic" education by which he means one that elicits a variety of interpretations, encouraging students to discover and create diversity of meanings in the texts they study..

Kaplan's reinterpretation of religion for democracy has a pragmatic goal. Kaplan recognizes, no less than Fromm, the dangers of modern freedom. He claims that the "machine economy" has threatened human security and the sense of personal worth. Out of the insecurity this economy produces, Kaplan asserts, people have been "seized with a craving for protection from exploitation and for security against unemployment and starvation."[34] Kaplan reinterprets Jewish religion as a means to train people the positive use of freedom that can combat this malaise. Education as technical training cannot, he thinks, respond to the modern crisis. Attempts to enable individuals to cope with modernity by manipulating machines, in his view, only lock them more securely into the cycle of dependency and despair of the "machine economy." In contrast, he claims that a religious education utilizes all its resources to teach an approach to life. It cultivates what he calls "the habits of moral responsibility and good will" which alone can avert the catastrophe threatening democracies.[35]

---

[33] Hartman, *Saving the Text*, p. 17.

[34] Kaplan, *Judaism Without Supernaturalism*, p. 88.

[35] *Ibid.*, p. 84.

Kaplan argues that every educational system has, in fact, a "two fold aim: the growth of the individual and the welfare of the community."[36] These two aims, however, do not contradict one another. They are natural complements. While American education tends to stress the former in its secular schools, religious schools should inculcate the latter. They do this, according to Kaplan, not by teaching a different curriculum than the public schools but by teaching it in a different way. Kaplan advises Jewish schools to adopt the same subject matter as that taught in the public grade schools and high schools. It should teach those subjects, Kaplan argues, as the material upon which youth can construct a responsible ethics. The task of Jewish education, in his view, is to use the curriculum of general education "as a base for those human and spiritual values which would relate these students to the task of building the better world to be.[37]

This vision of education synthesizes the criticism that education must focus on personal development with a passionate concern for the content that is studied. Kaplan recognizes the continuity between modern methods of study, particularly those of the universities, and the approach he associates with Judaism. Such education encourages social conscience and affects daily living because it addresses the central concerns of democratic society. When human beings seek education, when they strive to satisfy their curiosity and actualize social values, they participate in the divine process of furthering salvation, of enabling people to reach their full potential. Thus Kaplan's

---

[36] Kaplan, *Future of the American Jew*, p. 481.

[37] *Ibid.*, p. 389.

pedagogy envisions democracy and religion joining forces to create opportunities for personal development and self-fulfillment.[38]

Drawing on the resources of Judaism, Kaplan shows that a free society demands just that educational openness and applicability characteristic of Jewish pedagogy. He emphasizes the universal significance of "wisdom," of "Hochmah," as both a method and a content with which human being must be passionately engaged, just to retain their humanity.[39] Judaism specifically, but religion in general as well, contributes to education in a democratic society by constantly renewing a passionate concern both for the content studied and the methods used in that study. Judaism shows its attention to the social order no less by a demand that its books be given an honored place in the curriculum than by its stimulation of an ardor for learning. Kaplan's portrayal of Jewish interests in learning suggests a valuable prophetic model for social involvement. Kaplan finds in Jewish education a training for that spontaneous living which Fromm considers essential in a democracy.

Education for Democracy

This practical agenda of reinterpretation that Kaplan offers takes shape in his vision of religious education. Kaplan laments that American education focuses so completely on the individual that it ignores the needs of civil society itself. He complains that whether liberal or traditional the secular curriculum "has stressed the individual at the expense of the social,interest." This tendency cultivates a selfishness that impairs the welfare of the society.

---

[38] See ibid., pp. 67. 68, 86, 120 and *idem., Judaism Without Supernaturalism*, p. 110; *Questions Jews Ask*, pp. 84, 87, 94, 103; *Meaning of God*, pp. 26-30, 82-83.

[39] Barbara Ann Swyhart, "Reconstructionism: 'Hochmah' as an Ethical Principle," *Judaism* 24:4 (1977): 436-445.

The power that education provides an individual, Kaplan laments, tends to be used for "personal ends," for private benefit, rather than for the good of all.[40] Perhaps, by its very nature, civil education must focus on such personal uses of education. Democratic society, however, requires that its members learn the necessity of a wider scope of concern. Religious education in a democracy should teach that lesson. Jewish education, for example, should have as its goal, Kaplan avers, training students "to regard all power which the individual possesses and acquires as misused, unless, it is somehow shared with all mankind."[41] Without religion's training in values, democratic education tends to destroy itself from within.

Kaplan reports on a survey that revealed the appalling ignorance of American college students about American history. He finds the survey itself disturbing--it assumed that the knowledge needed for good citizenship consists of a series of facts rather than in a world view conducive to democratic values. In contrast, Kaplan insists that the true test of the students would be an examination of their attitudes.[42] How might students cultivate such a democratic world view? Kaplan reviews the traditional Jewish love of learning and discovers that its success lies in its educational method, in the way it *used* classical sources rather than in the content of those sources. He recognizes that the Jewish contribution lies both in its specific content and in its method of employing that content. He argues that the religious nature of Jewish education stems not from "the presumed supernatural source of its subject matter" but from seeing such study as "character training to enable the Jew

---

[40] Kaplan, *Future of the American Jew*, p. 483.

[41] *Ibid.*, p. 484.

[42] *Ibid,*. pp. 493-494.

to do his share toward the making of a better world."[43] The methods used in studying texts are critical factors for improving learning generally. The significance of religion in education lies in its vision of the method and purpose of study, a method that Kaplan discovers in Judaism. The success of a religious tradition lies in precisely its ability to transmit this vision by interpreting its classic texts in a modern way. Kaplan devotes his reinterpretation of Judaism to achieving this goal.

Kaplan's Pedagogy for Democracy

Kaplan envisions a democratic pedagogy in America infused with the values of Judaic religion. Kaplan sees religion as a socializing instrument within an individualistic society. Its task, therefore should be to help mold the educational system.[44] Education for democratic life, according to Kaplan, must inculcate the skills students need so they can distinguish between times calling for passion and those calling for reason. That task requires the educator to face new challenges. Traditional pedagogues, in his view, merely transmitted facts and truths. The new teacher that Kaplan envisions must perform a different function. Kaplan describes two functions that this teacher performs. The teacher makes students aware that the tradition has developed in stages, that it is a dynamic, living organism. Secondly, the teacher stimulates students to play their own part in shaping and developing that tradition, advancing it beyond its present stage. Kaplan calls this dilemma, that of transmitting a dynamic process rather than a fixed content "one of the most perplexing problems in education" since it requires those who receive the material taught

---

[43] *Ibid.*, p. 488 (see the discussion, pp. 480-516).

[44] *Ibid,*. pp. 518-522.

to participate in the forming of that very material.[45] His program of education, of reinterpreting religious tradition for a democracy, addresses that very difficult problem. That solution appears as distinctively "postmodern." Kaplan demands that students regard the Bible and Jewish subjects in just the way that Daniel Boyarin suggests. For Boyarin, "The text of the Torah is gapped and dialogical, and into the gaps the reader slips, interpreting and completing the text in accordance with the codes of his or her culture."[46] Kaplan's ideal student grows to self-realization through grappling with such a demanding text. Education is "salvific" in Kaplan's sense because it indirectly leads to actualizing the individual and preserving the society. Since the interpreter cannot help but infuse social values from a distinctive culture in the process of reading, both Kaplan and Boyarin are confident that engagement with the texts will lead to a preservation of the "religion" of those texts, restructuring them to fit a new context. The utilitarian aspect of Kaplan's Judaism, that it enhances the ability of the American community and its members to survive, is subsumed under the interpretive trops given by a free environment and the contextual sensitivity that Kaplan's view of the American crisis reveals. Kaplan may have misunderstood which interpretations worked most effectively in that crisis. His technique, however, articulated a relevant soluton to the American dilemma based on a postmodernist awareness of how to use words to achieve one's aims.

---

[45] Kaplan, *Judaism Without Supernaturalism*, p. 14.

[46] Daniel Boyarin, *Intertextuality and the Reading of Midrash* (Bloomington: Indiana University Press, 1990), p. 14.

Chapter 8:

Progress and American Religion

The Test of American Democracy

A justly famous passage by Walter Benjamin catches the disillusionment with progress that marks contemporary thought.[1] He describes the angel of history which he finds portrayed in a Paul Klee painting. The angel is turned toward the past. It wishes to stay and repair the ruins of paradise. A storm, however, catches the wings of the angel and will not allow it to perform this task of restoration. It "propels him into the future to which his back is turned" and flings the debris of Eden's destruction into an ever increasing pile of junk. That storm, Benjamin wryly remarks, is "progress." For Benjamin progress is "myth," that is, the ever recurring return of the same, which only appears to be different. In the modern world, innovation is expected; novelty is predictable; progress *is* return. Humanity, Benjamin laments, departs reconciled from its past gaily, because it never realizes that it treads a well worn path. In fact, he counters, progress disguises the terror, the horror of human change. Benjamin even calls the concept of progress "the figleaf"

---

[1] Walter Benjamin, *Illuminations*, edited and with an Introduction by Hannah Arendt. Trans. Harry Zohn (New York: Schocken, 1968), pp. 257-258.

covering people's aversion to change.[2] Contemporary thinkers tend to agree with Benjamin and to regard progress and change with a dubious glance, aware that its mythic power robs time of its significance.

American experience, no less than American thinking, reinforces this skeptical view of progress. Since the 1960s, American thinkers have discerned a crisis in American life. Americans, unaccustomed to failure, have been forced to reconsider their self-understanding. Already in 1966 the Jewish theologian Richard Rubenstein observed this mood. He noted the charmed life of American foreign politics and suggested the salutary effect of defeat. "The real test of America will come," he noted, "only when the going gets rough, when we experience, as has every other nation in history, the bitterness of defeat."[3] The ensuing decades confirmed Rubenstein's intuition. Americans try to cope with their failures, of their loss of power, of the defeat of their ideals, their armies, and their economy in the world community. As they cope, they develop new perspectives on reality and on religion.

Robert Bellah notes a shift in religious thinking in America that reflects this changed reality. Some Americans abandon their traditional religions, looking eastward to Asia or inward to personal enlightenment. Others work to change the traditional religions, to make them more responsive to the new crisis. At one time advocating a type of "utilitarian individualism," these religions now, according to Bellah, have cultivated an "openness to the needs of the contemporary world." The advancing experience of modernity transforms the optimistic and individualistic perspective of American religion

---

[2] See Susan Buck-Morss, *The Dialectics of Seeing: Walter Benjamin and the Arcades Project* (Cambridge, MA: The MIT Press, 1989), pp. 252-260, 277-283.

[3] Richard L. Rubenstein, *After Auschwitz: History, Theology, and Contemporary Judaism*. Second Edition (Baltimore: The Johns Hopkins University Press, 1992), p. 256.

into a more pessimistic, but broadened, one.[4] The American world view once embraced the ideas of progress and liberalism without question. In the wake of failure and disappointment, Americans are reevaluating that view of reality.

The contemporary temperament inspires a different type of theology from traditionalism and a very different politics. Rubenstein draws a connection between this collapse of theology and the rise of so-called "liberation theology." Liberation theology, he notes, refuses to relegate salvation to a divine act for which humanity must wait passively. Liberation thinkers read the Bible, which, Rubenstein comments, often records a rather unedifying tale of the struggle for power, as an imperative to action. They also translate theology from the world of ideas into the world of deeds. Because, he suggests, theological abstractions often bear little resemblance to the realities they purport to express, liberation theologians reject an abstracted philosophy. Instead, he comments, they turn to experience as the only true guide to truth. Rubenstein reflects on the fact that neither biblical tales nor speculative thought, but rather engaged activity confirms religious beliefs. For modern liberation theologians, he remarks, "Faith is no longer validated by the conviction that it is objectively true but by the theologian's concrete experiences in community with the poor."[5] Realism replaces an earlier speculative philosophy; activism takes the place of contemplative thought. This new attitude in theology requires Jewish thinkers to revise their presentation

---

[4] Robert N. Bellah, "New Religious Consciousness and the Crisis of Modernity," in *Varieties of Civil Religion*, by Robert N. Bellah and Phillip E. Hammond (San Francisco: Harper and Row, 1980), p. 186; see the entire essay, pp. 167-187.

[5] Richard L. Rubenstein, "Liberation Theology and the Crisis of Western Theology," in Richard L. Rubenstein and John K. Roth, editors, *The Politics of Latin American Liberation Theology: The Challenge to U.S. Public Policy* (Washington:Washington Institute Press, 1988), p. 76.

of Judaic religion. Older theological terms require a new interpretation, an interpretation "in a modern key" that strikes a responsive cord with contemporary Jewish experience.

Salvation in a Modern Key

Contemporary Jewish thinkers confront secularism and the American experience of failure. They lament the limitations these place on theology, but accept those limitations as essential in a modern perspective. Thus the Jewish theologian Eugene B. Borowitz expresses the dilemma of the modern Jew.[6] He acknowledges the virtues of modernity. Modern civilization has inculcated equality, liberty, and freedom. These ideals, Borowitz believes, serve humanity well. Nevertheless after emphasizing the indelible influence of modernity on Jews today and its heritage of autonomy, Borowitz returns to what he calls "my more characteristic tentativeness," and voices doubt about its virtues.[7] Throughout his writing Borowitz recognizes the crisis of modern secular culture. While warning against the temptation to reinstate naive belief as a response to that crisis, he tempers modernity with a skepticism born from a respect for the traditions of the Jewish people. Secular autonomy, faith in progress, and liberation from restraint must give way, he feels, to a balanced approach to life.

Jews, according to Borowitz, like many who once shared a common vision of progress and social evolution, no longer feel confident that humanity grows toward self-perfection. Borowitz, however, also contends that Jews

---

[6] See Eugene B. Borowitz, "Autonomy versus Tradition," in his *Exploring Jewish Ethics: Papers on Covenant Responsibility* (Detroit: Wayne State University Press, 1990), pp. 165-75 and the following essay, "The Autonomous Jewish Self," pp. 176-192.

[7] *Ibid*, p. 192.

cannot retreat to a premodern naiveté. He notes that Jews can no longer simply reiterate "classic Jewish faith." Jews holding that faith, he argues, were "so dependent upon God and God's saving power they seemed to have forgotten how to help themselves." Borowitz thinks that most modern Jews insist on taking responsibility for their own success or failure. He, therefore, concludes that the modern urge toward autonomy requires Jews to rethink their reliance on divinity.[8]

Rubenstein provides a similarly tempered response to the crisis of modernity based on this lack of trust in a deity. Since God no longer plays a determinative role in achieving human salvation, Rubenstein calls on religion to reevaluate its message. While admitting the devastating theological effect of the absence of God, he refuses to celebrate that absence. Whereas the Christian advocates of the "Death of God" claim that they have discovered a key to freedom and release, Rubenstein is more skeptical. Those who proclaim the freedom to do anything in a world bereft of divinity, he warns, are like Hitler--seeking a return to infancy. Given the dangers of the modern period, Rubenstein turns to religion for protection. In the time of the "Death of God," he warns, people need religion more than ever before. They must use what he terms the "inherited myths, rituals and traditions of our communities" to help "share our predicament." While he does not think that religions can "solve" the dilemmas facing humanity, he hopes that they can help people become more aware of those problems.[9] Rubenstein, no less than Borowitz, urges a cautious theology. He advocates the norms and disciplines of traditional Judaism not because they win a reward from a powerful deity

---

[8] Borowitz, *Exploring*, p. 171.

[9] Rubenstein, *After Auschwitz*, p. 264; see the entire essay, "Death-of-God Theology and Judaism," pp. 247-265.

ready to intervene in history, but for more pragmatic reasons. He argues that those norms and disciplines enhance life here and now. He makes several claims for them: they bind an individual to a nurturing community, they help individuals confront their own essential nature, they aid people in understanding their potential and limitations. These realistic pleasures in Rubenstein's view, should supplant the more illusory ones promised by secularism and traditional religion alike. He recognizes the disillusionment with which many moderns view secular society and calls on religion to help people come to face to face with that reality. Religion offers a mode by which to test one's perception of reality. Kaplan does not deny the fact of illusion; he recognizes no less than existentialists that human beings construct their own truths. He insists, however, that religion has as its purpose enabling people to live productively with this knowledge.

Philosophy and Modern Disillusionment

Both Borowitz and Rubenstein affirm aspects of traditional Judaism despite their full recognition of the power of modernity. They do so because they conclude that modernity fails to fulfill the promises of progress and increased humanitarianism it once offered. For contemporary Jews, the events of the middle part of the twentieth century make such a conclusion inescapable. The caution with which Eugene Borowitz and Richard Rubenstein approach modernity represents a new trend in Jewish thinking. It also represents a new way of understanding the philosophical tradition which modernity inherited. Nineteenth century and early twentieth century Jewish theologians embraced modernity and progress as harbingers of a better world. From the nineteenth century onward, Jewish thinkers reinterpreted their tradition in the light of modernity. This tendency has aroused the ire of critics who claim that modernization impairs the essence of religion.

Leo Strauss advanced the cause of conservative religion as early as 1952. Lecturing to an audience of Hillel students at the University of Chicago, Strauss decried the modern obsession with "progress." He contrasted the modern penchant for change and development with the nostalgic longing for a return to the perfect past that he found in the Hebrew Bible. The modern view fails to measure up to the classical perspective. Anticipating (although in some way also responsible for) the tidal wave of conservatism to follow some twenty-five years later, Strauss identified a growing recognition of this truth, a growing disillusionment with the idea of progress. Moderns find their lives in disarray according to Strauss because they can no longer count on human progress. He even traced the problems of contemporary life back to the modern fixation on progress. "The contemporary crisis of Western civilization," he claimed, "may be said to be identical with the climactic crisis of the idea of progress in the full and emphatic sense of the term."[10] Humanity today, Strauss cautions, recognizes the inevitability of change and also its ambiguousness. Contemporary people recognize that change can bring moral, social, and economic decline as well as improvement. He also claims that they know that change can mean disaster no less than triumph. The crisis of Western Civilization as Strauss diagnosis it, arises from the recognition that change brings problems as well as benefits. Those who invest this civilization with religious significance, he implies, find their hopes shattered by disillusionment; they feel the pain of recognizing the impotence of a once all-powerful god.

---

[10] Leo Strauss, "Progress or Return? The Contemporary Crisis in Western Civilization," *Modern Judaism*, 1 (1981), p. 27; see the entire essay pp. 17-45.

Jewish theology in particular feels this pain. Strauss noted that all modern forms of Jewish religious thinking take the thought of Baruch Spinoza as their point of departure. Spinoza, separating himself from Jewish religion, even before the Jewish community separated him from themselves, embraced rationalism and liberalism. He insisted that philosophers could survive only in a nation that regarded theology as politics, not as truth. Later Jews accepted this separation of functions. Religion adapts to the social reality; it does not attempt to shape a view of the world. Rationalism alone determines truth and falsity. Jewish thinkers, following Spinoza, relinquished their right to dictate morals to society. This capitulation to rationalism undermines any possibility for success such efforts might have. Strauss recognized that "post-critical" Jewish theologies, such as the existential philosophies of Martin Buber and Franz Rosenzweig, confront this problem but concluded that they fail to solve it.[11] Jewish thinkers have the difficult task of affirming the relevance of an ancient tradition in a modern world. Not surprisingly, therefore, they show the dynamic possibilities for change within that tradition. With the growing suspicion that change does not entail progress their tactic backfires. A realistic Jewish theology must show the enduring value of Judaism in times of change whether that change entails progress toward a better life or a decline into disaster. The modern temperament with its negative attitude toward progress rejects the rigorous and optimism of an earlier rationalism.

Mordecai Kaplan and the Modern Predicament

Kaplan, as noted earlier, affirms the divine as a power that aids humanity in its quest for salvation. He makes that idea the cornerstone of his

---

[11] *Ibid.*, pp. 22-24.

philosophy. Because his thought motivates people to work for salvation, he claims, it represents an advance over premodern theology. Kaplan stipulates salvation as the realization of human potential and defines God as the force that enables that realization. Not only does he agree with Spinoza that any definition of God must include the dimension of divine salvific power but he makes that dimension primary and joins Spinoza in a utilitarian approach. He considers "salvation" the most important category in theology because ethics depends upon it. Kaplan defines God in terms of the human experience of self-transcendence since he holds that modern Jews can build a relevant ethical system on such an experience. Because salvation refers to a this-worldly personal self-actualization, the search for salvation, according to him, entails actions that transform society and its members.

He rejects any religious concept that undermines transformative efforts and a view of salvation that ignores the human role in achieving it. From Kaplan's perspective social ethics serves to validate life's aims and goals; personal ethics projects a paradigm legitimating life's worth. He construes the religious vision as a cultural program that unites personal and social goals in a coherent purpose. From this standpoint Kaplan rejects a purely psychological or individualistic approach to religion. Certainly religion expresses personal convictions as "the psychic manifestation of the will to live"[12] He also feels, however, that an exclusively psychological interpretation of religion misses the point. He argues that only social action, only civil concerns, satisfy the personal need for worth and value. With this conviction in mind, Kaplan called the traditional idea of heaven "not only an astronomical fiction but also a psychological absurdity." The traditional view according to Kaplan stresses

---

[12] Kaplan, *Future of the American Jew*, p. 172.

supernatural grace. The individual is a passive recipient of a free gift from the divine. He considers this view one in which individuals find salvation alone, by themselves, in isolation. Salvation, as Kaplan understands it, requires human action in civil society since human beings are inherently social. Kaplan explains both personal and social ethics in a view of God as the source of human self-perfection. Salvation, to be meaningful, must be attained by a practical program.

The Realism of Kaplan's Reconstructionism

Kaplan believes that his Reconstructionist Judaism offers such a program. He exalts his philosophy not as the "true" philosophy but as a useful one that can "influence the conduct of people" because it verifies human ideals.[13] In this view the practical meaning of God depends upon human intellectual effort in constructing a viable God-idea. He judges the value of theology by its consequences for human ethical living and civil justice. Apparently, Kaplan has accepted the model of progress that Walter Benjamin declared a myth and that Strauss decried. He falls into the modern trap of exalting change.

Kaplan denies that he has overlooked the major philosophical problem facing modernity. Contemporary critics of Kaplan's thought, however, consider his theory hopelessly inappropriate for the pessimistic realism of contemporary Jews. One critic reviews the findings of modern science with their emphasis on indeterminacy as the surest refutation of Reconstructionism: "Since the Reconstructionist view of naturalism is so extremely naive and

---

[13] Kaplan, *Greater Judaism*, pp. 457-459, 473, 490-491.

outdated, nothing but failure was to be expected..."[14] Kaplan's understanding of salvation seems tied to a liberal theory of human progress. Several critics claim that such a theory while presumably utilitarian at one time, no longer correctly assesses the reality of human experience. They charge that this humanistic liberalism undermines the credibility of Reconstructionist theology and its ability to help Americans cope with their crisis of hope.

A sketch of Kaplan's thinking seems to justify this conclusion. Kaplan enthusiastically embraces the idea of progress. He hails it as the touchstone of civilization and Jewish religion. He argues that any future development of Judaism must make this principle paramount. Characteristically, Kaplan claims that "No civilization can afford to become a final and closed system of life. Continuous progress must henceforth be its ruling principle."[15] This remark seems an uncritical endorsement of progress. A careful reading, however, shows the subtlety of Kaplan's thought. He does not accept things the way they are. He argues for a religion that creates progress, that enhances changes that ameliorate life but rejects those that do not.

He explicitly denies that religion must naively accept everything modern. Confronting modernity means challenging it and testing it, not merely agreeing with its presuppositions or conclusions. Kaplan does not insist that everything modern is valuable. He does demand that a religious critique of modernity use a language relevant to modern life. The vocabulary of modern religion should make contact with the vocabulary of contemporary human beings. Religious insights enrich modernity with a wisdom that Kaplan considers "tested in the crucible of a rich and variegated experience." Those

---

[14] Eliezer Berkovits, *Major Trends in Modern Philosophies of Judaism* (New York: Ktav, 1974), p. 190.

[15] Kaplan, *Greater Judaism*, p. 453.

insights cannot improve human life, however, if expressed in an antiquated language that conveys only nonsense to a modern ear. Kaplan calls for a Judaism "viable in the present-day" but not for a Judaism that uncritically approves of everything contemporary.[16] Such a qualified acceptance of progress developed as Jews responded to modernity.

Kaplan's Religion of Progress

Kaplan's view of religion fits the call for a return from progress even while Kaplan's theology exalts progress. Kaplan revitalizes Jewish symbols and practices by showing how they can mobilize human resources to improve life. He returns to the tradition to refashion it into a rational tool suitable for modern Jews. Several elements combine in his programmatic returning to classical Judaism. He admits that he imputes to the tradition a view apparently at odds with its inner spirit. He then shows how that spirit in fact points beyond the literal meaning of the religious texts within which it is embedded. Then he applies those texts in their newly discovered spirit to the experience of modern life. His interpretation of biblical religion for modern Americans shows how tradition provides a vocabulary by which, after the world becomes uncertain, people "begin anew the process of learning to be human."[17] That readjustment often depends on creating a new way of understanding existence. Kaplan insists that only those able to use that new theological vocabulary can communicate in the wake of world transforming changes. Such changes have occurred in modern times, and he offers the language of Judaism to Americans as a way of coping with the transformations of modernity.

---

[16] Kaplan, *Judaism Without Supernaturalism*, p. xiii.

[17] Kaplan, *Not So Random Thoughts*, p. 3.

Kaplan's method of coping with modernity responds to the critique of conservatives by combining rationalism with respect for tradition.

Kaplan considers the biblical idea of an ordered universe the most important contribution Jews have made to the idea of progress. Before that contribution, humanity viewed the world as filled with arbitrary forces, acting out of whim, unpredictable and incomprehensible. Jewish monotheism introduced a principle or order, a sense of purpose and meaning, a unity of intention that gave humanity a firm basis on which to build its life. The idea of progress Kaplan contends, depends on "a movement from the notion that the world is governed by arbitrary whim to the realization that this is a law-governed world."[18] He shows how that idea dominates modern science. Scientists, he avers, must assume a lawful universe if they are to draw conclusions from their observations of the past and to make predictions about the future. The advances of physics could not take place were scientists to doubt the predictability of their results. Religion, Kaplan continues by analogy, provides the same foundation for drawing conclusions and making predictions about human life. The Bible, according to Kaplan, provides social science with the same lawfulness that physics offers to natural science. In his view the Bible supplies an "insight into the inherence of law in the art of living together" essential to developing any social structure.[19] Religion provides the basis for salvation by teaching how society may organize itself to make best use of the laws governing human behavior.

Kaplan emphasizes the social nature of progress. He understands the biblical story of Israel's escape to freedom as a paradigm of salvation in the

---

[18] Kaplan, *Meaning of God*, p. 316.

[19] *Ibid.*, p. 317.

modern world. He associates a love of freedom with the story of the Israelite exodus from Egypt, a demand for justice with the prophetic stand against false worship, a call for human self-improvement in the biblical view of repentance. The biblical view of history teaches Kaplan the lawfulness of human social living. The prophets show him that no existing social structure exemplifies that lawfulness perfectly. The prophets, Kaplan argues, realized the imperfections of their own community. Although theirs was a "traditional" community governed by sanctified laws, Kaplan claims that the prophets dared call for change: "refusing to regard God as the author of social practices and standards merely because they were accepted as authoritative."[20] Kaplan portrays the prophets as radicals who challenged those who deified the status quo. He also considers them conservatives who recalled their society to its earlier ideals. In his portrayal, then, the prophets were radicals in their call to alter the institutions of society because they were conservatives who held to the old values that animated the nation. Kaplan's own social program combines the demand for radical change with a respect for a tradition of social ideals and values derived from the past.

Kaplan claims that all human beings need the same dedication to ideals that characterized the prophets. Human nature, he thinks, requires a sense of transcendence, a feeling of serving ends that go beyond pragmatic usefulness. The term God as Kaplan uses it refers to that aspect of human nature which yearns for a more than practical meaning. He interprets theology as an expression of humanistic striving. Kaplan notes that "it is part of our nature to have purposes in life." He sees in religious traditions an accumulation of ideals that project a plan for fulfilling human goals. He affirms the necessity

---

[20] *Ibid.*, p. 323.

of creating such a compendium of ideals as "an indispensable part of the process by which our long-range purposes are realized." The idea of God so understood implies human purposefulness and, Kaplan claims, thereby makes explicit two basic biblical principles: that human beings must follow exalted laws if they are to live together harmoniously and that they must be prepared to change existing laws when they fail to meet the standard set by their highest values.[21] The divine has both a progressive and conservative function. It works to remind human beings of the unattainable ideals for which they are striving, and as such it portrays a vision toward which they should progress. Nevertheless, the idea of the divine as a principle of inevitable failure, of unpredictable changes, and of the infinite ignorance of human beings, tends toward a conservatism. The status quo may be oppressive and backward. Believers can take heart: all this will also pass and change. God's presence reminds them that so-called institutions of power will wither by themselves and precipitate that alteration which no intentional action accomplishes alone.

Religion as a Conservative Force For Progress

For Kaplan, civilization requires religion to teach it these lessons. Kaplan considers humanism incapable of stimulating idealism or advocating change. Instead, he charges, humanism accepts the status quo as the highest stage of human development. As Kaplan construes humanism it exalts the present condition of humanity, and when that condition reveals itself in all its degradation, humanists retreat to pessimistic despair. He describes such disillusioned humanists as frustrated and without motivation for changing the world. Therefore, he concludes, humanism alone "cannot regard the ought as more than idle fancy, and the hope of a better world as anything more than

---

[21] *Ibid.*, p. 325.

a mirage." Kaplan contrasts humanism to biblical religion, correctly stripped of its parochialism. He claims that the Bible represents the most realistic hope for modern civilization.[22] Kaplan, thus, agrees with Strauss: modernism alone is bankrupt. He takes this analysis one step further. He claims that Jews who capitulate to modernity abandon their distinctive contribution to the world. He regards Jews who retreat from the world and withdraw to their pre-modern tradition as even more dangerous. He charges that they have betrayed their most holy task. Since God for Kaplan represents the forces working towards human self-development, a Judaism that ignores the development of other human beings has betrayed God. Kaplan's adaptation of the biblical view of history modifies its parochialism while retaining enough of its specifically religious characteristics to counteract the problematic skepticism of modernity. He modifies the idea of "progress" and shows how the "evolution" of religion actually represents changes in the outward expression of an unchanging view of reality. Various biblical concepts find new significance when reconstructed in the light of the problems of modern society. Kaplan's exposition of the idea of covenant, central in the Hebrew Bible, illustrates how his thought is both conservative and oriented to progress.

The Progress of Covenant as a Conservative Ideal

The biblical view of history emphasizes the lawfulness of human social interaction. Practically, that view produced an extensive code of law, presented in the Bible as a contract or covenant binding the Jewish people to God. Kaplan considers the covenant idea an important basis for modern Jewish living. He considers many of the specific convenantal rules established

---

[22] *Ibid.*, p. 326; see the entire section "Why humanism is not enough," pp. 320-329.

by the Bible instructive. Nevertheless, he admits that the Bible shows its antiquity by couching those rules in an authoritarian language. To meet this objection, he offers a program of reinterpretation. Kaplan wishes to preserve the potential implicit in the biblical concept of covenant while removing its anti-democratic elitism.[23] In its supernaturalist form that concept does indeed inculcate the parochial self-interest that Kaplan describes. That paradigm draws on a purportedly ancient story. God, according to the tale, rescued a motley band of slaves, provided them a religio-political constitution (the covenant) and led them into a promised land where they might actualize that constitution in their daily life. God's providential care singled out this one group from the rest of humanity, performed supernatural miracles for it, and authorized its religious law. This covenantal legislation institutes the rule of ethical standards rather than of arbitrary whim as the basis of society.

Kaplan describes the evolution of Jewish theology as a gradual movement toward ethical universalism. Biblical Israel, he thinks, sought to unify a disparate social group. Originally biblical religion, in Kaplan's reconstruction, thought of God as the national God of a particular culture. This "henotheism" distinguished between God's concern for one group of people and divine displeasure with other cultures. Later biblical thought, Kaplan continues, evolved the idea that covenant was "the consecration of the nation to universal ideals which...would ultimately issue in an integrated cooperative human society."[24] This ideal challenged the nation. It forced citizens to think about global concerns and develop an inclusive ideology. As Kaplan interprets it, this covenantal idea still possesses importance today. It

---

[23] See my study *Covenant and Community in Modern Judaism* (Westport, CN: Greenwood Press, 1989).

[24] Kaplan, *Meaning of God*, pp. 101-102.

reminds people of "the nation's responsibility for contributing creatively to human welfare and progress."[25] The covenant idea, in his historical review of biblical evolution, grew from a parochial and chauvinistic concept into a universalistic ethical ideal.

Kaplan associates the idea of the chosen people with an early stage in Israel's development. It took shape in the idea of a special contract binding the Jewish people to its ideals. This concept made those ideals so real and palpable that Jews were ready to die for them. The self-presentation as a group with a special commission and purpose enabled the Jewish people to survive in times of crisis. Later, however, Kaplan shows that the idea no longer served merely utilitarian purposes. It became a means by which Jews made their lives more ethical. As members of a chosen people with a special charter and set of guidelines, Kaplan argues, Jews learned to restrain the free use of power. The concept of the chosen people, understood as a function of covenant, established limitations on raw power as an intrinsic good, as a force for human improvement in itself. In this way "Religion progresses and religion ceases to be utilitarian and becomes ethical."[26] This ideal, Kaplan thinks, served the Jewish people well in premodern times. In contemporary life, however, the concept needs revision. American pluralism goes even further than biblical covenantalism. As Kaplan understands it, American democracy substitutes a civil covenant for a divine one and thereby makes the ideal of a chosen people not only unnecessary but also pernicious.

This sketch of the development of the idea of covenant leads from one religious insight to another, with America at the pinnacle of that evolution.

---

[25] *Ibid.*, p. 102.

[26] Kaplan, *Greater Judaism*, p. 197.

The tale of humanity's progress, Kaplan feels, displays the ever-expanding covenantal program that, unlike the plan of the biblical God who elects Israel, includes all humanity in its dialogical parameters.[27] Kaplan's celebration of this development suggests a naive hopefulness foreign to the realism of modern conservatives who offer more pessimistic judgments concerning civil life.

This acceptance of progress only appears to affirm the optimistic model of social evolution. While Kaplan rejects an authoritarian covenant as inconsistent with modernism, he advocates the concept as a progressive goad to American self-understanding. He does not regard progress as inevitable and actually requires the religious concept because he distrusts humanity to achieve covenantal community on its own. Kaplan urges America to progress toward the fulfillment of that pluralistic community first intimated by the biblical ideal of covenant. America fulfills the divine plan insofar as it provides the means by which people actualize their potential. This view combines a creative conception of progress with the traditional values of covenantal religion. Kaplan does not insist that change always entails progress. He calls change progress only when it transforms a parochial idea into a more inclusive one. Were covenant to change from a protection of human interests into a threat to those interests, he would oppose the change. In the idea of covenant, as in the idea of biblical history, Kaplan shows himself more a conservative than a radical. He does not embrace progress for its own sake. He takes one aspect of modernity--its ecumenical structure--and then infuses it with the ancient concept. He modernizes the tradition only so it can then transform modernity. Kaplan, therefore, does not romanticize modernity. He recognizes

---

[27] Kaplan, *Religion of Ethical Nationhood*, p. 70.

its limitations and calls upon religion to reshape modernity so that it more truly advances human life and humane causes. He does this through his transformation of traditional religious categories.

The Relevance of Covenant For American Democracy

Kaplan recognizes the validity of the covenant as a traditional symbol in Jewish life but he transforms an idea that emphasized Jewish particularity into an idea that stresses universalism and an ethical acceptance of social responsibility. Thus, he declares, the covenantal idea expresses the duties a society owes to its members. Creating the concept of a constitutional limitation on governmental power, ancient Israel, he avers, forced leaders to bear the responsibility for improving human life. He sees the welfare state as the modern equivalent of covenant: "The sense of the nation's responsibility for contributing to human welfare and progress in the light of its own best experience becomes the modern equivalent of the covenant idea."[28] Kaplan bases his hope that the biblical idea of covenant can create a modern pluralistic community on his trust in American democracy. The American environment, he feels, offers a context in which the idea of covenant, no longer tied to parochial nationalism, can encourage diversity, cooperation, and the free exchange of ideas among all members of the community.

The modern ideal of covenant finds its fullest realization for Kaplan in American pluralism. Kaplan describes democracy as a pluralistic environment in which every citizen participates in several cultures simultaneously. While one "American culture" unites the citizens into a single community, the several particular cultures strengthen and enrich the whole. Were Jews or

---

[28] Kaplan, *Meaning of God*, p. 102.

Christians to sacrifice their individual loyalties in favor of some broadly defined Americanism, Kaplan thinks that they would be "anti-social" and destructive to American life. Democracy, he holds, requires both the adherence to a common set of values and the creativity of affirming the value individual cultural legacies.[29] He claims that the values uniting Americans transcends the differences between the different individual religious communities. While Judaism and Christianity do indeed exclude one another, the American ideal of pluralism includes both of them.

Kaplan argues this case because American democracy cannot, by its nature, interfere with private beliefs. Yet human beings, at least for Kaplan, require religious commitments. America, for Kaplan, needs the particular religions from which its citizens derive their spiritual values. He claims that the dialogue among the specific religions creates the conditions for human self-improvement desired by the American community generally.[30] Out of this dialogue Kaplan combines the hope born from recognition of progressive universalization of an idea with a realistic vision of life. Covenant, as Kaplan understands it, limits human destructiveness, provides an appraisal of humanity noting its failings, but offers a framework within which increasingly inclusive communities may make use of these insights. Such a view of progress actually entails a growing acceptance of a conservative understanding of human nature and destiny. In this way Kaplan's "progressive" view of salvation criticizes the status quo even advancing a realistic view of the inadequacy of human intentionality. in some small measure. Kaplan's progressive conservatism has the advantage that Jonathan Culler associates with Deconstructionism. It raises

---

[29] Kaplan, *Questions Jews Ask*, pp. 31-32.

[30] Kaplan, *Greater Judaism*, pp. 460-462; compare p. 477.

just those questions which may be irrelevant for "normal" communication or ordinary social behavior. It looks not to a program for progress or a plan for social change. Instead it asks those quiries that investigate the dynamics of changing, that wonder how it is possible for social development to occur at all. It studies the mechanics of social dynamics. In this way, Kaplan's politics, like Culler's literary approach, introduces that measure of "paranoia" which he considers "essential to the just appreciation of things."[31] While accepting the unchanging nature of human beings and human society, Kaplan stimulates his followers to ask questions and demand an understanding of just those activities which make change necessary and inevitable.

---

[31] Culler, "In Defence of Overinterpretation," p. 113.

PART IV: THE SURVIVAL OF JUDAISM IN DEMOCRACY

Chapter 9:

Freedom in Jewish Worship and Prayer

The Problematics of American Jewish Worship

Worship and ritual in a democracy takes on certain problematic elements. The ideas and values accepted as normative and unquestioned find confirmation not in the particular actions of separate groups, but in great corporate activities. The civil events of presidential inaugurations, memorial celebrations, and national holidays fulfill the need every society has for structuring events in which reality functions as theory says that it should. With public life satisfying the need that private religions often served in the past, the individual religious traditions in America need to find some reason for existence, some inherent value in their ritual performances. The relationship between the powerful symbols and rituals of civil religion and the supplemental rituals of the particular religions gives many theorists cause for reflection. The variety of civil religious forms in the United States makes the difficulties of the particular religions especially great.[1]

A general theory of ritual might help place this dilemma in perspective.[2] Several theorists emphasize the behavioral element in religious ritual. They claim that while theory emphasizes thought, ritual consists of action, of what people do. Ritual appears as "thoughtless deed" in such a construction. The dichotomy between deed and thought, action and theory, however, tends to produce an untenable tension. That tension leads to attemps to unify thought and deed on a higher level. That attempt itself, however, often fails and Catherine Bell claims that "In the end, a model of ritual that integrates opposing cultural forces becomes homologized to a mode of theoretical discourse that reiterates the dichotomy" which it tries to overcome.[3] Her solution is to avoid making a definition in the first place. She advocates "deconstructing" the cultural logic of ritual by focusing on its political and social strategies. What does ritual do in the struggle for power that makes up human society?[4] Such a question makes sense when applied to Mordecai Kaplan's reconstructing of Jewish ritual. He uses the traditional forms of Judaism to provide an opportunity by which people confront the powers and structures of their lives and emerge stronger from that confrontation. Naturally he himself encountered opposition as he deconstructed the tradition.

---

[1] See the discussion in Bellah and Hammond *Varieties of Civil Religion*.

[2] The brief survey that follows draws on, but does not accept all the particulars of, the detailed and instructive discussion of Catherine Bell, *Ritual Theory, Ritual Practice*, (New York: Oxford University Press, 1992).

[3] Bell, *Ritual*, p. 32.

[4] *Ibid.*, p. 80.

Mordecai Kaplan's Practical View of Jewish Religion

In 1945 American Orthodox Judaism began to display a "more aggressive attitude and program" than ever before. While the Conservative Movement's Jewish Theological Seminary expanded its scope into a "University of Judaism," Orthodoxy's Rabbi Isaac Elchanan Theological Seminary and Yeshiva College launched a similar plan. Another sign of this Orthodox resurgence came in June when several leading Orthodox Rabbis issued an edict of excommunication (a *herem*) against one of the leading teachers at the Conservative Seminary, Rabbi Mordecai Kaplan. The rabbis castigated Kaplan for editing a new Sabbath prayer book expressing what they called "atheism, heresy, and basic disbelief in the basic tenets of Judaism." They consigned his prayer book to flames and prohibited its use in Orthodox synagogues.[5] Kaplan was anathema as a threat to traditional power.

This reaction by Orthodox leaders expresses a frequent objection raised against Kaplan's thought. Critics often argue that his reconstructionist theology leaves little room for genuine prayer. Charles Liebman, for example, remarks that while Kaplan offers a "justification" for prayer, he fails to motivate worship. Jews who already have the impulse to pray can, according to this view, find in Kaplan's philosophy a rationale for their action. Jews who have no such impulse will not, Liebman suggests, be inspired with one by reading Kaplan.[6] One reason often given for Kaplan's lack of motivating power derives from his view of God. Kaplan's transnatural divinity seems impervious to human prayer. A humanistic religion has the power to stimulate personal

---

[5] See Joshua Tractenberg, "Religious Activities," *The American Jewish Year Book 5706 (1945-46)* Volume 47 (Philadelphia: Jewish Publication Society of America, 1945), pp. 215-216.

[6] Liebman, "Reconstructionism," p. 102.

self-improvement. A humanism which "has so tightly defined God in terms of the human" that it leaves no room for divine response cannot stimulate worship. Even Steven T. Katz, who understands Kaplan's intentions, declares that his actualization of them falls short; his reconstructions of Jewish practice may appear rational, but they are untenable. Katz affirms that rationalism views prayer as superstition and calls the attempt to justify worship through elaborate rationalizations a dishonest "charade." He proposes the modern dilemma and asks "how can we go on with *tefillah* (prayer) and ritual, Mordecai Kaplan's illogical "reconstructions" notwithstanding?"[7] Kaplan's theology seems ill constructed to revive Jewish worship.

Prayer and Reconstructionist Judaism

Chapter four mentions Kaplan's concern with liturgy and his pedagogic approach to Jewish prayer. His impetus to such liturgical creativity was not only exegetical but rational. Prayer for him teaches worshipers a more accurate view of the world. Kaplan claims that his view of divinity as the sum of diverse forces working for human salvation satisfies the need for a universal philosophy of history. Human history as he interprets it consists of efforts to attain "salvation," to enable all humanity to reach self-fulfillment. The tale of humanity's progress as Kaplan tells it displays the unfolding place of "nature's God" that, unlike the plan of the biblical God who elects Israel, seeks to actualize the potential of every human person. Kaplan describes nature's God as the accumulation of possibilities for human self-development. He argues that the God idea understood in this way unifies rather than divides

---

[7] Katz, *Historicism*, p. 50.

cultures.[8] A new view of the divine will overcome apparently intractable conflicts which separate one religious group from another.

In contrast to the supernatural view of God espoused in the Bible, Kaplan holds that a transnatural definition of deity leads to the recognition that religious worship and practice fulfill human needs not divine ones. From a personal perspective, he posits, rituals provide an opportunity for self-development. Worship, for Kaplan, is not theurgic but rather a complex of symbols by which people learn to recognize their own potential. A transnatural God as Kaplan describes this idea represents the forces that help people develop their talents. The religious practices he associates with such a God provide opportunities to exercise those talents. Kaplan judges the value of a ritual by its ability "to activate the better part of us, our latent potentialities for what is fully human."[9] Rather than act as magic to help the vulnerable protect themselves, Kaplan asserts that rituals become tools by which self-actualized human beings develop their own skills and abilities.

To be a Jew in Kaplan's terms means to celebrate the human ability to make choices, to act creatively. As Katz recognizes, Kaplan understood that one part of his theological task involved cultivating prayerfulness. He actively sought to awaken the spirit of worship among modern Jews. Marc Lee Raphael correctly notes that Kaplan's liturgical efforts attempted to make prayer more compelling in an irreligious age. His radical innovations that included changing the traditional prayers, adding new liturgical pieces from Hebrew literature, and eliminating untenable ideas were intended "to arouse religious emotion in those who felt services provided little emotional

---

[8] Kaplan, *Religion of Ethical Nationhood*, p. 70.

[9] Kaplan, *Judaism Without Supernaturalism*, p. 49.

impact."[10] His search for freedom in worship entails creating new forms of personal expression no less than making choices concerning traditional prayers and liturgical forms. Contemporary Reconstructionists maintain that tradition. They use liturgical images that Kaplan might reject, they include texts from the Jewish mystics that might perplex rationalists, but their intention remains that of Kaplan. Some who use this new liturgy do so because of its "mythic and poetic power to move us." Others fuse the "counterculture" and Jewish mystical language. In both cases Reconstructionists agree with Kaplan that the literal meaning of these texts "cannot in rational terms be true." They disagree about which "terms should predominate in our lives--particularly in our religious language" because they judge the Jewish audience of prayer differently. In this way Reconstructionism, precisely by disagreeing with Kaplan's specific suggestions while agreeing with his intention, continue his innovative tradition. They prove "more venturesome" in the realm of liturgical innovation and "more creative" in their use of theological language than other American Jewish movements because they retain his combination of conservatism and daring.[11] The continuing concern of Reconstructionists testifies to Kaplan's emphasis on renewing prayer as an essential activity of Jewish life. Through creative decisions shaping Jewish liturgy, analysts note, Reconstructionists celebrate personal freedom as a path to personal self-fulfillment. Rather than celebrating the sacrifice of the individual to society, liturgy expresses a commitment to discovering the personal meaning of life.

---

[10] Raphael, *Profiles in American Judaism*, p. 183.

[11] Arnold Eisen, "American Judaism: Changing Patterns in Denominational Self-Definition," in Peter Y. Medding, ed., *Studies in Contemporary Jewry VIII: A New Jewry? America Since the Second World War* (New York: Oxford University Press, 1992), pp. 37-39.

Mordecai Kaplan and the Philosophical Problem of Prayer

Kaplan's approach to religion in a democratic society emphasizes its rationality, its contribution to the social well being of a liberal state. This utilitarian explanation, however, neglects many of the specifically religious aspects of Judaism. Kaplan recognizes that a Jewish religion bereft of its cultural distinctiveness cannot survive. He values that survival not just for the benefits democracy derives from Judaism, but for the worth inherent in Judaism itself. He turns to the past for instruction. The philosophical approach of Moses Maimonides, for example, appears to prefigure modern rationalism. By rejecting a personal and responsive deity, however, it seemed to stifle genuine prayer. Marvin Fox explains how Maimonides, seeking to reconcile his legal and philosophical works, struggled with the meaning and significance of prayer.[12] As a philosopher, Maimonides denied that God could change, that any creature could affect the creator. He, therefore, could not explain the appeal to petitionary prayer prevalent in Jewish sources. He also emphasized the divine transcendence to such an extent that he denied humanity any positive knowledge of God. Human beings might know what God could not be, they could negate certain attributes as fitting for divinity. They could not, however, gain enough positive knowledge to praise God in the language of affirmative attributes.

Maimonides solved his problem by interpreting prayer and the commandment of worship in a non-literal way. It is "one of a number of sets of commandments whose main concern is to implant in us a deep commitment

---

[12] Marvin Fox, "Prayer and the Religious Life," in his *Interpreting Maimonides: Studies in Methodology, Metaphysics, and Moral Philosophy* (Chicago: University of Chicago Press, 1990), pp. 297-321.

to sound doctrine."[13] Nevertheless, Maimonides at times seemed to imply a more conventional view of prayer. His life was filled with personal piety; he "engaged in prayer in ways that go far beyond the fixed statutory requirements."[14] As a human being and philosopher he balanced his intellectual and personal needs against each other. He did not intend his conventional and philosophical views of prayer to be mutually exclusive. There are certain "necessary beliefs" that cannot be justified by reason that are, nonetheless, essential for every religious person. These beliefs are "necessary...in the significant and admirable sense that no religious person can do without them, however sophisticated he or she may be."[15] Even Maimonides, the model Jewish rationalist, admitted the necessity for prayer as an expression of a person's humanity. How much more should moderns recognize this fact.

The dynamic interplay between philosophical understanding of the "God-idea" and pietist interaction with the divine occurs within traditional Jewish liturgy. That liturgy often begins by addressing God with an immediate appeal, such as "Blessed are You, O Lord." It then continues by alluding to the divine in the third person, such as "the one who causes the evening to descend." This dualism arises from the combination of intellectual and emotional elements found from the very origins of traditional Jewish liturgy. As Jakob Petuchowski has pointed out, the prayers developed in the rabbinic House of Study (*bet hamidrash*) are couched in the third person. The rabbis expressed a reflective mood comparable to the philosophical attitude of

---

[13] *Ibid.*, p. 311.

[14] *Ibid.*, p. 319.

[15] *Ibid.*, p. 321.

Maimonides. Petuchowski also notes that these same rabbis continued to use the immediate, second-person, form of address found in other Jewish prayers. He concludes that normative prayer balances the reflective and the devotional, the meditative and the petitional. The crisis of modern prayer, as he sees it, arises because Jews no longer know how to keep the tension alive, how to maintain both third person and second person prayers as equally valid.[16]

Kaplan agrees with this analysis. His first step in renewing prayer focuses on the interplay of philosophy and piety in worship. He affirms this necessity for personal piety and, explicitly, claims to have learned it from Maimonides and the controversy surrounding his philosophy. He, however, reverses the paradigm: it is not that a religious person cannot dispense with prayer that goes beyond philosophy. Rather, Kaplan claims that a philosophy which does not allow for prayer, that does not point beyond its own limitations, is unworthy of the religious person. He accepts as legitimate only that philosophy alone which "is compatible with prayer and worship." Certainly, Kaplan admits, as with Maimonides, some philosophies may be incompatible with superstition and popular belief. He does not, however, consider that fact of determinative force.

Popularity, he insists, is not the test of a philosophy. Instead he claims that such a test lies rather in its affinity for true religious living. Theology, he thinks, depends on its fruits, that is on its ability to stimulate individual piety. Kaplan will not accept any philosophy of religion no matter how sophisticated that cannot motivate worship.[17] He achieves his integration of philosophy and piety by stressing how worship becomes a living force for

---

[16] Jakob J. Petuchowski, *Understanding Jewish Prayer* (New York: Ktav, 1972), p. 62-63.

[17] Kaplan, *Questions Jews Ask*, pp. 86-87.

human development. Kaplan's emphasis on a naturalistic view of divinity has, as one of its important elements, a realistic appraisal of prayer. Kaplan recognizes that the problem with prayer is not merely the liturgy but also the nature of the divinity to whom worshipers address prayer. He accepts as valid only a conception of God that acts "not only to permit, but to necessitate, worship."[18] He demands an idea of the divine which makes prayer an active and essential part of how people improve their world.

The Traditions of Prayer

Kaplan argues that this positive influence of prayer owes much of its effectiveness to the traditional forms in which it appears. His affirmation of tradition, however, differs from the pietism of many other modern traditionalists. They too recognize the crisis of modern worship, but they seek to answer it by returning to an earlier mode of piety. Some modern Jewish thinkers attempt to revitalize Jewish prayer by returning to a more supernaturalist and less philosophical view of the divinity. Kaplan disagrees with those theologians who exalt "faith" over reason, claiming that they act deceptively. He argues that those who embrace "contemporary existentialist conceptions of God" do not really intend to affirm an antirationalist position. None of them, he avers, "would go so far as to imply that prayer can be a means of ending a drought, or that it can cure cancer and pneumonia." They preach a faith that transcends common sense but they act as if the normal laws of cause and effect always maintain.[19] The stimulus to action that Kaplan affirms is not belief in a particular idea of God. He trusts rather in those

---

[18] Kaplan, *Future of the American Jew*, p. 184.

[19] Kaplan, *Questions Jews Ask*, p. 87.

practices which reinforce a belief and instill a sense of piety. He calls on modern Jews to create a new environment for prayer which will call forth those actions which belief alone cannot stimulate. What is necessary, Kaplan claims, is not a new consciousness but a new instrument for prayerfulness. He defines the problem as "how to elicit from Jewish life the spirit of personal religion which would be in line of continuity with the highest manifestations of personal religion in our past."[20] A valid solution to the religious malaise of modernity for Kaplan depends on establishing the positive aspects of tradition, using them in appropriately modern ways, and advancing beyond rather than returning to earlier Jewish forms.

Since, for Kaplan, the purpose of prayer is to actualize an awareness of the worshiper's participation in the power that God provides, tradition legitimates itself by enabling such awareness. One way that Kaplan conceives of prayer fulfilling this role is through its evocation of past human experience. As an expression of tradition, prayer, he believes, reminds worshipers of opportunities seized by past generations and points them toward the same opportunities in the present. He avers that traditional liturgy continues to be relevant in Jewish life. "Traditional forms," he declares, "should be retained, wherever these have something of positive value to contribute..."[21] One contribution he thinks derived from using familiar forms is psychological. Traditional Jewish prayer, Kaplan avers, helps people regain self-confidence in times of trouble. Prayer and praise, he comments, possess "the psychological effect of exorcising the dread of the terrible consequences" of

---

[20] Kaplan, *Future of the American Jew*, pp. 135-136.

[21] *Ibid.*, p. 49.

some suspected sin.[22] Praise of God in Kaplan's philosophy points to unexpected sources of personal renewal existing in the world. Kaplan suggests that the traditional liturgy consists of prayers praising God not for the sake of flattering the deity but to restore personal self-confidence. Such prayers, he claims, function "to arouse in ourselves the will and the courage to avail ourselves" of those opportunities for improvement found within human beings and the world.[23] Traditional forms of worship as Kaplan understands them serve modern Jews by helping them mobilize the resources at their disposal.

The Creative Elements of Liturgy

Kaplan, however, also admits that traditional liturgy alone cannot succeed in the task of creating legitimate prayer. He recognizes that both Jewish worship and Jewish religion need, in his words, revitalization. He calls upon Jewish leaders to set about that task of revitalization. He demands that they not only rethink the meaning of prayer but also that they create new liturgical forms. He points to the "tremendous amount of work" he thinks necessary for reevaluating Jewish liturgy and "for replenishing it with new prayers arising out of the experiences of our age..."[24] Kaplan's rationale for this work, for the necessity of creating new prayers, lies less in the traditional liturgy than in the changed religious situation. Jews need, he insists, to reconstruct their communal life in order to make it conducive to the message of prayer. They need, Kaplan argues, to create a context which stimulates a movement away from the individual ego to consciousness of communal

---

[22] Kaplan, *Meaning of God*, p. 151.

[23] Kaplan, *Questions Jews Ask*, p. 457.

[24] *Ibid.*, p. 460.

responsibility. The new prayers Kaplan seeks are not merely expressions of a person's consciousness. The ones he envisions are expressions of awareness that one consciousness reaches out to another, that human beings depend on other people, that no one is isolated but that the universe offers a community of cooperation in the process of amelioration of reality.[25]

Kaplan's View of a Personal God

Critics claim that Kaplan's view of the divine leaves little room for a personal relationship with the divinity. Some argue that his defense of the Jewish relevance of his view of the divine falls short. In Jewish tradition, these critics argue, God's creative act emphasizes both the unity of the creator in contrast to the diversity of the creation and the purposefulness of the Creator: the creation reveals the personal involvement of the divine with the creatures. Eugene B. Borowitz, surveying contemporary Jewish thought, criticizes Kaplan's view of God on the grounds that it contradicts these two principles.[26] In the first case, Borowitz claims, Kaplan's God is unified only in human consciousness. The objective manifestations of God occur as "disparate objective realities." This objection, however, misunderstands Kaplan's view of the transcendent nature of divinity. While the various "attributes" of God appear as diverse phenomena for Kaplan, the "nature" of God, as the source of meaning in human life, remains constant.

Borowitz raises a second, and more damaging, objection. Kaplan's view of God fails to function adequately because it lacks personality. "Can man

---

[25] *Ibid.*, pp. 248-262.

[26] Eugene B. Borowitz, *A New Jewish Theology in the Making* (Philadelphia: Westminster, 1968), p. 111 = his *Choices in Modern Jewish Thought* (New York: Behrman House, 1983), p. 111.

take personally an impersonal God?" Borowitz asks. Kaplan certainly agrees that the God-idea functions to affirm human personality. Has he inconsistently removed from his own theology the potential of such a function? Borowitz claims that "Kaplan's rebuttals have not been convincing to many..." Nevertheless, those rebuttals do suggest how a functional and transnatural definition can ensure the place of personality in the world. Kaplan suggests that "will of God" refers to the sense of transcendent that permeates such a programatic system. God as creator in this view refers to humanity's ability to construct a universe only by elevating a general principle to unify experience. Kaplan therefore concludes that personality consists of just such a principle that unifies the various efforts made to attain self-fulfillment.[27] This theology of the divine personhood, Kaplan declares, corresponds both to reason and its demands and to tradition and its images.

Kaplan considers his theology more practical than that of his rivals. What could be more personal, he wonders, than a divinity who provides the means by which people transform their lives. Theological language as he understands it shapes the experience of nature, artistic works, and other people and thus affects human lives. Kaplan, therefore, declares that "A God who makes a difference in one's personal life should be designated as a personal God.[28] Kaplan offers those practical means by which Jews might recognize the difference that God makes to their personal life. He seeks to structure the experience of Jewish practice and worship to transform the personal consciousness of every Jewish participant. He advocates using a type of utilitarian calculus in determining which parts of tradition a person should

---

[27] Kaplan, *Greater Judaism*, p. 459.

[28] *Ibid.*, p. 104.

maintain (although he emphasizes that ethics and not "utility" serves as his model, most utilitarians would see the ethical as but a more rational understanding of what is useful). Through this new type of revitalized ritual, he contends, not only do Jews help themselves but they also help "the American people as a whole out of the present world wide religious predicament." Kaplan considers his approach to Jewish practice the key, not only to Jewish welfare, but to the welfare of humanity as a whole.[29]

Such personal selectivity, Kaplan holds, demands a communal setting that permits and encourages freedom of choice. Kaplan's commitment to American Democracy shapes his view of Jewish practice. He understands its explicit aim as that of helping each individual pursue a path toward personal fulfillment. This humanistic intention shows that Jewish ritual has a universal dimension--that of actualizing the truly human. Animating that aim, however, and lying hidden behind it, he discerns a more specifically Jewish concern. Kaplan, like cultural Zionists such as Ahad HaAm, recognizes in worship and ritual a means for maintaining the survival of the Jewish people. This unstated but pervasive aspect of Jewish practice means, he thinks, that the politics of worship is not international but national, not universalist but particularist. He takes as his particular task reconciling this fact with the modern perspective.

The Particularism of Jewish Worship and Ritual

At first glance Kaplan would seem to reject Jewish ritual and practice as an expression of Jewish parochialism. Kaplan's view of Jewish practice, however, reflects his own life experiences. He uses American democracy as a model for any future Judaism and therefore accentuates pluralism and

---

[29] Kaplan, *Judaism Without Supernaturalism*, pp. 98, 115.

diversity, recognizing the voluntaristic nature of American Judaism as a positive feature. He claims that "voluntaristic Jewish religion, which is likely to be diverse in belief and practice, can enhance the Jewish way of life in Israel and in the Diaspora."[30] This view of religion as a voluntary and pluralistic phenomenon leads him to interpret covenant as a basis for diversity and individual autonomy. Kaplan roots his insistence that Jewish religion allows for pluralism in a humanistic understanding of the idea of covenant. Covenant, he argues, commits the Jewish people to "ethical nationhood."[31]

Kaplan charges the Jewish community with a parochial attitude that destroys its inner coherence. Jewish leaders, he thinks, exacerbate the problems of living in a pluralistic society by requiring uniformity of Jewish living. Kaplan traces the problem to its roots in Jewish history. Biblical heroes, he thinks, emphasized religious conformity and created a philosophy to "convince those who disagreed of the truth" of a particular creed or version of religion. The internal conflicts described in the Bible, as Kaplan interprets them, arise from a contentious claim that God demands one and only one type of worship.[32] Biblical religious practice in Kaplan's view seeks to satisfy a demand of an authoritarian deity. This belief, he argues, leads to the conclusion that divergence from that practice leads to divine displeasure. Traditional religion, as Kaplan pictures it, rejects deviation from the divine norm and excludes those who deviate from the community (much as the Orthodox leaders excommunicated Kaplan). Yet, Kaplan holds, modern Jews no longer follow any single order of observance. Pluralism and diversity of

---

[30] Kaplan, *A New Zionism*, p. 105.

[31] Kaplan, *Religion of Ethical Nationhood*, p. 10.

Kaplan, *If Not Now*, p. 111.

practice, he observes, have replaced uniformity. Insisting on uniformity he asserts, destroys communal solidarity rather than strengthening it.[33] Inescapably, he thinks, one must conclude that the biblical approach can only lead to Jewish conflict and hostility as one group of Jews regard another as unauthentic. A modern religion, in his estimation, succeeds only by showing how diversity strengthens group identity rather than weakens it. Kaplan rejects a view of God as an authoritarian tyrant demanding one and only one way of response claiming that it alienates most modern Jews. Jews, Kaplan avows, will accept Jewish religion only when it shows how Jewish history, destiny, and civilization help them achieve personal goals while maintaining their ties with a wider society.[34]

Kaplan's Solution to the Problem of Prayer

Kaplan's program for renewing Jewish develops in three stages. The first is philosophical: Kaplan offers a naturalistic understanding of how prayer does indeed make a difference in the world. Kaplan's naturalistic definition of God "as the power that creates and determines the conditions" by which human beings may improve their lives may seem impervious to prayer. Kaplan, nevertheless, does emphasize the value of worship. Worship for him directs a person's attention to the possibilities available for self-improvement and improvement of the world. By reminding people how they can bring their lives into harmony with that "power," Kaplan claims, worship enables them to "achieve abundant and harmonious" success.[35] Prayer, in his understanding

---

[33] Kaplan, *Judaism as a Civilization*, p. 215.

[34] Kaplan, *If Not Now*, pp. 67-68, 79.

[35] Kaplan, *Future of the American Jew*, p. 49.

of it, transforms life by mobilizing the resources on which an individual can draw. The universe, he claims, responds to human initiative. Stupidity, ignorance, dishonesty, and hate, he avers, breed failure, exploitation, and destruction. In contrast, he thinks, intelligence, knowledge, honesty, and love breed success, cooperation, and progress. Science, he asserts, reveals that theurgic prayer cannot manipulate the world. The universe, for Kaplan, remains indifferent to supernatural appeals. He does not deny, however, that the universe responds to prayers which alter human consciousness, which leave a person better prepared to utilize the possibilities for good inherent in any situation.[36] Such prayer, Kaplan admits, strengthens human beings and endows them with capabilities of changing reality. Whereas theurgic prayer seeks to alter the universe directly through words, what Kaplan calls legitimate prayer, alters the world indirectly, by using words to change the human worshiper.[37]

Secondly, Kaplan renews prayer by strengthening its most basic mechanism: the use of words. Prayer accomplishes its transformation through its use of words. Kaplan, as is clear in his affirmation of tradition as well as in his transformation of tradition's meaning, defines prayer as an act of thought, an intellectual dialogue. The intellectual dialogue occurs, he claims, within the worshiper; it confronts one part of a person's self with another part. Kaplan characterizes these two elements within each person in terms of a conflict between self-interest and public interest. He views tradition as an essential instrument for moving the individual from selfishness to social consciousness. He argues that prayer, like all human reflection, "is essentially

---

[36] Kaplan, *Greater Judaism*, pp. 481-482.

[37] Kaplan, *Questions Jews Ask*, p. 244.

a dialogue between our purely individual egocentric self and our self as representing a process that goes beyond us."[38] Through the words of prayer, Kaplan explains, worshipers transcend their usual limitations. Kaplan's idea of God, that of a transcending power, communicated through the liturgy, is thought to empower worshipers and liberate them to change the world. From Kaplan's perspective a vital liturgy fulfills this liberating function. He claims that it works toward an indirect transformation of reality through changing the way human beings think of themselves and orient themselves toward the world. People change reality when they change their attitudes.

Finally, as a social context in which this self-transformation takes place, prayer in Kaplan's system reflects the values of the civilization within which the worshiper resides. Kaplan insists on the public nature of personal growth. "Prayer," he argues, "is improved not by liturgical change but by communal association."[39] The environment of prayer, Kaplan declares, its aesthetic setting, provides that sense of being with others that lifts people out of their selfishness. Kaplan focuses his call for new liturgy on this motivational aspect of worship. He denies that liturgical alterations are mere decorative gestures. Symbols, rituals, and music should in his reconstructed Judaism reflect aesthetic standards not because they are "sensuously pleasing" but because as a means of arousing actions and stirring responses they are "appropriately expressive of religious values" and awaken a sense of religious community.[40] This instrumentalism explains why Reconstructionists today can combine a seemingly strange agenda that consists of both contemporary and traditional

---

[38] *Ibid.*, p. 105.

[39] Kaplan, *Meaning of God*, p. 261.

[40] Kaplan, *Future of the American Jew*, p. 52.

elements. The use images of the divine fitting for a pluralistic society augmented with pagan symbols that "their parents and grandparents rejected as outrageous literalism or anthropomorphism." By so doing, they assert the primacy of the function of prayer over the forms that it may take.[41]

The Sabbath and Kaplan's View of Prayer

Jewish practice, then, no less than Jewish belief appears as an instrument cultivating such responsible behavior in Kaplan's system. One example of the transformation of tradition into modern and humanistic terms occurs when Kaplan associates his definition of God's role in salvation with the Jewish experience of Sabbath worship. The Sabbath for Kaplan represents the "resources that inhere in the world" upon which human beings draw in realizing their potential. The Sabbath, as Kaplan reads the tradition, celebrates creation, not as a fact in the past but as a continual process supporting human efforts at self-fulfillment.[42] Kaplan hails the Sabbath as a transformation of an ancient theurgic practice into a modern commitment to humanism.[43] He traces how the Sabbath grew from a pagan ritual borrowed from Babylonian religion into an expression of Jewish religion. He thinks that its celebration took root in Israel by imposing personal and social obligations as a means of protecting citizens from the wrath of arbitrary deities. Originating as a day of ill omen, Kaplan claims that it restricted human behavior. As Judaism transformed the holiday, Kaplan continues in his analysis, it came to symbolize the creative aspect of life as against the destructive and cultivated in every Jew "a

---

[41] Raphael, *Profiles in American Judaism*, p. 194.

[42] Kaplan, *Greater Judaism*, p. 470.

[43] See Kaplan, *Meaning of God*, pp. 40-61, 90-103; *Judaism as a Civilization*, pp. 443-447; *Judaism Without Supernaturalism*, pp. 50-54.

renewed faith in the creative possibilities of life."[44] This change of meaning makes the Jewish Sabbath more in keeping with Kaplan's view of divinity than its original meaning suggested. Linking his definition of God with Sabbath observance enables Kaplan to maintain continuity with the Jewish tradition and its classical views of divinity while creating the communal environment needed to stimulate piety within individual Jews.

Kaplan, for example, argues for the philosophical rationality of the Sabbath. The Sabbath, like all Jewish folkways, in his view, serves to advance human life, to realize human potential, to lead people to fulfilled lives; in a word it is "an instrument that we may employ to advantage in our pursuit of salvation."[45] The Sabbath, as Kaplan interprets its ultimate meaning in Judaism, does not represent an irrational view of life, it does not reinforce a theurgic understanding of the world. Kaplan notes that Jewish tradition has exalted the Sabbath as a "foretaste of the World to Come." He points out that various maxims associated with the Sabbath suggest the necessity for human beings to take a hand in their own salvation. He recalls the rabbinic teaching that one eats on the Sabbath only if one has prepared ahead of time. He therefore contends that there is a "this-worldly" aspect to the Sabbath that makes it a rational, not supernatural ideal.[46]

Kaplan, in this way, turns traditional Jewish sources into instruments of the modern consciousness. He shows how the words and ideas associated with the Sabbath in those sources reinforce his interpretation. Thus he compares Exodus and Deuteronomy and their different justifications for the Sabbath

---

[44] Kaplan, *Meaning of God*, p. 92.

[45] Kaplan, *Judaism Without Supernaturalism*, p. 58.

[46] Kaplan, *Greater Judaism*, p. 76.

commandment.[47] Exodus focuses on the experience of creation and human participation in the sanctity God provides for that act. Because God rested from creation, so too human beings rest from their creation. The Sabbath as Kaplan understands this aspect of its meaning reinforces commitment to creativity and "a heightened sense of its sacredness." That holiness and sense of the sacred he insists was expressed in specifically Hebraic ways. Deuteronomy, Kaplan notes, associates the Sabbath with Israel's Exodus from Egypt. From this he draws the conclusion that the particular history of the Jewish people shaped how the Sabbath celebrates human creativity. Kaplan uses this as an example of how tradition links a person to a specific culture, to a definite past. The Sabbath laws, according to Kaplan's reading of Deuteronomy, are reminders of each Jews's "relationship to the civilization in which he participates."[48] In his discussion of the Sabbath, as in his study of prayer generally, Kaplan shows how the forms of tradition rescue people from a feeling of despair and disillusionment. By combining sensitivity to human creativity with the social setting that stimulates that creativity, the Sabbath tradition, Kaplan believes, awakens Jews to their potential. He concludes that "through our observance of the Sabbath we shall come to know God as the source of our salvation, of that state of being in which all our powers are harmoniously employed in the achievement of worthwhile aims."[49]

---

[47] For a discussion of the significance of this difference, a brief reference to Kaplan and a longer study of Abraham Heschel's interpretation of the Sabbath, all in the context of Judaism's contribution to the civil order, see my *Judaism and Civil Religion*. South Florida-Rochester-Saint Louis Studies on Religion and the Social Order vol. 3 (Atlanta, GA: Scholars Press, 1993), pp. 60-57.

[48] Kaplan, *Meaning of God*, p. 92.

[49] *Ibid.*, p. 103; the entire discussion runs from pp. 40-104.

Kaplan follows what he sees as the lead of Deuteronomy in emphasizing the creative aspects of Sabbath worship: the Sabbath serves human needs, it offers an opportunity for "the complete development of the imaginative arts and religion".[50] With that goal in mind, Kaplan evolves a modern approach ritual. He refuses to abandon the Sabbath because he claims it has an enduring usefulness--both for "the spiritual life of our people and of mankind." He admits that some Jews may need to fulfill every aspect of Sabbath observance to feel the complete benefits of the day. He suggests, however, that what they really cherish is the way that obedience to Sabbath regulations creates a community that reinforces their personhood. Kaplan notes that these laws enforce an egalitarianism in which master and slave, male and female, rich and poor join in common activities for an entire day. Obeying those laws, he conjectures, reminds individuals of their greater potentials but also binds them to the social whole. As such the Sabbath, he thinks, proclaims the hope for a new, cooperative society. Kaplan interprets the Sabbath laws as instruments meant to create a community in which all "collaborate in the pursuit of common ends in a manner which shall afford to each the maximum opportunity for creative self-expression."[51]

While non-Jews from the time of the Romans onward considered the Jewish sabbath a symbol of exclusivity and Jewish separateness, Kaplan finds in it the will to universalism and community. He interprets its practice as a symbol of how society can provide the framework within which individuals pursue singular paths to self-fulfillment. The Sabbath offers society a symbol of its solidarity and a means to affirm and reconfirm that solidarity. The

---

[50] Idem., *Judaism as a Civilization*, p. 443; see the discussion through p. 447.

[51] Kaplan, *Meaning of God*, pp. 53-54.

Sabbath, as Kaplan understands it, creates and sustains the community that practices it. Kaplan recognizes the personal benefits of the Sabbath as the basis of its appeal to the individual whose salvation it enhances.

Despite its benefits, however, Kaplan knows that modern Jews find the Sabbath antiquated and unattractive. He realizes that they need a hermeneutic for recognizing within the traditional forms the actual benefits of the Sabbath and so seeks to provide that hermeneutic. He uses the language of pragmatism as that hermeneutic. Thus he evokes a social occasion for the Sabbath. He locates its observance within community. He urges Jews to acknowledge that "a Sabbathless people cannot possibly cultivate the life of the spirit."[52] To preserve the spiritual basis of Judaism, to retain its hold on the Jewish people, Kaplan works to renew the Sabbath. The same motivation stimulates his varied attempts to reconstruct Jewish practice. These attempts are not as "illogical" as Steven T. Katz thinks. They are rather part of a coordinated program to maintain Jewish religious life within the modern democratic state. They affirm that creative use of freedom without which a democracy cannot survive. They do so precisely because they make use of the opportunity to choose one's heritage, to decide which elements of that heritage are most valuable, and to reinterpret the meaning of those elements. The Sabbath is indeed a symbol of "salvation," that is, of that freedom for personal development essential in a liberal democracy. It represents salvation not as achieving some supernatural value but as an opportunity for personal growth. This construal of traditional observance shows how Kaplan eschews prayer as a petition for personal goods and understands it, instead, as an opportunity for reflection on life and on the variety of meanings possible in existence. This view of liturgy strikes many

---

[52] Kaplan, *Greater Judaism*, p. 487.

resonant chords with postmodernist reflections of worship. He moves beyond petitionary prayer in its supernaturalist sense but also moves toward the "symbolic sense" rather than the "literal sense" of the texts of the classical liturgy.

Kaplan's "Prayer Without Demand"

Kaplan transforms the Sabbath from a behavioral act with specific theological meaning into an opportunity for reflection on the possibility of all meaning. In his hands the Sabbath becomes a tool for deconstructing the normal world of human limitations, the very world that makes ritual itself possible. The Sabbath confronts the worshiper with the need to choose how to view the world, it demands that each person reconstruct reality anew, it becomes a challenge to perception, not a confirmation of it. This approach to prayer and ritual agrees with the analysis given by Emmanuel Levinas.[53] Levinas emphasizes that prayer does not seek to transform God or theurgically make demands on God. Rather prayer creates an opportunity where one gains awareness of the Other. Prayer changes the worshipping subject not the object of prayer. Where as the subject often construes its meaning as existence "in itself" or "for itself," prayer reverses this priority. In prayer the subject exists for the Other. "Prayer," Levinas comments, "never asks for anything for oneself; strictly speaking, it makes no demands at all, but is an elevation of the soul."[54] This rejects petitionary worship for the sake of symbolism; literal meaning gives way before the hidden significance of a text.

---

[53] See Emmanuel Levinas, "Prayer Without Demand," in *The Levinas Reader*, ed. Seán Hand (Oxford: Blackwell, 1989), pp. 227-234.

[54] *Ibid.*, p. 232.

Prayer makes ritual itself no longer a human creation or a continuation of daily consciousness. Using kabbalistic references and focusing on the writings of Hayyim Volozhiner, Levinas show how through prayer worshipers confront the false visions of themselves and their world. This understanding of ritual accords well wit h Kaplan's reconstruction of Jewish liturgy. Liturgy no longer has a meaning in and of itself; prayer no longer supports the usual structures of belief in which people entrap themselves. Prayer for Kaplan as for Levinas liberates from the self-contained world human beings construct and demand a freer reconstruction. While Kaplan's formulation sees this liberation within the context of American life, as part of the American quest for new thinking, higher horizons, and self-renewal, it also uses ritual as the means for deconstructing itself and its presuppositions.

Chapter 10:

Interpreting the Jewish Tradition

Language, Tradition, and Postmodernism

When postmoderns, particularly those influenced by Structuralism, approach a traditional text they do so to decode the system of meaning no less than the specific meanings involved. Reinforcing the claim of Harari mentioned above, Jonathan Culler contrasts Richard Rorty's distinction between using texts and interpreting them and his distinction between "understanding" what texts mean and "overstanding" texts to discover *how* they mean. He declares that the purpose of literary study is not only to "develop interpretations (uses) of particular works but also acquire a general understanding of how literature operates."[1] Different theorists argue the nature of that mode of operation. Umberto Eco, for example, agrees that in theory symbols and images have infinite meanings. He claims that the symbolism found by medievals in biblical texts were meant not to exhaust the meaning of those scriptures, but rather to suggest the limits of human knowing. These writers used symbolism to "make rationally conceivable the

---

[1] Culler, "In Defence of Overinterpretation," p. 118.

inadequacy of our reason and of our language."[2] The purpose of a symbol is to teach humility. Eco claims that postmodern Deconstructionists have failed to learn such a lesson. By celebrating the infinitude of meanings possible in words, they forget that every text comes to set boundaries on that possible infinity. He calls for "a contextual disambiguation of the exaggerated fecundity of symbols."[3] Interpretation, on this account, should teach the discipline that textualization places on all possible meanings.

In contrast, Geoffrey Hartman sees in symbols a "surplus" that testifies to the inadequacy of the very limits which Eco celebrates. Studying a text or a tradition should entail discovering that surplus so as to undermine faith in the limited vehicle that transmits it. The student of a text should excavate for the "stubborn surplus capable of motivating a text or being remotivated by it."[4] A text is a cipher, a peculiarly powerful puzzle, that calls forth myriad responses. Hartman points to Walter Benjamin's fascination with names and anagrams generally and with particular reference to his discussion of a picture by Paul Klee, as an "example of how autobiography is determined by the idea of a hidden—spectral or specular—name."[5] Tradition, like literary or pictorial art, represents a surplus to be revivified.

Joseph Blau, reflecting on what makes American Judaism American, suggests certain characteristics of Jewish religion in the United States which call forth a response closer to that of Hartman than that of Eco. Blau isolates

---

[2] Umberto Eco, *The Limits of Interpretation* (Bloomington, IN: Indiana University Press, 1990), p. 11.

[3] *Ibid.*, p. 21.

[4] Hartman, *Saving the Text*, p. 15.

[5] *Ibid.*, p. 112; see the entire essay pp. 112-117.

"voluntaryism" as the primary force operating on American Jews--the "market-place" mentality in which the individual shops for a religious home and "pluralism, potestantism, and moralism" as secondary aspects of American Jewish religiousness.[6] The creativity of the individual is paramount. While certain contextual elements of American life may, secondarily, play a role in how the individual views Judaism and selects which Jewish elements to appropriate, the freedom of selection is granted pride of place. A postmodern awareness of the infinity of possible meanings in a text legitimates this personal liberty. Mordecai Kaplan recognizes the necessity for such justification for treating Jewish tradition as the source for infinite diversity. He does, secondarily, point to certain elements in the tradition that appear singularly relevant for modern American Jews. His major concern, however, is to validate an unlimited variety of responses, to teach Jews how to discover the "surplus" in traditional forms so as to deconstruct their apparent inflexibility and reawaken them, thus remotivating tradition.

Jewish Identity and the Jewish Languages

Kaplan approaches Jewish particularism from a democratic perspective. His view of the divine leads to a theory of worship which justifies a specific cultural expression as a means to achieve personal liberation. His theory of the interpretive process expresses a similar emphasis on democracy. Judaism, he claims, recognizes the value of interpretation because of its peculiar linguistic heritage. The biblical record, he contends, distinguishes among ethnic groups on the basis of their languages. He cites Genesis 11, the story

---

[6] See Joseph L. Blau, "What's American About American Judaism?" in Jacob Neusner, ed. *The Challenge of America: Can Judaism Survive in Freedom?* (New York: Garland, 1993), pp. 30-40.

of the Tower of Babel, to show that languages perform a double function: they promote social solidarity and separate one culture from another. Possession of a specific language, Kaplan comments, enables "individuals of a nation to enter into communication with one another", and, at the same time, develops a "consciousness" of one people "as distinct from other peoples."[7] According to him, socialization depends on combining these two processes. Without the ability to communicate, people would be locked in an isolated solipsism. Without their sense of group identity, however, people would lose their distinctiveness and forget the value of individual differences. From the connection between these two uses of language, Kaplan draws the conclusion that people must learn to extend their concerns beyond those of their immediate family. In this way he thinks, language socializes individuals to a group of others. He considers language a conventional construction of a particular community which creates social boundaries. The fact that language and ethnicity are interrelated, Kaplan claims, demonstrates that peoplehood is not a "natural" phenomenon but rather a social creation. Peoplehood, he argues on the basis of the linguistic evidence, is "not the product of any hereditary tendency or instinct, but of historical circumstances."[8] The process of socialization, he maintains, involves first a movement beyond family and self toward the communal body. Secondly, he continues, language consists of signs and symbols derived from the past. Language, Kaplan remarks, "brings in its train a whole complex of elements" that point backward in time. The specific vocabulary, idioms, and usages of a language point, he contends, to a "heritage which is transmitted from generation to generation." He

---

[7] Kaplan, *Judaism as a Civilization*," p. 190.

[8] Kaplan, *Future of the American Jew*, p. 84.

conjectures that a unity with the past that extends beyond contemporary experience arises from a shared linguistic tradition.[9]

Judaism, he believes, shares this common use of language, but with a difference. Jews, before any other cultural group, Kaplan avers, experienced language conflict. Jewish history as Kaplan describes it created a linguistic challenge for Jews. Even in their earliest cultural period, he suggests, the Jews suffered exile and were forced to adopt a second language. During the postexilic period of biblical Judea, Kaplan contends, Aramaic and then Greek succeeded in displacing Hebrew as the daily language of the Jewish people. Yet Kaplan argues that such displacement did not lead Jews to abandon speaking Hebrew. Jews, he notes, created a diglossia in which one language was adopted for certain situations and another used in alternative circumstances. Thus "Judaism," Kaplan states, "has not been monolingual...Instead of having one language to give it individuality, it has always had two."[10] According to this paradigm Jews used two languages, one for communication with the non-Jewish world and one for interJewish communication. Jews, according to Kaplan's telling, communicated with non-Jews using the common languages of the cultures in which they lived. In contrast, he states, they expressed their desire for salvation, their hopes for self-fulfillment, in a liturgical language, that of Hebrew.

According to Kaplan, the use of Hebrew reminded Jews of their loneliness, of being strangers in a foreign country. He observes that Jews, wherever they settled, no matter how congenial the host culture in which they lived, always created a special language of their own that would reconstruct

---

[9] *Ibid.*, p. 85.

[10] Kaplan, *Judaism as a Civilization*, pp. 191-193.

a spiritual homeland. They combined hebraic elements with the vernacular of the lands of their dispersion. Various religious practices reinforced this tendency to develop a particular culture of their own. Jewish liturgy, he suggests, offered a supportive communal reality in the midst of a sea of alien culture.[11] Without recourse to that language, he maintains, Jews remain isolated from their civilization. Kaplan contends that they need Hebrew as a cultural possession which creates the bonds of community that provide the social confirmation essential for salvation, and thus a manifestation of the divine. Lacking cultural ties with others, he cautions, Jews cannot find fulfillment and are bereft of contact with the divine. Without the sense of communal solidarity that Hebrew supplies, he warns, Jews cannot overcome their estrangement from others and therefore "their craving of communion with God remains unsatisfied."[12] Maintenance of cultural identity requires the use of such specifically Jewish expressions as Hebrew, Kaplan argues. He, therefore, supports the preservation and cultivation of Hebraic culture.

With that understanding of the power of Hebraic culture in mind, Kaplan insists that knowledge of Hebrew is essential for every Jew. He looks to the past to confirm this claim. In the past, Kaplan argues, the Hebrew language was not relegated, like Latin, to a pedantic elite who used it to control access to knowledge. Instead, he claims, it pervaded the most important spheres of human life: intimate family affairs, ceremonies of personal maturation, national survival. He draws the conclusion that this democracy of knowledge evolved because of the essential nature of Hebrew for Jewish survival. He remarks that of the various Jewish languages "Hebrew

---

[11] Kaplan, *Meaning of God*, p. 263.

[12] *Ibid.*

has been by far the more indispensable one" since it has preserved the Jewish sense of "historical continuity and present solidarity" (the two functions of socialization that language normally serves in a civilization).[13] Jews who forfeit this socialization, Kaplan argues, will experience frustration and a sense of "remoteness and irrelevancy" in Judaism. Estrangement from the Jewish tongue leads, he claims, to alienation from the Jews and their civilization.[14]

The centrality of the Hebrew language as a sign of Jewish distinctiveness, as a symbol of the Jews' contribution to whatever general culture they share, plays an important role in Kaplan's reconstruction of modern Judaism. He considers learning Hebrew an emotional prerequisite in the creation of Jewish identity. Through its instrumentality, he thinks, Jews experience "intimacy with Jewish life." Without the empathetic ties established by use of Hebrew "as a living vernacular," Jews who look for a "rational justification for being a Jew" will, he conjectures, only deceive themselves.[15] Nevertheless, he realizes that the language is a medium and an inspiration-not an end in itself. An irrational Judaism, he argues, cannot survive in the modern world. Kaplan augments his exaltation of Hebrew as a linguistic tradition with a reinterpretation of Jewish sources so that modern Jews will find them rational and compelling.

Kaplan's View of Biblical Religion

Kaplan's attitude toward tradition is both respectful and challenging. Mel Scult comments that Kaplan certainly "used the Bible as a point of

---

[13] Kaplan, *Judaism as a Civilization*, p. 193.

[14] *Ibid.*, pp. 452, 483.

[15] *Ibid.*, p. 452.

departure" for his own thinking, but that "making the text relevant was his ultimate, but not his sole, purpose" in biblical studies. Kaplan sought an honest understanding of the biblical perspective. While eventually noting the modern importance of the Bible, he began by appraising its objective characteristics and their difference from modern sensibilities.[16] He describes his technique as one of demythologization which recasts the language of supernaturalism into a humanistic key. Whereas the Bible speaks in terms of what the divinity demands of human beings, Kaplan seeks a modern approach interprets it in terms of the way the divinity serves human needs. This apparently radical change, he asserts, actually reflects the concerns of the Hebrew Bible itself. When understood in its own context, he explains, the Hebrew Scriptures introduces humanistic interests into religion. Whereas other religions focused on specific parochial needs, the Bible, according to Kaplan, pays attention to those universally human needs common to all people. Kaplan seeks to interpret the Bible so that this aspect of its teaching becomes clear.[17]

Mel Scult clearly recognizes that Kaplan engages in an act of translation. He does not, Scult claims, so much alter the biblical message as recast it in a modern language. His approach as Scult presents it is "functional" since he worked to translate "archaic notions into contemporary terms." Kaplan reconstructed the biblical texts so that the animating ideas behind them could be applied in modern life. He saw that application as critical rather than as a capitulation to modernity. He did not interpret the Bible to assimilate it to the modern climate but so that it could better criticize modernity. In this way, as Scult puts it, Kaplan's hermeneutic reveals him to

---

[16] Scult, *Judaism Faces the Twentieth Century*, pp. 246-247.

[17] Kaplan, *Religion of Ethical Nationhood*, pp. 17, 43, 47.

be "a rebel against modernity."[18] His attachment to the mythic world of the Bible shows his ambivalence toward the lure of contemporary secularity.

Of course, Kaplan makes concessions to the vocabulary of modernity. Jewish survival, he clearly fears, depends on the development of a religious philosophy congenial to the modern temperament. He contends that a modern Judaism cannot exist unless it makes use of the most recent discoveries. It must, in his words, "assimilate the best in contemporary civilization."[19] He notes that modern culture permeates every aspect of human existence. He sees radical change taking place "in the entire gamut of human living except in religion." Kaplan cautions the religion which fails to adapt to the language of modernity modern temperament fails to attract followers. More importantly, however, he fears that the vacuity of a religious message couched in irrelevant language leads to its ineffectiveness in cultural life. Since such a religion speaks a language no longer comprehensible, Kaplan argues that it no longer helps human beings improve their lives. To regain its usefulness, he demands that religion adjust to the realities of contemporary thinking.[20]

That usefulness, however, as Kaplan understands it, works against the very modernity it employs in its self expression. Traditional images, according to Kaplan, continually challenge a changing world in the way that America's basic documents, the Declaration of Independence and Constitution, continually recall Americans to their basic beliefs. Kaplan agrees that America's basic

---

[18] Mel Scult, "Kaplan's Reinterpretation of the Bible," in Goldsmith et. al, eds., *The American Judaism of Mordecai M. Kaplan*, p. 313; see the entire essay, pp. 294-318; compare chapter 9: "Torah and Salvation: Interpreting the Bible," in his *Judaism Faces the Twentieth Century*, pp. 240-253.

[19] Kaplan, *Greater Judaism*, p. 452.

[20] Kaplan, *Judaism Without Supernaturalism*, p. 5.

document retain their significance through a process of continual reinterpretation. He also claims that they curb possible excesses and enable Americans to balance progress and affirmation of ideals that do not change. So too, Kaplan argues, Jews understand their status and purpose through their relationship to the Bible. That text, Kaplan admits, no less than the basic texts of America, have different meanings today than they did at their inception. He also asserts that it corrects an uncritical acceptance of change as progress, just as America's legal process prevents radical revolution in political life.[21] Biblical symbolism remains important today, Kaplan suggests, for the same reason it remained functional in the past: it provides guidance in the present together with continuity to the life of the Jewish people. By maintaining a connection with the Jewish heritage, he observes, modern Jews avoid cutting themselves off from their roots. Using the Bible as an anchor to the past, he urges them to challenge the secular implications of modernity that threaten to overtake their lives.[22] Revelation, as Kaplan understands it, provides American Jews with a unique perspective from which to criticize and evaluate contemporary civilization. Kaplan translates from the prophetic and rabbinic religious idiom into a modern language that can revitalize the critical force of Jewish religion.

The Prophetic View of Revelation

God as revealer, Kaplan teaches, provides that social organization necessary for human self-actualization. The term God, for him, refers to a human fact: human beings within a social setting discover their individuality.

---

[21] Kaplan, *Judaism Without Supernaturalism*, p. 35.

[22] Kaplan, *Future of the American Jew*, p. 451.

He construes the term "miracle" to apply to the surprise people feel when discovering that obedience to an external code, acceptance of communal structures, and recognition of social interdependence leads to greater self-expression. Referring to God as the source of revealed laws, of halakha, according to Kaplan's interpretation, affirms that individuals potentiate their unique personalities more fully when acting within a social tradition than when standing outside of it. Kaplan's God of revelation confirms observance of law as a means for personal development. To speak of God in his terms means to advocate obedience to social norms as the route to human freedom.

The content of divine revelation in Kaplan's thought emerges from the interplay between traditional symbols and images on the one hand and personal frustrations on the other. The content of revelation, according to him, transcends the specific details found in any revealed text. The content as he understands it consists of an awareness of the human condition, the experience of frustration and ignorance arising from an honest view of reality. Kaplan also attributes to it the personal resolve that follows such an awareness. Not only does revelation in Kaplan's philosophy convey the terror of the sublime but it also provides people with the courage to persist life in the face of that terror. Kaplan traces the history of revelation as an ongoing development of the idea of the divine presence. He describes how Jews in different generations understood the divine differently. He affirms these differences as natural and positive. God in the Jewish tradition, he asserts, appears in both the despair that confronts human hopes and in the persistence that transcends despair. Belief in Kaplan's God of revelation implies a faith in the human ability to face disillusionment and inevitable limitations without thereby undermining the human will to survive.

Kaplan judges the authenticity of a revelation on the basis of its account of human nature as transmitted in a public and social tradition. Revelation, as a concept, means for Kaplan more than mere personal insight. Kaplan defines as revelation an idea of the human condition transmitted across generations. Kaplan's God as the source of revelation stands for the power of transmission that humanity possesses. Kaplan's belief in revelation affirms that human societies have the power to pass down a vision of reality from one generation to another. Affirming that belief declares humanity capable not only of withstanding the realization of its limitations but also of communicating to others that realization and an appropriate response to it.

This view of revelation as the basis for a social unity, Kaplan argues, finds confirmation in the approach of the Hebrew prophets. Kaplan associates his approach with that of the prophets. The biblical prophets, he contends, did indeed criticize their people. He describes them as denouncing the flaws in public worship and all forms of immorality. Nevertheless, he claims, the prophets maintained their connection with the Jewish people. Whatever their criticism, the prophets, at least as Kaplan portrays them, affirmed the value of the Jewish tradition. While the prophets rejected the common assumptions about religious practice, Kaplan remarks that "it would never have occurred to them to exempt themselves or their people from ritual observances as such." The prophets, according to Kaplan, respected tradition because no prophet "could not permit himself to be cut off from the particular people into which he was born."[23] Revelation in his theology becomes a means of affirming the particularity of a specific cultural community. Moving beyond the anonymous uniformity of modern democracy, biblical religion as expressed

---

[23] Kaplan, *Questions Jews Ask*, p. 229.

by the prophets as interpreted by Kaplan legitimizes those social identities created by the voluntary associations necessary in a democracy.

The Midrashic Interpretation of Revelation

Not only the prophets, according to Kaplan, but the rabbinic teachers, the heirs to the prophets, share this view of revelation. Their mode of interpretation of religious tradition, he allows, differs dramatically from philosophical rationalism and from the presuppositions of democracy, drawing as it does on models of Greek rationalism. Still, he insists, it complements rationalistic views espoused by a democracy. Kaplan, while not rejecting Greek rationalism, claims that American politics requires the passion and commitment only possible on the basis of religious faith. He notes that the Greek and Jewish views of reality differ and identifies that difference with the Jewish belief in God. Whereas the Greeks take a pragmatic view of society, the Jews, according to Kaplan, emphasize the transcendent responsibility that binds one member of society to all others. The Israelites, unlike the Greeks, he argues, founded social obligation on individual need. "The Hebrews," Kaplan writes," stressed involvement with the nation as the most effective source of control and satisfaction of human needs." He continues by suggesting that the Israelites rooted the value of the individual in a transcendent idea--that of God. Each person was needed by society just as each person needs society because "all were regarded as dependent upon the one God, the Creator of the world, its King and Savior."[24] Faithfulness to tradition, viewed this way, requires a double faithfulness--to the society as a whole and to the individual as well.

---

[24] Kaplan, *Religion of Ethical Nationhood*, p. 28.

The test of such faithfulness, for Kaplan, is not blind acceptance of revelation but a philosophical and utilitarian analysis of it. He insists that biblical thought does have a pragmatic philosophical purpose--to describe as fully as possible the interdependency of individuals and the society to which they belong. Tradition supplies that description, he thinks, because it provides individuals with a sense of the community while simultaneously restraining the community from infringing on the rights of the individual. He holds that that understanding of tradition creates a philosophy of political life. The human being exists within society, Kaplan asserts, more especially, within a particular cultural social group. Human beings, he claims, exercise their talents together with others; they do not develop their abilities in isolation. Kaplan sees this social tradition as the unalienable ground for every person's deployment and development of capabilities. Without being rooted in a specific cultural setting, he contends, people cannot realize their inner potential. Religions like Judaism and Christianity, he observes, contribute to democracy through their distinctive civilizations, each of which adds a political component essential to civil life. Kaplan, therefore, promulgates a particular political agenda. He insists that "every cultural or religious group should be permitted to function as the milieu in which the individual's rights to life, liberty and the pursuit of happiness may be realized."[25]

Kaplan recognizes the religious basis for such a claim. Kaplan construes one meaning of the term "God" as a metaphor for the human ability to utilize the social setting as an opportunity for personal creativity. The metaphor portrays a single being, an individual whose will and concern ensure individuals of the possibility for self-realization. Kaplan admits that the

---

[25] Kaplan, *Future of the American Jew*, p. 148.

personal attributes given to the divinity are essential ways of communicating, metaphorically, the positive potential within any society for unlocking personal potential. He recognizes the power and value of that metaphor. He cautions, however, against taking it literally. Kaplan prefers to speak of God as a metaphor for that lawfulness, resourcefulness, and humanitarian impulses that make personal life possible. To believe in God in Kaplan's way is to affirm the possibilities for human achievement. To speak of God is to refer to that aspect of human experience "which impels us to grow and improve physically, mentally, morally, and spiritually."[26] Biblical images, such as that of Abraham, perform the same function. Because, like a post-modernist, Kaplan emphasizes words, symbols, and their varieties of meaning, he uses the biblical material for contemporary purposes. He sensitively evokes new understandings from old texts through a hermeneutics directed not so much at what is "modern" as at what is humanly accessible.

Abraham as Jewish Ideal in Kaplan's Theology

Kaplan examines the biblical text to show how modern Jews can reject traditional religion without rejecting the images and symbols it contains. When interpreted from a modern perspective, he argues, contemporary Jews can find in it the same guidance as their forbearers. Kaplan understands himself as part of the interpretive tradition by which Jews have read the Bible from earliest times. Hellenistic Jews, he notes, cloaked the Bible in Greek garments; medieval philosophers clothed biblical religion in rationalism. Modern Jews, he continues, can provide the Bible with a contemporary dress -- that of humanism. His humanistic rather than theocentric reading of the Bible enables

---

[26] Kaplan, *Judaism Without Supernaturalism*, p. 110.

modern Jews to affirm their tradition rather than reject it. Kaplan assures such Jews that by approaching the Bible from his perspective they can appreciate their ancestral text and its significance.[27]

Kaplan's efforts at biblical interpretation show his determination to remain within Jewish tradition, despite the radical nature of his theology. He counts himself in the heritage that traces itself back from the present to the originators of Judaism. From the biblical injunction "Look unto Abraham your Father (Isaiah 51) through modern interpreters whom Kaplan cites, Jews have found in the first patriarch a model for their own religious thinking. Kaplan continues that tradition.[28] He reads Abraham's story not as an example of biblical supernaturalism but as a model of transnatural theology, transposing it "from the key of the ancient mode of thought, which was God-centered, to that of the modern way of thought which is man centered."[29]

Kaplan restricts his interpretation of Abraham to remarks on selected stories from the biblical corpus. He ignores many of the stories and focuses on those most amenable to his anti-supernaturalist interpretation. Three stories in particular occur frequently in his writing: Abraham's defense of Sodom and Gomorrah (Genesis 18), the *Akedah* (the binding of Isaac, Genesis 22), and Abraham's commission by God with its attendant change of name from "Abram" to "Abraham" (Genesis 17). The first seems particularly congenial to a humanistic theology. The story tells how God consults with Abraham before punishing the two evil cities of Sodom and Gomorrah. While Abraham has a personal stake in the outcome of this consultation, his nephew Lot being

---

[27] Kaplan, *Future of the American Jew*, p. 378.

[28] Kaplan, *Greater Judaism*, pp. 211-212, 237-238, 260-263; compare the discussion in Scult, "Kaplan's Reinterpretation of the Bible," p. 311.

[29] Kaplan, *Future of the American Jew*, p. 263.

a resident of Sodom, the story focuses on Abraham's humanistic concerns. Abraham argues against the injustice of destroying entire cities just because some members within it are wicked. More radically, he argues that the presence of a minimal number of righteous should weigh more heavily than a preponderance of sinful people. God listens to Abraham and allows his arguments to prevail. This tale of a human victory over the divine has clearly humanistic implications. As the Bible tells it, the story retains several "supernatural" elements: God destroys the cities in miraculous fashion, angels perform unnatural feats, God exhibits a superhuman power. Nevertheless, it provides a likely occasion for experiencing the importance of human beings for the divine.

Kaplan recognizes these elements in his discussion of the tale.[30] His most insistent interpretation, however, emphasizes Abraham's universalistic concern. Kaplan remarks that the story of Abraham, like that of Job, focuses on the question of theodicy. How can God, being just, punish the innocent? As in the story of Job, Genesis 18 questions God's nature. Can God fulfill the function of ensuring "responsibility as law and order" while inflicting pain on the righteous? Kaplan answers this question by showing its irrelevance. The Bible, he conjectures, does not focus on what God can or cannot do. It describes instead the process by which judgment is reached. Its intention is not to justify divine actions but to provide a guide to human beings seeking to create a well working society. Kaplan suggests that the purpose of the story is to show that God's righteousness appears in the *process* of determining justice, not in the final decision. God, according to Kaplan's reading of this

---

[30] See Kaplan, *Ibid.*, pp. 98-99; *Meaning of God*, p. 182, *Religion of Ethical Nationhood*, pp. 32, 37; *Future of the American Jew*, pp. 231-232; *If Not Now*, pp. 120-121.

tale, ensures justice by demonstrating the correct procedure any judge must use to reach a valid verdict.[31]

A contrast with the Book of Job suggests a second aspect of this story. Not only does it indicate concern with theodicy, with an understanding of the process of justice, it also projects a view of the scope of justice. Like Job, Abraham is skeptical of God's justice. As in the story of Job, God's justice resides not in *what* occurs but in *how* God acts. Kaplan notes that Job questions God because he himself experiences evil, is the victim of pain. Abraham's motivation transcends personal self-interest. Abraham pleads for the entire population of the cities, not just for those whom he knows are innocent.[32] Kaplan notes that "A less spiritual character...would have rested content with God's having saved Lot and his family." The story as Kaplan tells it focuses attention away from the parochialism of supernaturalist religion and emphasizes universalism. The biblical stories about Abraham, Kaplan avows, exemplify a philosophy of history that advances from one ethical stage to another with increasingly inclusive concerns. The stories, according to Kaplan's exegesis, show that human beings continually refine the process of justice so that it becomes less and less an expression of parochial self-interest and more and more an affirmation of universal human values.[33]

Kaplan's interpretation of Genesis 18 focuses on universal ethics derived from a religious philosophy of history. His interpretation of Genesis 22, the

---

[31] Kaplan, *If Not Now*, p. 121.

[32] Modern interpreters of the Bible would disagree with Kaplan's analysis. See the discussion in Laurence A. Turner, A., "Lot as Jekyll and Hyde: A Reading of Genesis 18-19," in *The Bible in Three dimensions: Essays in celebration of forty years of Biblical Studies in the University of Sheffield*, David J. A. Clines, and Stephen E. Fowl, Stanley E. Porter, eds. (Sheffield: Sheffield Academic Press; 1990), pp. 85-101.

[33] Kaplan, *Future of the American Jew,* pp. 232-233.

story of the binding of Isaac and Abraham's willingness to sacrifice his son to the divine whim, focuses on personal experience. The story tells how God "tested" Abraham by calling on him to sacrifice his son as a burnt offering. At the final moment, however, the story tells that an angel intervened to stop the murder. Henceforth, biblical religion rejected the practice of child sacrifice. Theologians have long been fascinated with this story.[34] It resembles other stories, like that of Agamemnon in Greek lore, where a man must sacrifice a beloved child. It differs from those stories in dramatic ways. It seems at odds with much of the ethical and humanistic aspects of the Bible, yet it provides the New Testament with a major theme and an example of ideal faith. Kaplan follows a well traveled road when he seeks to interpret the meaning of this perplexing text.

Kaplan interprets Genesis 18 in a straightforward, rather literal way. He provides little background to the story or discussion of its literary development. For Genesis 22, however, he feels compelled to offer such a discussion. He calls the tale a "myth" that arose to express a tension within ancient Jewish experience. Kaplan admits that this "bizarre" tale requires explanation because it combines an emphasis on blind obedience with an ethical prohibition against child sacrifice.[35] The story, he explains, arose when the Israelites stood at the crossroads of their development. They lived at a time when, according to Kaplan, religion demanded absolute devotion to God combined with an absolute respect for human life. Kaplan remarks that "out of the tension between those two conflicting attitudes" the myth of Genesis 22

---

[34] The tale also puzzles biblical scholars; see Francis Landy, "Narrative Techniques and Symbolic Transactions in the Akedah," in J. Cheryl Exum, ed., *Signs and Wonders: Biblical Texts in Literary Focus* (np: The Society of Biblical Literature, 1989), pp. 1-40.

[35] Kaplan, *Religion of Ethical Nationhood*, pp. 37-38.

arose.[36] He views it as an expression of a duality present throughout human culture. He takes it as testimony to a generally human experience, not to a historical event that occurred centuries ago.

The story, as Kaplan interprets it, reveals the traces of ancient Israel's changing sensibility. He uses the biblical tale to show how religion responds to new personal experiences. Kaplan glories in the complexity of the narrative. Biblical critics delight in showing the multitude of strands interwoven in the stories of Abraham. While they take this complexity as a sign of multiple authorship, Kaplan understands them as testimony that as people learn to value one set of concerns (that for human life) they displace older ones (in this case, that of absolute devotion to the deity). Like the author of this story, Kaplan suggests, modern Jewish leaders should facilitate the transition from one moral system to another. Abraham is portrayed, according to Kaplan, as evolving from a primitive state of willingness to sacrifice his son to a more advanced recognition that such an act contradicts God's desires. Ancient Israelites, Kaplan avers, needed the model of Abraham to legitimate their own religious advances. Modern Jews, he contends, need similar models for their own transition from supernaturalism to a transnatural theology. Kaplan uses the authors of Genesis 22 to illustrate the consequences of a transnatural view of divinity. The picture of God changes in the text, Kaplan argues, in accordance with changing realizations of human needs. The story, Kaplan realizes, occurs in the context of various "tests" that Abraham encounters. After each such test, Kaplan observes, the authors show Abraham emerging stronger and more self-confident. Transnaturalism, he comments, recognizes this process: rather than identify God with a static set of

---

[36] *Ibid.*, pp. 38-39.

commandments, it sees God as the process by which cultures and individuals recognize new demands facing them in their struggle for self-fulfillment. Biblical stories, in Kaplan's transnatural perspective, illustrate how God functions in this way.

The Bible presents Abraham as an individual struggling for self-actualization. It also presents him as a symbol of the nation of Israel. Genesis 17 tells how God renames the hero "Abraham." The patriarch's original name "Abram" refers to his exalted status. His expanded name refers to his national potential: he is to be a "father of many nations." Kaplan interprets the story of this change as one which emphasizes the social dimension of religion. He concludes from this tale that religious leaders should not restrict themselves to personal concerns but rather help stimulate growth and change within the group that they lead as a whole. Kaplan interprets Abraham's name as the symbol of a new life and new beginning. Abraham as an individual and the Jewish people as a whole undergo a series of transformations of which Genesis 17 is only a symbolic intimation. The people of Israel, like its putative founder Abraham, exchanges old names for new ones, old ways for new ways, old perceptions of the deity for more advanced ones.

Kaplan notes a startling fact. Not only human leaders such as Abraham undergo a change of name. Even God, he remarks, undergoes a similar change of name in several biblical stories. Kaplan draws an amazing conclusion from this occurrence. The Bible, he declares, recognizes that theology must change, that religion must grow and develop. Stories about the changing name of the deity and of religious leaders legitimate, in his view, the continuing self-transformation of Jewish religion. Thus he announces to contemporary Jews that "We have nothing to fear from metamorphosis. That, indeed, is how we began our career as a people."[37] While a supernatural deity appears unchanging and unchangeable, Kaplan's transnatural deity does not dread such evolution. As human needs develop, according to Kaplan, so people discover new sources and resources for their satisfaction. God's function, he insists, does not alter; the realities associated with that function must evolve with human needs. Kaplan's transnatural theology, as exemplified by Abraham, conceives of social identity as a process of growth and diversity, not of static conformity to an authoritarian order.

Kaplan's Justification of Jewish Sacred Texts

Kaplan's description of Abraham paints an attractive model for modern Jews. Kaplan succeeds in advancing a view of Judaism that responds to the problems he discerns in biblical religion. A critical look at his exegesis, however, shows that Kaplan strains the meaning of the biblical text. At times he draws conclusions from a simple reading of the narrative (Genesis 18); alternately, he relies on historical studies and a literary analysis of the development of the Bible (Genesis 22); in still other cases (Genesis 17) he takes a biblical passage as a mere point of departure, a suggestive stimulus for his musings. He neglects the entire narrative cycle that frames each of these passages and never confronts the comparative Ancient Near Eastern material which gives them significance. His biblical comments remain at a homiletical and sermonic level, lacking the rigor of a scientific study.

Kaplan's willingness to resort to such homiletics reveals the strength and weakness of his method. He succeeds in addressing the problems of a clearly defined constituency: one that accepts the modern scientific world view and

---

[37] Kaplan, *Future of the American Jew*, p. 539.

wants to reconcile it with respect for traditional Jewish sources. Within that context transnatural theology fulfills the criteria Kaplan sets for it. A contemporary Jew, however, can raise questions about Kaplan's thought. The problems that prevented many Jews from accepting Judaism in the past no longer present insuperable obstacles. A modern approach to religion often includes the experiential and ethical dimensions Kaplan suggests without being determined by sheer human needs. Jews have discovered the limitations of humanism, the ineffectiveness of a humanly generated system of values to authenticate ethical behavior. While Kaplan affirms God's presence in the personal possibilities open to every individual, many Jews do not know where to look to discover such possibilities whether aesthetic, intellectual, or practical. While Kaplan conceives of God as strengthening people in their attempts for self-actualization, many Jews are in search of self. While Kaplan's God points to ways of developing an ethical nationhood, many Jews despair of politics and of their own potential to influence political life. Without returning to the authoritarian deity that Kaplan associates with biblical religion, these Jews seek a theocentric religion for guidance in their lives.

Acknowledging Kaplan's legacy does not entail accepting his transnatural theology as an answer to modern problems. The response most loyal to his intent is that of living as a modern Abraham prepared to discover new meaning in Judaism by reconsidering the facts of the Jewish past and the realities of the modern present. Kaplan denies that his technique is arbitrary since no text can be read without interpretation. The superficial sense of a text inevitably distorts it: "The meaning of any passage in the Bible is not what the surface reading of it seems to convey, but what the interpreter reads out of or into it."[38] Kaplan's own thinking is susceptible to the same type of reading. While rejecting his specific interpretations of the Bible, a modern follower of Kaplan may accept the lesson he teaches concerning responsive reading of texts and the qualities necessary in any modern hermeneutics.

---

[38] *Ibid.*, p. 452.

Chapter 11:

Salvation and Jewish Identity

History, Halachah, and Prophecy in Postmodern Reflection

Geoffrey Hartman begins his reflection on the thought of Derrida by considering the writings of the modern Jewish theologian Franz Rosenzweig.[1] Rosenzweig emphasizes the need to move from the general to the specific, from life to death as he puts it. Religion, Hartman suggests, had "deferred" its knowledge of the whole and settled either for negative theology or for making the ultimate negation, death, the purpose of existence. If every individual must die, then the individual must be subsumed into a greater, eternal, universal. Philosophy provides death with its antidote--give up individuality and immerse the self in that which transcends mundane life. Rosenzweig finds the price to pay for immortality too high. He demands that history, the individual, and not only the unchanging universal receive a reprieve from death. He declares as his manifesto "into life." That emphasis intended to dispute philosophy's love for the universal and to root reality once again in the historical, in the specific. Yet Rosenzweig failed to achieve his

---

[1] Hartman, *Saving The Text*, p. xvii.

aim. His vision of Judaism was that of the "eternal people." He left history and its specificity and life to Christianity. Hartman concludes that this failure shows how history collapses all distinctions;"Jewgreek" or "Greekjew" as Joyce describes Bloom is all that is left. The story of Abraham collapses into the story of Odysseus. Everyone's adventures are those of Ulysses; everyone's child is Isaac.

Alexander Altmann explains Rosenzweig's dilemma more contextually. For Rosenzweig, Altmann suggests, history is identified with Christianity. The struggle between Christendom and Rome was not only the model but also the essence of history as he saw it.[2] The context in which Rosenzweig lived and its basic myths determined his approach to history and life. Those living in a different context would need to approach the revitalization of religion differently. A postmodernist would use the specific to generate not a single universal but an infinite plurality of possibilities. Josúe Harari notes the power of such an approach. A text always takes shape in a particular time and place, congealing a rich deposit of sedimentation into a single concrete form. The postmodernist critic engages in "desedimentation" that dissolves the final product into its composite parts. By doing this it permits "what was already inscribed in its texture to resurface."[3] This liberation of potentials from their imprisoned state provides an answer to the inevitable "death" that history entails without lapsing into a universalizing mode.

Mordecai Kaplan uses this technique of desedimentation rather than Rosenzweig's existentialism as he seeks to rediscover the meaning of

---

[2] See Alexander Altmann, "Franz Rosenzweig on History," in Paul Mendes-Flohr, ed., *The Philosophy of Franz Rosenzweig* (Hanover: University Press of New England, 1988), pp. 124-137.

[3] Harari, "Critical Factions/Critical Fictions," p. 37.

"salvation" for American Jews. He needs to balance American individualism with the communal identity of Jewish belonging, the defined nature of tradition with the limitlessness made possible by postmodern reading. As he sees it a Jewish view of salvation must contend with three sedimentary deposits: that which crystalized in the idea of the "chosen people," that evidenced in Jewish law, and that formed out of prophetic visions of the ideal. In every case he takes what appears as a complete, unified, and self-contained theological value and shows how it generates variety and limitlessness. While in its classical expression the idea of the chosen people identified salvation with the triumph of one specific nation, Kaplan discovers in the fundamental idea of covenant an impetus to compromise, re-evaluation, and process. Salvation as understood through covenant takes shape in a community willing to engage in an ongoing self-reflection and self-transformation. Covenant religion demands flexibility.

Kaplan recognizes that such an idea contrasts with the traditional view identifying covenant with a set of rules and obligations derived from "Moses at Sinai." To make his view of salvation plausible he must show that it encompasses an interpretation of *halakhah*, of Jewish law. Again he takes the crystalized tradition as a point of departure. Subjecting it to the disintegrating flame of analysis, he sees in it an open process. The leaders of the Jewish people, who "sit in Moses' seat," should be, like Moses, revolutionaries who continually challenge the people with new ways of acting, new perspectives on human behavior and values, new models of living. Kaplan finds such leaders not in the religious functionaries such as rabbis but in Zionist leaders and in American Jewry's lay organization. The promise of these new leaders is that they will generate a process of communal development and change, an infinite variety of Jewish alternatives. Finally Kaplan focuses on the "messianic" visions of the biblical prophets. He begins by suggesting that psychological and contextual elements shaped the prophetic visions. He continues by showing how attention to the detail of prophetic texts, such as that in Isaiah 6, leads to a deconstruction of the vision itself. In each of his treatments of traditional Jewish views of salvation Kaplan moves from the finished product--the doctrine of the chosen people, the corpus of law making up the *halakhah*, the biblical canon of the prophets--and generates instead an open idea liberating alternatives rather than restricting them by confining these aspects of religion to narrow definitions.

Kaplan and the "Chosen People"

Kaplan believes that religion's most important task involves projecting a view of the world, establishing a sense of the order of the world in which human beings live. Religion, he imagines, enables a person to move beyond the struggle to survive as an end in itself to an understanding of life in the service of values and ideals that transcend life. Religion, according to Kaplan, undergoes a predictable evolution. He thinks that it develops from a magical superstition to a philosophical monotheism. It advances beyond philosophy, according to him, and becomes ethical when it provides a sense of universal meaning that lifts its members beyond their parochial boundaries. That meaning comes, he says, from discovering the way every human life is interwoven with "ever-increasing webs of relationship with the rest of reality."[4] A religion, as he understands it, must continually re-evaluate its philosophy of life, its understanding of the purpose of human existence and its conception of the patterns governing that existence. Kaplan insists that only

---

[4] Kaplan, *Greater Judaism*, p. 468.

an acceptable, believable, and ethical philosophy of history can legitimate a modern religion. All such philosophies of history depend on the point of view of their creators and must be periodically exchanged for more effective and persuasive ones.

A religion such as Kaplan envisages must contend with one central difference between the modern and premodern religious environment: ecumenism.[5] Biblical religion, Kaplan believes, emphasized the exclusive history of the Jewish people and explained the importance of Judaism in terms of that history. Kaplan realizes that most ancient peoples presented themselves in such a way. He acknowledges that traditional religions see themselves as recipients of a special revelation and place their history at the center of human development. Nevertheless, he considers this view no longer tenable. The idea is now, in his words, "an anachronism" the luxury of which no civilization can afford in an interdependent world.[6] Because cultures need one another, Kaplan argues, concepts of cultural superiority undermine a group's ability to survive in a pluralistic context.

This approach underlies Kaplan's analysis of what he finds to be a peculiarly pernicious idea in biblical religion -- that of the chosen people. Biblical religion, he explains, considers Jewish history the unfolding of a divine plan. In it, Kaplan avers, God seeks to use humanity to create an ideal world. Kaplan claims that according to the biblical story, after experimenting with others, God decides that the Jews alone are capable of fulfilling the divine purpose. Kaplan opines that this religion fostered "an ethnic consciousness, which for intensity and far-reaching consequences in their lives,

---

[5] Kaplan, *If Not Now*, p. 111.

[6] Kaplan, *Judaism Without Supernaturalism*, p. 69.

was without a parallel in the life of any other people."[7] In biblical times, Kaplan reflects, providing an excuse for the origins of this concept, Jews needed an incentive for survival. Even after the biblical period Kaplan understands why Jews might cherish such an idea. During periods of persecution, he allows, the Jewish conviction of chosenness inspired heroic loyalty to Judaism. In the modern context, however, Kaplan argues that the idea only exacerbates intercultural hostility, warfare, and competition. With this in mind, he rejects the biblical claim to Jewish chosenness. He legitimates only that idea of God which brings unity and harmony out of the divisiveness of contemporary life. Modern religion, he insists, must devise a philosophy of history that "imposes on its adherents loyalty to a universally valid code of ethics."[8] Because Kaplan thinks that biblical theology emphasizes parochial history and therefore contradicts the ethical impulse of modern religion, he cannot affirm its continued relevance. Despite this rejection of biblical belief, however, Kaplan contends that Jewish particularity has a place in the modern world. Through constructing a laboratory for democratic living, Judaism, he asserts, provides a vital demonstration of the communal search for salvation. From its original idea of chosenness, he avers, the Jewish people can evolve a more adequate concept of religious vocation that will legitimize its continued existence as a distinctive group in the modern world.

Zionism and Kaplan's Prophetic Covenant

This view of religion as a voluntary and pluralistic phenomenon leads Kaplan to find a source of Jewish unity that does not conflict either with

---

[7] Kaplan, *Greater Judaism*, pp. 34-36.

[8] Kaplan, *Future of the American Jew*, p. 220.

diversity or with individual autonomy. Recognizing that, historically, the biblical idea of covenant had once cultivated diversity, Kaplan proposes that world Jewry once again perform a public and voluntary act by which they would bind themselves to Jewish identity. He calls for a modern reaffirmation of this covenant, a new covenant that will emerge from a world Jewish conference. He contends that such a conference could be the beginning of a new dynamic Jewish life. He calls it a "unique expression of religion under freedom."[9] His program for Jewish renewal in general and especially Zionism reflects the evolution of Kaplan's covenantal thinking. Kaplan's realistic approach to Zionism insisted on the creation of an ethical communal democracy. Kaplan recognizes that Jews often "paid only lip service to naturalism and democracy" and he offers a rigorous blueprint for a new Jewish society.[10] This democratic covenant associated with Zionism is dynamic rather than static. Kaplan understands it as a mechanism for contnual change in which the Jewish people transforms itself and legitimates that change.

In connection with his practical approach to Jewish social organization, Kaplan offers an extended explanation of the biblical view of covenant. He interprets the notion as one based on an affirmation of human initiative. When a community asserts that its identity derives from a covenant agreement, Kaplan explains, it claims that communal unity springs neither from accidental traits (such as birth or geography) but from a self-conscious, voluntary, decision. Jewish communal identity, insofar as it remains true to what Kaplan considers the symbolic meaning of covenant, affirms the freedom of individual Jews. Kaplan believes that loyalty to this community reflects personal

---

[9] Kaplan, *Judaism Without Supernaturalism*, p. 234; compare p. 155.

[10] See the discussion in Jack J. Cohen, "Reflections on Kaplan's Zionism," in Goldsmith, et. al, eds., *The American Judaism of Mordecai M. Kaplan*, pp. 401-414.

decision-making and voluntary association with a group and its ideals rather than blind "ancestor worship" or nationalism. Jewish peoplehood, understood in Kaplan's way, is a unique type of social organization, indelibly democratic. In contrast to other, more authoritarian forms of social unity, its very nature depends upon choice and intellectual assent.[11]

Kaplan applies this biblical model to modern Jewish life in his "covenant proposal."[12] Jews, as individuals and as a people, must enter into a new communal agreement. The various Jewish agencies -- whether Zionist or religious -- should, he thinks, form a communal and democratic body. He calls on this body to formulate and ratify a new constitution for the Jewish people that would transcend loyalty to any particular political state, but which would organize local, national, and international Jewry into a coherent unity. This rather ambitious program depends upon a general awareness of the unity of the Jewish people combined with an acceptance of difference and diversity within that people. Kaplan roots his insistence that Jewish unity allows for pluralism in a humanistic understanding of the idea of covenant. Covenant, he argues, commits the Jewish people to "ethical nationhood."[13]   Therefore, he demands the creation of a new Jewish order, one based upon voluntaryism rather than authoritarianism. He holds that only such a voluntary Judaism will enable the Jewish people to survive in modernity:

---

[11] See Kaplan, *Judaism as a Civilization*, pp. 258-259; *Judaism Without Supernaturalism*, pp. 155, 230-236; *Questions Jews Ask*, p. 50.

[12] See Kaplan, *Judaism Without Supernaturalism*, pp. 192-205 for the explication of the "covenant proposal;" other treatments of the same idea can be found in *A New Zionism*; *If Not Now*, p. 23; *Future of the American Jew*, pp. 54, 114, 392; *Questions Jews Ask*, pp. 48-50, 402.

[13] Kaplan, *Religion of Ethical Nationhood*, p. 10.

"The Jewish people, in our day, will be reconstituted as a law-making body, only when a sufficient number of affirmative Jews become convinced that there are need and room in Jewish life for a modern type of democratically instituted law."[14]

Kaplan's Call For New Leaders

Kaplan's program of covenantal voluntarism takes the biblical idea and liberates it from the crystalization it underwent in traditional Judaism. Covenant, as he interprets it, becomes a plan for continual desedimentation of possibilities within Jewish religion. Such an ideal program, however powerful it might be in theory, depends upon a responsive leadership for its practical realization. The reality of Jewish politics, for Kaplan, makes such leadership difficult to attain. In fact, Jews in the State of Israel have not achieved the goals that Kaplan set. Kaplan himself lamented that from at least two perspectives that State fails to live up to his covenantal model. Kaplan often criticizes the Zionist view of the Muslim Arab population in Israel. The lack of democratic outreach to the non-Jewish Arab population constantly concerns him. His views, like those of a few other Jewish thinkers, probably appear too "idealistic" in their hopes for democracy and voluntary cooperation. Nonetheless, they are important symptoms of the false consciousness that political realism often engenders. As Jack J. Cohen puts it, Kaplan stands in the "noble but ineffectual tradition" of Zionists such as Ahad HaAm and Martin Buber who opposed taking pride in the conquest of a national soil. With these others, Kaplan demands that leaders "accept the responsibility that their sovereignty be morally defensible."[15] With this in mind

---

[14] Kaplan, *Future of the American Jew*, p. 54.

[15] Cohen, "Kaplan's Zionism," pp. 412-413.

Kaplan attributes the modern malaise of Jews in the Jewish state to its lack of humanistic leaders. Kaplan does not castigate Jews for their arbitrary ways. Instead, he castigates authoritarian leaders.

A second symptom Kaplan sees of such short sighted leadership lies in the narrow view of Jewish religion authorized in the State of Israel. For political and practical reasons, Israel favors the Orthodox movement within Judaism. It discriminates against the non-Orthodox movements making them and their leaders marginal in Israeli society. This state-supported discrimination conflicts with the pluralism inherent in Kaplan's vision of democracy. Kaplan, therefore, castigates the leaders of Zionism for leaving the seeds for such a development uncultivated. Were Zionists to recognize the interconnection of all Jews, the interdependency of diaspora Jews and Israelis, and the dynamic qualities of Judaism as an ideology, then Kaplan suspects they would be able to create just those institutions he envisions; they would help transform Judaism in the modern world just as the framers of biblical covenant transformed their ancient Near Eastern environment. Zionists disappoint Kaplan because they fail to institute the communal democracy he envisions. Zion, however, is not Kaplan's only hope. He sees in American Jewry an equally promising opportunity for covenantal Judaism.

In several places Kaplan writes about the humility of Moses, the founder, he says, "of a civilization that still lives."[16] This hero, whom Kaplan notes is called "rabbenu," "our teacher," introduced a revolution in religious thinking and living. He did so because, as the humblest of all, he learned from others. As one of a long series of "younger sons" who eventually triumph (Kaplan notes the examples of Isaac, Jacob, and Joseph as well as

---

[16] Kaplan, *Future of the American Jew*, p. 279; compare pp. 216 and 317 and *Meaning of God*, p. 231.

Moses), he willingly listens to what others teach. When his disciple, Joshua, seeks to reserve prophecy for his master, Moses rebukes him. The true leader is open to the wisdom of others, is ready to heed alternative programs, is prepared for change. Kaplan deconstructs the Moses of tradition from an authoritarian figure who gives the law to a postmodernist willing to tolerate a cacophony of meanings.

Halakha and a Defense of Jewish Parochialism

Moses, in the tradition, appears as the source of Jewish law, of those revealed directives given at Mount Sinai. Kaplan concedes that "The most difficult obstacle to be overcome in the reinterpretation of the Jewish tradition is no doubt the dogma that the Torah is supernaturally revealed."[17] The ideal to which Jews strive has been, traditionally, confined to the specific dictates of that supposedly supernatural Torah. Kaplan opposes the static identification of Jewish practices with any one set of regulations. He sets as his task the opening of the gates of interpretation which, while not closed in theory, were in actually shut before the innovations of modernity. Yet Kaplan admits that specific practices and performances that distinguish Jews from non-Jews play an essential role in the diaspora. He defends American Jewish particularism because it can facilitate such organization. Kaplan's defense of Jewish particularity derives from the potential for democracy within what appears at first glance as an exclusivist ethics. Jewish tradition clearly divides its ethics between the rules meant for all humanity, the laws given to Noah and through him to every human being, and the rules given to Jews alone, the halakha, the six hundred and thirteen commandments that Jews are to follow. Kaplan's

---

[17] Kaplan, *Future of the American Jew*, p. 381.

understanding of the meaning of Torah suggests a new way to revive halakha as a means to ethical responsibility. Jewish law, Kaplan argues, works toward the goal of achieving human self-fulfillment. The structures of the halakha, he argues, provide a democratic forum within which individuals explore possibilities for action. In his view of the halakhic process, every Jew contributes to the growth of Jewish law because the true legislating authority in Judaism, from his standpoint, is the Jewish people as a whole. He calls for a restructured Jewish community with the power to enact meaningful and modern legislation which would demonstrate the creative possibility of a tradition renewing itself from within. Participation in Jewish law-making, Kaplan hopes, will teach each Jew the importance of personal decision making, offering each Jew an opportunity to grow in democratic responsibility.

Kaplan does more than refer to the humanistic aspects of this legalistic tradition. He notes that the potential within the halakhic system has been untapped in modernity. Indeed, he recognizes forces within modern Jewry that work against the humanistic aspects of Jewish law. Kaplan, therefore, calls upon world Jewry to organize itself as a collective body and renew the halakhic process in modern times.[18] His approach embodies a positive view of halakha within Judaism since it provides the mechanism for creativity.[19] Naturally Kaplan also recognizes the limits of traditional halakha in solving the problems confronting modern Jews. He admits that even the most liberal interpreters of Jewish orthodoxy emphasize an authoritarian rather than

---

[18] See Cohen, "Kaplan's Zionism, pp. 429-535.

[19] See Meir Ben-Horin, "Perspectives on Halakhah" in *Jewish Civilization: Essays and Studies 2 Jewish Law*, Ronald A. Brauner, ed., (Philadelphia: Reconstructionist Rabbinical College, 1981), pp. 112-121. Compare in the same volume Ira Eisenstein, "Mordecai M. Kaplan and Halakhah," pp. 145-154.

democratic model of decision making. The value of Jewish legislation for Kaplan lies in its reinforcing a theological contention: through social institutions God enables each human person to develop and potentialize selfhood. Halakha provides one mechanism by which the individual, as part of a group, grows to fulfillment.[20] This emphasis on law as the basis for personal development might seem paradoxical. Indeed, Mel Scult highlights the contradictory elements within Kaplan "the innovator, the rejector of tradition" who was also "very straitlaced in his moral convictions." He notes that Kaplan saw the discipline imposed by social regulations as an aid to personal development. "Although a thoroughgoing modernist himself," Scult maintains, "Kaplan had a keen sense of the destructive aspects of modernism."[21] Kaplan's advocacy of a constraining halakha, of a return to tradition as a restraint on chaotic freedom has both a conservative and post-modern aspect to it. The numinous expresses itself not only in moments of insight but in actions of obedience to external rules and obligations. The social order need not appear as an obstacle to spirituality but as its carrier.

In Kaplan's theology halakha reveals God's presence as a transformative force within society and the human environment challenging people and impelling them toward self-fulfillment. Viewing God this way reconciles the traditional emphasis on halakha with Kaplan's modern understanding of divinity as a continuing and revolutionary presence. Not only historically but presently too, Kaplan argues, human beings discover themselves through obedience to rules and norms that govern their lives. God, at least as Kaplan

---

[20] See the following essays in Brauner, ed., *Jewish Civilization*: Jack J. Cohen, "Toward An Ideology for Post-Halakhic Jews," pp. 127-143; Mel Scult, "Halakhah and Authority in the Early Kaplan ," pp. 101-110; and Charles E. Vernoff, "Toward a Transnatural Judaic Theology of Halakhah," pp. 195-205.

[21] Scult, *Judaism Faces the Twentieth Century*, pp. 266-267.

understands the term, reveals divine power by the persuasive function such rules play in human self-development. Just as no human community in the past could survive without structures and institutions of social life, so too, Kaplan argues, those today need a similar framework for themselves. His modern theology, like that of traditional theology, legitimates laws and rules as divinely sanctioned. He justifies acquiescence to social structures on pragmatic grounds. Human beings, he insists, cannot actualize their hidden potential without the protection that such structures offer. Structure calls forth anti-structure. In this way Kaplan anticipates the theory of Victor Turner. Turner sees the ritual process as a reminder that structure and antistructure, society and community, are in constant dialectical relationship with each other. He contends that studying society as a process rather than as a produce will "enable us to concentrate on the relationships, existing at every point and on every level in complex and subtle ways, between communitas and structure."[22] That, for Kaplan, is precisely the role of the structures of Jewish law.

Since "God" is but another symbol for "self-actualization" in Kaplan's system, his assertion that belief in the divinity sanctifies social norms and also undermines them at the same time is hardly inconsistent. The operation of Jewish law, halakhah, Kaplan thinks, illustrates his point. Through halakha, according to Kaplan's thinking, Jews can establish a balance between structure and antistructure, between law as a framework accepted by the individual and legal decisions as the result of individual decision making. He sees this dynamic dialectic present in Jewish theological ethics and applicable not only to Jews but to every human community. Kaplan envisions Jews teaching, by example, the dialectics of a humanistic ethics. He considers this exemplary

---

[22] Victor Turner, *Dramas, Fields, and Metaphors: Symbolic Action in Human Society* (Ithaca: Cornell University Press, 1974), p. 52.

teaching a major contribution Jews and Judaism can offer to American life. To achieve this aim, however, Kaplan reinterpreted and reconstructed the traditional halakhic system of Jewish life. The halahkic pattern that he advocates draws on but is not identical to that of the tradition.

Adapting Traditional Halakha

Kaplan defines halakha broadly. Any self-legislated set of actions falls within its boundaries. In this sense artistic expression may be a form of halakha. Kaplan integrates the demand for this artistry with his entire program for a new Jewish legislation.[23] Kaplan understands art as an expression of the reconciliation a person feels toward life. He claims that it puts into practice the theological recognition that human beings must transform the dross of existence into beauty.[24] In contrast to Kaplan, Jewish tradition usually regulated such artistry to a secondary role. Tradition considered the halakha primary: Jews should obey the *mitzvot*, the commandments as they are given. Nevertheless, Kaplan recognizes, the tradition does call on Jews to "beautify" the commandments by giving their obedience an artistic value. Celebration of the holidays follows a halakhic mandate; sanctifying those holidays with specially designed ornaments adds a beautifying touch. On the Sabbath Jews chant a prayer over wine to initiate the holiday. Beautifying the Sabbath entails creating an artistic goblet for the wine. Kaplan uses this aspect of Jewish custom as the basis for his own understanding of Jewish law; he retains these observances as distinctive Jewish norms of behavior.

---

[23] See Kaplan, *Future of the American Jew*, pp. 351-355.

[24] *Ibid.*, p. 118.

Jewish tradition, however, provides a different interpretation of these customs than Kaplan does. It calls them *aggada* and refers to this tendency toward artistry in condescending fashion. Judah Goldin traces that condescension back to the earliest rabbinic materials. He notes the instruction to "keep to the four ells of the halakhah" and concludes that, put "bluntly," it means that "Haggadah is not important." The practical impulse in Judaism often disparaged the theoretical attempts to explaining the reason and significance of observances. Theological musings were secondary to behavioral instructions.[25] Kaplan agrees with the tradition's de-emphasis on the aggada. This agreement limits Kaplan's effectiveness in reconciling modernity and the traditional claims of revelation. How can revelation demonstrate its authenticity when science disputes its conclusions and daily experience refutes its view of the meaning and destiny of human life.

Kaplan cites Hayyim Nahman Bialik's essay on the need to revive halakha in the modern world. Like Bialik, Kaplan feels that moderns often escape to aggada without sufficient recognition of their obligations for action. He translates the last section of Bialik's essay comparing halakha and aggada approvingly as a spur to create a new halakhic model for modern Jews. He uses Bialik's call for halakha to reinforce his own summons to serious Jewish activism.[26] Kaplan's citation of Bialik's essay on halakha and aggada reflects accurately its rejection of pure theory. Bialik directed his criticism to those who sought art for its own sake.[27]

---

[25] See Judah Goldin, "The Freedom and Restraint of the Haggadah," in *Midrash and Literature*, Geoffrey H. Hartman and Sanford Budick, eds. (New Haven, CT: Yale University Press, 1986), pp. 57-76.

[26] Kaplan, *Judaism Without Supernaturalism*, pp. 175-176.

[27] An excellent study of Bialik's view of aggada and halakha throughout his corpus and its

(continued...)

Kaplan misrepresents Bialik, however, when characterizing the essay as a description of the *conflict* between the two. Bialik recognizes the need for balancing the practical and the theoretical. Kaplan's own approach to Jewish liturgy reveals a similar practical combination of idea and expression. Perhaps no where does Kaplan reveal this combination better than in his approach to women in Jewish ritual.[28] Kaplan notes that Jewish tradition excludes women from various important functions and explains this exclusion as a result of historical conditioning. He suggests that as that history has changed, the status of women should change as well. It has not, and in the modern context, Kaplan can only interpret that lack of change as treating women as inferior. Originally, Kaplan concedes, the exemption of women from Jewish legal practice "was no derogation of their status." In the contemporary world, however, he asserts that it can be interpreted as nothing else. The creation of a covenantal Jewish community must involve what Kaplan calls "creative adjustment" and therefore extend equality to women.[29]

In his practical activities as a rabbi Kaplan matched his theory with deed. Learning from the example of his father who had caused a scandal by educating his daughter, Kaplan actively worked for female equality. He insisted on mixed seating, with men and women worshiping together, in his Society for the Advancement of Judaism. He instituted the Bat Mitzvah, a ceremony for women parallel to the male maturation ritual of the Bar

---

[27](...continued)
relationship to opposing views such as those of Micha Yosef Bin-Gorion is found in Isaiah Rabinovitch, "Struggles Between Halakha and Aggada" in his *Roots and Trends: Essays on Literature* [Hebrew] (Jerusalem: Bialik Institute, 1967), pp. 219-259.

[28] See the essay by Carole S. Kessner, "Kaplan and the Role of Women in Judaism," in Goldsmith, et. al, eds., *The American Judaism of* Mordecai M. Kaplan, pp. 335-356.

[29] See Kaplan, *Questions Jews Ask*, pp. 230-236.

Mitzvah. He deliberately decided to apply all the requirements of the male ceremony to the female ritual in contrast to other "liberal" attempts that introduced a similar, but diluted, form of the ritual for young men.[30] Kaplan argued that such rituals provide the incentive women need for lives of piety. Such feminine piety, he claimed, "will speed the redemption of modern Israel."[31] Kaplan recognizes the importance of integrating women into a modern Judaism and uses ritual as a means of achieving this goal.

Theology and Practice in the Formation of Community

Kaplan applies his covenantal model of Jewish community to all aspects of Jewish ritual practice, not just to the question of the rights of Jewish women. His new approach to Judaism as an exercise in democracy requires new guidelines for Jewish behavior. Kaplan demands that Jewish practice be revised through a voluntary, democratic process. He claims that the formation of a new covenantal constitution will solve the dilemma of Jews who reject an imposed tradition by providing a new democratic source of those laws which govern Jewish living.

When outlining the elements required by his proposed covenantal constitution, Kaplan insists that there must be "unity without cultic uniformity."[32] This insistence reflects a reality of modern Jewish life. Kaplan's insight that religion must be pragmatic finds support in contemporary Jewish behavior. Jews follow only those religious practices that translate into personal

---

[30] Kessner, "The Role of Women in Judaism," p. 351.

[31] Kaplan, *Future of the American Jew*, p. 412.

[32] Kaplan, *Religion of Ethical Nationalism*, p. 11.

significance.[33] Jews become uncomfortable with those practices that seem to thwart or even reverse modern efforts at self-development. The transformation of Jewish practice for the sake of pragmatic ends--whether done consciously or unconsciously--presents a problem for both traditionalists and non-traditionalists. Traditionalists must cope with the necessity for change despite their commitment to continuity with the past. Non-traditionalists must discover a means of ensuring their continued links with a historical identity despite their acceptance of changes in religious practice.

Kaplan's view of Jewish practice generally emphasizes this double contribution that religion makes to individual development and that the individual makes to humanity. He argues that religious practice and symbolism binds an individual to a particular social group. According to his philosophy, an individual learns to share with others, to place the group at the center of personal concern. The individual, Kaplan feels, learns that self-actualization becomes impossible unless done within and for the sake of a larger unit than the self. Religion, as Kaplan uses the word, teaches that life is worthwhile not only by stressing the importance of the individual, but, more concretely, showing how the individual is important for the group.[34] This altruism, he feels, expresses itself most clearly when individuals act not merely for the good of their parochial group, but for all humanity. He does not consider the two types of motivation mutually exclusive; by acting for the sake of one's own community, he argues, one not only increases the possibility of self-actualization but also advances the good of the human community. Society

---

[33] See my study *The Ecumenical Perspective and the Modernization of Jewish Religion* (Chico, CA: Scholars Press, 1978).

[34] See Kaplan, *A New Zionism*, pp. 98, 112, 115; *Greater Judaism*, pp. 453, 468.

and individuals are not competitors but co-workers in the attempt to improve human life.

Kaplan notes the interaction of benefits--an individual's altruism influences the local community, but also humanity at large. He argues that the group serves the individual. Not only does he think that religion identifies the individual with the community, but also that it gives the community the task of serving the individual. Kaplan explains the function of communal worship as serving two purposes: that of selecting and symbolizing those elements of reality that help one attain certain ideals and that of identifying oneself with a community that holds those ideals. Such self-identification, according to him, includes a recognition of the obligations an individual owes to society. These obligations become compelling, Kaplan argues, only if the society supports individual growth. Such a symbiosis indicates to him that the society itself is to be judged--by virtue of the ideals it holds and the way in which it serves individuals who seek to realize those goals. Kaplan contends that a religion serves its members through symbols and rituals that satisfy their spiritual needs and that also bind them to society.[35]

Kaplan's approach to the problem of religious practice tends to be concrete and practical. He urges that individuals accept those "rites and symbols" having personal meaning, reserving the right to reject meaningless ones. This approach will create a "voluntaristic Jewish religion" that is "diverse in belief and practice." He realizes that this call if heeded will result in ritual diversity and destroy any uniform code of Jewish behavior. That consequence seems a price worth paying since, not only does he find the idea of an absolutely uniform code of Jewish practice unrealistic, but he feels that

---

[35]   Kaplan, *Judaism as a Civilization*, p. 347; *If Not Now*, pp. 38-39; *Future of the American Jew*, p. 418.

differences "in personal taste, aptitudes and interests renders it undesirable." Jewish communal life, Kaplan asserts, would become less able to respond to individual needs were it to impose a single standard of ritual practice.[36] Since rituals lead from the past to the future, from the static to the dynamic, Kaplan insists on destabilizing the *halakhah* and showing its potential for stimulating diversity rather than reducing the infinite to a single system.

Community, Salvation, and Prophetic Hope

Kaplan's view of American Jewry seems, perhaps, utopian. He envisions a Zionism that transcends parochial national interests, a democratic process in Jewish organizations that defies the logic of power politics, and a sense of peoplehood that stimulates individual development. His theology, however, is not as naive as it might appear. It rather sees the virtue of religion to lie in its appeal to the ideal as a criticism of the present. He uses the language of democracy against itself, as a critique of its self-satisfaction. He shows how the biblical texts perform a similar function. Prophetic writers often portray a vision of the ideal, of a utopian hope. Nevertheless, they undermine the picture they evoke. Kaplan draws attention to the way in which biblical passages actually work against themselves and lead to a desedimentation of the infinite possibilities hidden by the reduction of the visions they report to a single written work.

He understands his own work to destabilize tradition as a continuation of prophetic Judaism. He recognizes that Israel's prophets made use of affective language to transform their community. As early as 1926 he points to the inadequacy of a purely rationalistic religion. Studying the prophetic

---

[36]   Kaplan, *Judaism Without Supernaturalism*, p. 116; *A New Zionism*, p. 92; *Future of the American Jew*, pp. 420-421--see the entire discussion on ritualism on pp. 413-428.

experience reflected in Isaiah 6, Kaplan notes its appeal to imaginative and emotional resources.[37] Kaplan considers the narrative in Isaiah and concludes that it reflects a prophetic vision, not a recollection of Isaiah's call to prophecy. Isaiah 6 relates how the young prophet was confronted by a vision in the Jerusalem Temple at the time when King Uzziah died (perhaps on the occasion of the coronation of a new king). God, imagined as a king holding court with the angels on high, seeks a messenger to send to Israel; Isaiah volunteers and finds his profession. The event, however, needs to be examined in detail.

Isaiah reports:

> In the year of King Uzziah's death I saw the Lord seated on a throne, high and exalted, the hem of his robe filled the Temple. About him were attendant angles, each had six wings: one pair covering his face, one pair his feet, one pair spread in flight. They called continually to one another: "Holy, Holy, Holy is the Lord of Hosts: the whole earth is full of his glory. As each one called the foundations of the threshold shook while the house was filled with smoke.

The overwhelming awe associated with this vision cannot be ignored. It should, however, be understood in context. Isaiah is not shocked that God should appear at the Temple but rather at the realization that God lies outside the Temple and that proclamations of God as the Lord of Jerusalem are misplaced. Indeed he discovers that it only takes God's shirt tails, the hem of the divine garments, to fill the Temple! This insight leads him to admit the inadequacy of his worship, his theology, his view of God. Only sinful lips

---

[37] See Mordecai M. Kaplan, "Isaiah 6:1-11," *Journal of Biblical Literature* 45 (1926): 251-259.

can so constrain God who is not within the Temple. This realization underlies his words of response:

```
Woe is me! I am lost, for I am a man of
unclean lips and I dwell among a people of
unclean lips; yet with these eyes I have seen
the King, the Lord of Hosts.
Then one of the seraphim flew to me carrying
in his hand a glowing coal which he had taken
from the altar with a pair of tongs. He
touched my mouth with it and said "See this
has touched your lips; your iniquity is
removed and your sin is wiped away. Then I
heard the Lord saying, "Whom shall I send? Who
will go for me? And I answered, "Here am I
send me."
```

Two points should be stressed about this text. First, Isaiah's initial response refers to his dissatisfaction with cultic performances. He does not declare himself a sinner nor does he declare the people to be sinners. He does not announce--in words that might be expected based on passages in Isaiah 1-5 that "I am a wicked man and I dwell among a wicked people." The passage focuses instead on what Isaiah has been **saying**. It is the confession of faith that he and his people have been uttering that is at fault. Kaplan understands his words with reference to the prophetic profession. He claims that the experience arises out of the facts of Isaiah's prophetic career. It grew out of the tension between his acceptance of tradition and his criticism of that tradition. The images he uses draw on the very religious sources against which he protests. Kaplan sees the vision as a psychological event occasioned by the internal conflict within the prophet's own mind.[38] The need for balance creates the psychological environment which stimulates an ecstatic vision. The

---

[38] *Ibid.*, p. 251.

description itself evokes a tension between the place of the vision, the Temple in Jerusalem, and its content, God stands outside the Temple, between the task of the prophet--to speak for God and act as a divine messenger--and the destiny of the prophet--to be misunderstood, ignored, and rejected. Here the inner workings of the text reveal the false polarities which inevitably undermine any single interpretation of meaning.

Secondly, God enables Isaiah to accept a task assigned to him by sending an angel to touch Isaiah's lips with a burning coal to cleanse him of guilt and sin. God has the obligation of preparing human beings to accept the ethical obligation that flows from an encounter with the Holy. Even with the experience of the Holy it might be impossible for a human being to be ethical, human nature might prevent the realization of the divine task. The experience of the Holy itself, however, purifies and makes it possible for human beings to respond when God requires a messenger.

Kaplan understands this aspect of the experience no less than the tension within the vision in utilitarian terms. He considers this experience as indirect utilitarianism at work. On one level the text concerns theological change, it demands a new understanding of the deity. On another level, however, it changes Isaiah's perception of what it means to be human. He suggests that ancient texts always attribute new views about human experience to the deity. "Any striking idea," he comments, "whether it dealt with some immediate personal concern or with some social problem" was considered a divine inspiration.[39] Here indirection takes the form of using theology to teach a social and psychological truth.

---

[39] *Ibid.*, p. 257.

The text continues with the details of Isaiah's task, details that portray and legitimate what, at first glance, appears to be an impossible duty: Isaiah has been doomed to failure. His task is to speak but to be misunderstood. He describes how God said:

> "Go and tell this people: you may listen and listen but you will not understand. You may look and look again but you will not know."
> ...Then I asked, "How long, O Lord?" and he answered "Until cities fall in ruins and are deserted...and until only a holy stump, a remnant remains."

While this text includes a hopeful message -- a remnant will remain -- it emphasizes the futility of Isaiah's mission. The task of being a prophet is deconstructed by the content of that task. The biblical text denies that it can function as a means of communication. What appears as a message turns out to be a wall of silence. Isaiah's task fails if he succeeds in warning the people. He succeeds only if he confuses them! Kaplan sees this announcement as a response to the psychological despair that affected the prophet in his ministry. The passage itself reshapes conventional thought so that apparent failure takes the form of success. Here the idea of the inevitable destruction of the nation of Judah took form through what Kaplan calls "a powerful imagination" into a "vivid metaphor" that he judges as "a genuine psychological experience."[40] Kaplan identifies this transformation of a realistic view of the communal crisis into a psychologically compelling image the prophet's contribution to society. It takes but some imagination to extend that function from the prophets through the mystical tradition to modern society. Jews today require leaders who, like Isaiah among the prophets, can refashion

---

[40] *Ibid.*, p. 259

their analysis of reality into a means of mobilizing the feelings of modern Jews. The Jew today, Kaplan suggests, needs a revisionist prophet like Isaiah who can take up criticism of the society, transform it into psychological experience, and convey it in poetic ways to the contemporary audience.

This approach reveals the postmodern impetus behind Kaplan's work. He tries to sensitize American Jews to the endless possibilities present when struggling with a tradition. Postmodernism has been defined as a rejection of authority, or better as a deconstruction of authority. The basis for orthodoxy discloses itself as pluralistic and variable. Touted uniformity reveals its diversity. Postmodernism, it is said, "refines our sensitivity to differences and reinforces our ability to tolerate the incommensurable."[41] Kaplan draws attention to the incommensurable, and he describes salvation as the discovery of that unbounded within the apparently limited and defined. Tolerating the incommensurable means discovering that it provides the tool for our liberation and salvation.

---

[41] See Jameson in Lyotard, *The Postmodern Condition*, p. xxv.

PART V: KAPLAN FOR THE POSTMODERN AGE

Chapter 12:

Kaplan Beyond Rationalism

Postmodern Anticipations in Kaplan

Kai Nielson accepts the postmodern recognition of layers of meaning. He denies, however, that they testify to an incommensurability that makes definitive statement impossible. He agrees that legitimating myths often reinforce oppressive social systems. Ideological beliefs undergird the repressive and coercive political bodies that govern society. Nevertheless, he argues, the solution of the postmodernist seems to extreme. To deconstruct these myths by positing an infinite and uncrossable gulf between meaning and text seems to him an overreaction. He questions "whether there are really such incomensurable abysses" as postmodernism delcares.[1] Umberto Eco seems sympathetic to this type of critique. He compares the current situation to that of the Middle Ages. There the problems of understanding the meaning of the Bible resolved itself into two alternatives: philosophy understood plurality of meaning by using a single, and logical standard; mysticism,

---

[1] Kai Nielson, *After the Demise of the Tradition: Rorty, Critical Theory, and the Fate of Philosophy* (Boulder, CO: Westview Press, 1991)

kabbalah, delighted in myth and declared that it was a gift from the divine. Thus he notes that while "symbolists...defined the ideal text as that which allows the most contradictory readings" the mystics claimed that "the Torah was open to infinite interpretations because it could be rewritten in infinite ways"[2] While he argues that both approaches reduced an infinite plurality by positing some form of limitation, the difference between the two forms is essential. The first uses logic to evaluate texts; the second refers to the divine as a rationale for generating more meanings from discrete texts. The latter, despite Eco, seems close to postmodernism.

The previous chapters have suggested that while clothed in modern garments Kaplan's thought reveals many connections to postmodernism. In two areas, however, Kaplan is distinctly "unmodern" and anticipates the postmodern. He rejects logic and philosophy as valuable tools in creating a viable religion. This present chapter investigates this antipathy toward the philosophers as a postmodern anticipation explicit in Kaplan. Kaplan also self-consciously prefers the mystics to the philosphers. Like contemporary postmoderns he privileges variety and diversity over definition and economy. He affirms an infinitude of meaning in preference to precision. The following chapter examines that aspect of Kaplan's thought which also anticipates the attraction to myth and kabbalah found among the postmoderns.

Criticism of Kaplan's Rationalism

A common critique of Kaplan's naturalistic theology complains that it ignores the transcendent dimension of human life. Many critics find the system of thought described in the previous chapters a distortion of the rich

---

[2] Eco, *The Limits of Interpretation*, p. 51.

mythic and emotional elements within Judaism. David Hartman's analysis of Kaplan's thought echoes this criticism. Hartman recognizes the many valuable aspects of Kaplan's philosophy of Judaism but concludes that his approach locks the divine and human "into the same anthropocentric framework" and fails to do justice to the fullness of religious experience. Hartman contrasts Kaplan's humanistic naturalism to the theology of Abraham Joshua Heschel, whose advocacy of the sense of the ineffable looks beyond human experience. He also notes the claims of Heschel's predecessor in the phenomenology of religion, Rudolf Otto, whose intuition of the idea of the holy recognizes the awe and mystery associated with religious experience. Hartman claims that both a study of religion in general and of Judaism in particular discloses the affective and suprarational aspects that inform human spirituality. The evidence these theorists provide suggests that too rigorous a rationalism overlooks the depth dimension of human religiousness.[3] Kaplan's functional approach to religion and theology apparently ignores the yearning for transcendence that motivates the religious quest.

Hartman concludes that Kaplan's approach to Judaism suffers on two counts. In the first place his absolute rationalism leads him to overemphasize traditional Judaism's reliance on supernaturalism. In several of his own writings, for example, Hartman emphasizes the dialectic between human creativity and divine authority. On the same grounds he charges Kaplan with reducing this dialectic to an unequivocal naturalism. In this way he characterizes Kaplan's presentation of the contradiction between the authority of divine revelation and the autonomy demanded by human reason as "incomplete and misleading." He states that "Kaplan weakened the dynamic

---

[3] See David Hartman, "Kaplan's Critique of Halakhah," in his *Conflicting Visions: Spiritual Possibilities of Modern Israel* (New York: Schocken, 1990), pp. 192-194.

tension underlying Judaism" by making too sharp a distinction between the roles of the divine and the human in the creation of Jewish religion.[4] Secondly, as intimated above, Hartman claims that Kaplan fails as a phenomenologist of religion and ignores the affective dimension of Jewish religion. Kaplan's exposition of Jewish teachings, according to Hartman, stresses the rational, the lucid, and the self-evident. As such, Hartman declares, these teachings obscure Judaism's recognition of its own limitations. Hartman affirms that Jewish religion retains a sense of ultimate mystery, of the boundary beyond which human knowledge cannot cross. He criticizes Kaplan's reconstruction of Judaism because it renders the entire meaning of Jewish religion in rationalistic, explanatory, and mundane terms. For Hartman this functionalism prevents Kaplan from intimating the ultimate mystery.[5] Hartman claims that Kaplan seeks to answer all questions, to provide an entirely rational explanation for all aspects of Judaism. Indeed, Hartman distinguishes Kaplan from medieval rationalists because those Jewish thinkers "never believed that their functional, anthropomorphic interpretations were exhaustive."[6] Kaplan, on this reading, differs from the medievals by a type of intellectual arrogance that prevents him from admitting ignorance.

These criticisms misunderstand Kaplan's approach to Judaism generally and his appreciation of the affective dimension of Jewish religion in particular. Kaplan approaches Jewish religion neither as an absolute rationalist nor as a phenomenologist, but as a utilitarian. He criticizes traditional Judaism not merely because it relies on supernaturalism, but rather because it cannot

---

[4] *Ibid.*, p. 202.

[5] *Ibid.*, p. 206.

[6] *Ibid.*, p. 191.

function effectively in the modern world. He deemphasizes the affective aspects of Jewish religion not because he rejects them but because emotional commitment cannot be commanded, it evolves as a by-product, indirectly stimulated through the persuasiveness of a tradition. Ironically, he criticizes the rationalistic tradition of the medieval period precisely because he claims that it is insensitive to the emotional and mysterious aspects of Judaism.

Kaplan and Utilitarianism

Studying Kaplan's thought in detail shows the fallacy of Hartman's critique. Emanuel Goldsmith recognizes the passion with which Kaplan embraced religion and the search for religious truth. He suggests that Kaplan offers "a Jewish version of what has been termed the 'religion of quest'." Kaplan is animated by passion and desire. He searches for truth and meaning, not for rationality alone.[7] Goldsmith accurately reflects the emotional depth of Kaplan's Judaism, his commitment to more than a merely philosophical or rational religion. Kaplan displays an enthusiasm for religious feeling. He looks beyond mere rationalism to advocate a commitment of self. His appeal to rationalism is mixed with not a little ambiguity. Mel Scult comments on Kaplan's appreciation of the mystical element in religion. He notes that Kaplan was "a rationalist who craved a religion that was understandable" but also "at the same keenly aware of the mystical tradition..."[8] He also suggests that Kaplan felt himself misunderstood by his contemporaries. He felt they never recognized the spiritual dimension to his thought. Kaplan, Scult says, was distressed when others charged him with a lack of spirituality. He

---

[7] Goldsmith, "Mordecai Kaplan," p. 20.

[8] Scult, *Judaism Faces the Twentieth Century*, p. 175.

considered the "will to divine presence and manifestation" an essential aspect of religion, its "ultimate unresolvable element."[9] Kaplan combined a modernist facade with a sensitivity to the depth dimension of human experience. Too often his critics stopped at the facade.

Several scholars recognize that a clue to Kaplan's ability to embrace both rationalism and mysticism lies in his early work on philosophical Utilitarianism, in particular the writings of the utilitarian philosopher Henry Sidgwick.[10] Sidgwick's utilitarianism adumbrates many of the themes that Kaplan would later raise in his writings on Judaism. Like Kaplan, Sidgwick emphasizes the evolutionary progress of moral and religious thought, its rooting in a social foundation, its functionalist approach, and the development of religion and its morality.[11] Sidgwick also anticipates Kaplan's enthusiasm for religion by admitting that he could never rid himself of the emotional component of faith. Human beings, he confesses, cannot build their lives on rational principles alone. Sidgwick believes that an appeal to the emotions helps reach rational moral objectives.[12] Kaplan and Sidgwick tend to agree in their analysis of religion. Kaplan goes further, however, and in his specific analysis of Jewish mysticism shows how the kabbalah actualized principles in their approach to Judaism. Studying Kaplan's attitude toward the kabbalah explicates both his passionate search for religion and his utilitarianism.

---

[9] *Ibid.*, p. 178.

[10] *Ibid.*, pp. 84-86 and Meir Ben Horin, "Ahad Ha-Am," p. 223.

[11] See Henry Sidgwick, *The Methods of Ethics*. Seventh edition. Foreword by John Rawls (Indianapolis: Hackett, 1981).

[12] See *ibid.*, and compare J. B. Schneewind, *Sidgwick's Ethics and Victorian Moral Philosophy* (Oxford: Clarendon Press, 1977).

Utilitarianism and Jewish Mysticism

Kaplan traces his utilitarian bias to aspects already present in Judaism. He avers that Hillel, the hero of rabbinic Judaism, and the kabbalah, the mystical tradition, both affirmed the functionalism that he espouses.[13] Kaplan explicitly affirms the value of Jewish mysticism. He claims that the kabbalah presented Jews with a means to maintain meaning and significance despite the adversity of history.[14] Jews possessed what Kaplan calls "legitimate mysticism." Such an approach does not depend on superstition or wishful thinking. Instead it appeals to the highest aspects of human thinking and aspiration. This mysticism teaches people to appreciate the sublime, to advance the cause of human life, to concretize the best in human hopes.[15]

This advocacy of kabbalah springs from Kaplan's utilitarianism. As late as 1973, he contended that what he learned from Henry Sidgwick was negative: that utilitarian reasons alone cannot motivate moral action.[16] Sidgwick's emphasis on *indirect* utilitarianism would require just such a denial. Only by making utilitarian ends appear as if they were meeting more subjectively important aims can the philosopher attain them. Kaplan recognizes that the Jewish mystics, used such indirect motivation in contrast to the philosophers and, therefore, approves of their medieval program. Kaplan's appreciation of medieval Jewish mysticism illustrates a utilitarian acknowledgment of the power of the indirect consequences of any action. Kaplan also follows Sidgwick in seeking to balance radical change and the

---

[13] Kaplan, *If Not Now*, p. 116.

[14] Kaplan, *Judaism As a Civilization*, pp. 270-271.

[15] Kaplan, *Questions Jews Ask*, p. 468.

[16] Kaplan, *If Not Now*, p. 56.

retention of tradition. Sidgwick advocates a balanced approach to social amelioration. The utilitarian, he insists, neither rebels against tradition nor accepts it uncritically. He warns against the temptation to discard laws merely because they are "not intrinsically reasonable," but he also cautions against a "superstitious" awe characteristic of "intuitional moralists" when confronted with a divine code.[17] Kaplan follows this balanced approach. He often accentuates the positive aspects of Jewish mysticism, noting its potential for revitalizing Jewish tradition. This recognition grows out of the same sensitivity to human emotion that Sidgwick confessed about himself.

One of Sidgwick's most startling pronouncements concerns the legitimacy of what he calls "religious fictions."[18] There are cases, he contends, when an abstract truth can be conveyed only by telling a historical fiction. He argues that Utilitarian principles do not demand absolute veracity. He suggests that circumstances determine how much of "true belief" one should communicate to others. Resort to less than complete veracity recommends itself when "important truths" can only be transmitted by enclosing them in a "shell of fiction."[19] These fictions not only convey a truth, they motivate action. That motivating effect legitimates the fictions. Sidgwick's view of human nature makes these fictions indispensable for moral life. He confessed the presence of "an indestructible and inalienable minimum of faith" without which human beings would be unable to act. Only a device

---

[17] See Sidgwick, *Methods*, p. 475.

[18] See Sidgwick, *Methods*, pp. 316-317; 448-449.

[19] *Ibid.*, p. 316.

such a religious fictions could appeal to that irredeemable core of irrationality in the human heart.[20]

Kaplan agrees with Sidgwick's principles, although his expression of them differs. He would never explicitly characterize religious views as "fictions." Nevertheless, he realizes that stories and beliefs motivate human action. Abstract truths may need emotive vehicles to activate them. Thus, he acknowledges the necessity for religious enthusiasm. He does indeed allow that the striving of the Jewish mystics testifies to a valid religious experience. He grants that "No religious experience is genuine without elements of awe and mystery," but merely stipulates that these should not lead to "occultism or supernaturalism."[21] This view adapts Sidgwick's intuitions. In medieval times the mystical stories about demons and magic helped motivate attachment to the Jewish people, in those times the narrative was "true" insofar as it functioned positively. Modern Jews, however, accept another story, another vision of reality. If they retain the external form of the older truth it becomes a fiction. To maintain the veracity of the Jewish story, Kaplan demands that the story itself change.[22] Mystics, Kaplan thinks, retain the flexibility necessary for such self-transformation. He rejects the Jewish philosophers because they appear too absolutist and unbending.

Kaplan's Ambiguous View of Jewish Philosophers

Kaplan's approach to the kabbalah depends on his prior rejection of Jewish philosophy. That rejection draws on lessons learned from Sidgwick.

---

[20] See Schneewind, *Sidgwick's Ethics*, p. 378.

[21] Kaplan, *Future of the American Jew*, p. 198.

[22] Kaplan, *Judaism Without Supernaturalism*, p. x.

Rationalism may, despite its correct intuitions of reality, Kaplan discovered from reading the Utilitarians, be socially harmful through the consequences of its teachings and, therefore, consistently refuses to absolutize human reason. He notes that the philosophers won little acceptance from the Jewish people in contrast to the mystics who commanded a popular following. He comments that "Unlike philosophy, whose study tended to alienate Jews of a reflective turn of mind from the Jewish tradition, mysticism exercised an attractive influence on them."[23] Like a utilitarian, Kaplan, rejects philosophies not because of their lack of truth but because of their indirect consequences on social life. The intended results of philosophy are, Kaplan thinks, salutary, but he cautions against the unintended consequences that act in contradiction to the philosopher's explicit desires. Kaplan views the philosophers with great ambivalence. He approves of a rationalistic approach to life. He disapproves, of a philosophy that, as a matter of practical results, undermines the possibilities for Jewish survival. The indirect effects of philosophy more than mitigate against the attractiveness of its rationalistic self-presentation.

This emphasis on indirect consequences of philosophy for Jewish survival explains the paradox of Kaplan's hostility toward medieval Jewish philosophers. He certainly affirms rationalism and attacks those who reject it out of hand. He approves of reason self-consciously harnessed for the salvation of the Jewish people. Kaplan's spiritual mentor, Ahad HaAm, held up Moses Maimonides as a heroic exemplar of the "Supremacy of Reason." Kaplan recognizes that the tradition of rationalism, in Ahad HaAm's hands, became a tool for Jewish survival. Ahad HaAm's advocacy of a "National Ethics," sought to provide thinking Jews with a realistic alternative to fideism.

---

[23] Kaplan, *Greater Judaism*, p. 124.

Baruch Kurzweil, a profound and religious Israeli thinker, points to the deep split within the modern Jewish soul. He criticizes various writers including Bialik and Ahad HaAm for secularizing Jewish tradition and injecting rationalism into the heart of faith. His analysis of modernity and call for a return to tradition stimulated Kaplan to defend Ahad HaAm. Kaplan notes in response the antagonism that traditionalists have often held toward rationalists. In particular he recalls the opposition of the French rabbis to Moses Maimonides. Kurzweil's attack on modern rationalists, Kaplan argues, represents a modern "anti-Maimunism," as inappropriate in the modern world as the anti-Maimunism of obscurantists in the middle ages.[24] Kaplan's defense points to Ahad HaAm's concern for Jewish survival, his ability to address the modern crisis of Jewish life by separating religion from the other aspects of Jewish civilization. Kaplan does not defend Ahad HaAm's Maimunism.[25]

Kaplan opposes the overly rationalistic approach Maimonides takes to Jewish tradition. He sees in Maimonides a type of reinterpretation of Jewish tradition that fails to further the survival of the Jewish people. Maimonides, he thinks, by transvaluating traditional concepts rather than re-valuating them as Kaplan advocates, weakens the power of Jewish religion. For Maimonides, as Kaplan understands him, Jewish ideas function as philosophical values; they reaffirm the exalted rationalism he inherited from the Greek and Arab thinkers who influenced him. This rationalistic function, according to Kaplan, contrasts

---

[24] See Mordecai M. Kaplan, "Anti-Maimunism in Modern Dress: A Reply to Baruch Kurzweil's Attack on Ahad Ha'Am," *Judaism* 4 (1955), pp. 303-12. Meir-Ben Horin clearly shows, "Ahad Ha-Am," 221-233, that
Kaplan was far from an uncritical disciple of this teacher.

[25] In fact, one could join Noah Rosenbloom and argue that Kaplan actually uses a rather anachronistic argument to defend Ahad HaAm as a Reconstructionist! see Noah H. Rosenbloom, *Studies in LIterature and Thought From the Eighteenth Century to the Present* [Hebrew] (Jersalem: Rubin Mass, 1989), pp. 265-266.

with the more practical functions the ideas served in their traditional form. Kaplan replaces Maimonides' approach with a translation of traditional concepts that keeps their original function in tact.[26] Understanding how Kaplan thought the philosophers mistranslated the tradition into rationalistic terms helps explain his preference for the Jewish mystics against the philosophers. He distrusts Maimonides' view of Judaism because he considers it an intellectual arrogance that threatens the persistence of tradition and the survival of the Jewish people.

Kaplan objects to Maimonides' excessive rationalism because of its effects on Jewish piety. While Kaplan thinks that a modern rationalist Ahad HaAm could self-consciously raise the question of Jewish survival, he claims that Maimonides as a medieval thinker could not. Medievals, he thinks, could only choose between faith in reason and faith in tradition. They faced an implacable dichotomy. They would, he felt, "render unswerving loyalty to tradition so long as they lack confidence in the ability of the human mind." When they become philosophers and "rely on their own thinking, they are inclined to challenge the tradition in which they have been brought up.[27] Medievals such as Maimonides were, in Kaplan's view, too naive to deal self-consciously with this problem.

Moderns, in contrast according to Kaplan, can learn to balance tradition and innovation, change and continuity, in their religious thinking. Kaplan wrote his critique of Jewish philosophy in a cultural milieu saturated with reverence for Maimonides. He did not fear that his criticism would undermine

---

[26] See Henry Morris, "Mordecai Kaplan's Criticisms of Maimonides' Reinterpretations," in Ronald A, Brauner, ed., *Shiv'im: Essays and Studies in Honor of Ira Eisenstein* (Philadelphia and New York: Reconstructionist and Ktav, 1977), pp. 269-276.

[27] Kaplan, *Greater Judaism*, pp. 113-114.

that respect. Naturally, his zeal for self-reflective thinking, for an approach to Judaism that, unlike Maimonides', would honestly portray itself as both deviating from the past and honoring that past, led him to exaggerate. Kaplan's Maimonides often looks like a caricature. Nevertheless, this caricature suggests the dimensions of Kaplan's demand that thinkers transcend the false illusion that they merely continue a tradition, when in fact they are shaping it. Perhaps Kaplan is overly critical of the great medieval philosopher, yet his criticism reflects the exaggerated praise which modernists often accorded to this early rationalist.

Kaplan's Critique of Maimonidean Philosophy

The image of Kaplan as a radical rationalist offered by critics such as David Hartman needs tempering in the light of this rejection of philosophical naiveté. Many modern Jewish apologists emphasize the rationalistic strand in medieval Jewish thought. Moses Maimonides appears as a cultural hero for several theorists of Judaism who recast him in their own image.[28] Kaplan, however, clearly does not accept this romantic view of Jewish philosophy. He appreciates Maimonides' efforts in their historical setting, but dismisses his views. Thus he claims that Maimonides' interpretation of the dietary laws "is scarcely worth considering."[29] He acknowledges that no one can "question Maimonides' genuine piety and belief in God or the greatness of his mind and character," but then proceeds to question the adequacy of his view of the

---

[28] See the review of previous literature as well as the discussion of Maimonides in Fox, *Interpreting Maimonides* and Menachem Kellner, *Maimonides On Judaism and the Jewish People* (Albany, NY: State University of New York, 1991). See also Kellner's "Reading Rambam: Approaches to the Interpretation of Maimonides," *Jewish History* 5:2 (1992), pp. 73-93.

[29] Kaplan, *Judaism as a Civilization*, p. 440.

divinity.[30] For Kaplan, who emphasizes the modern situation, Jewish philosophy suffers from its contextual limitations: it makes use of an outmoded science and self-consciously preaches an elitism that thwarts the articulated values of democracy. Kaplan's critique, however, goes beyond the obvious weaknesses common to all medieval traditions generally.

Jewish philosophers, Kaplan explains, faced the challenge of Jewish life in exile, in the diaspora. Kaplan understands this challenge to include three component parts: that of keeping alive a vital connection with Jewish national consciousness, of preserving a sense of the value and relevance of traditional Judaism, and of mobilizing Jewish resources to make the most of their present opportunities. The Jewish philosophers, Kaplan holds, failed in each of these endeavors. Their teachings led to an assimilation of non-Jewish culture and an undifferentiated humanism rather than an affirmation of Jewish national consciousness. Their emphasis on abstract thought devalued even if it did not specifically reject the inherited traditions of Jewish observance. Their rationalism encouraged an intellectualism and a withdrawal from the social and political activities of their times.

Medieval Jewish philosophers as Kaplan presents them tended to stimulate assimilation even when explicitly rejecting it. Kaplan explains the rise of Jewish philosophy as a response to the challenge of Arabic rationalism. When Muslims argued for the greater rationality of Islam, Jews, Kaplan avows, necessarily needed to respond by showing how Judaism exemplifies rational concepts. Kaplan applauds the intention of Jewish thinkers who sought to show that Judaism, no less than Islam, met the universal criteria for truth. He recognizes the advantage these thinkers provided to the Jewish community

---

[30] Kaplan, *Questions Jews Ask*, pp. 102-103.

when they "reinterpreted their religious tradition in more universal categories of philosophic thought."[31] Nevertheless, the implications of that rationalistic reinterpretation of tradition, Kaplan thinks, weakened Jewish commitment to what another philosopher, Judah HaLevi, called a "despised religion." If Judaism merely teaches universal truths, he insists, one need not maintain the particular expressions of Jewish life. The dietary laws and the use of Hebrew separate a person from the general community, and Kaplan suggests that the philosophers' universalism could not justify continuing those practices. The historical necessity that created the climate for philosophy, he remarks wryly, also ensured that philosophers emphasized the abstract and universal rather than the concrete ties to a particular tradition. The philosophical desire to rationalize Jewish religion, he charges, led Jews to adapt it to predetermined philosophical categories--a clear capitulation to assimilation, and their intellectual elitism estranged them from the Jewish masses. The self-conscious attempt to restore dignity to Jewish tradition actually, he thinks, backfired in an increasing alienation from it.

Kaplan laments that philosophy undermines the pious motives that encourage Jewish behavior. For example, he suggests that ever since philosophy "invaded" Judaism, simple prayer has been rendered difficult. Kaplan realizes, in ways that he thinks the philosophers did not, that any new conception of deity requires a new understanding of worship. He castigates Jewish philosophers for never turning as much attention to the practical problem of how to pray to their philosophic deity as to their description of that deity.[32] The philosophic view of God, Kaplan admits, purifies belief from

---

[31] Kaplan, *Meaning of God*, p. 347.

[32] Kaplan, *Meaning of God*, p. 33.

superstitious elements. Yet he also complains that such purified belief, by stressing abstractions, leaves little common ground between humanity and the divine. In Kaplan's view, philosophers like Maimonides misunderstood the dynamics of a living tradition. When Maimonides required Jews to abandon an anthropomorphic view of the divinity, Kaplan charges, he failed to realize that "viewed in historical perspective" anthropomorphism represents an important advance in religious thinking.[33] By associating the idea of divinity with human morality, Kaplan avers, religion enhanced its ethical dimension. While philosophically suspect, Kaplan claims that the traditional anthropomorphism of Jewish religion provides a realistic impetus to moral living. Jewish philosophers, he concludes, in their zeal for a unified system of Jewish thought, neglected to take into account the limitations of the Jewish people and the realism inherent in the tradition.

Kaplan also attacks the philosophers for their lack of self-criticism. Because they could not see the historical sweep of Jewish history, he charges, they assumed that their Judaism represented the only legitimate Jewish religion possible. This blindness to alternatives led the philosophers, he thinks, to misunderstand their own position in Jewish life. Medieval Jewish philosophers, he argues, underestimated their divergence from traditional Judaic religion. By seeking to reconcile Jewish texts with philosophical principles, the philosophers, he declares, in effect devalued those texts. By stressing a univocal and rational meaning in traditional Jewish thought, the philosophers, he thinks, narrowed rather than broadened the implication of traditional beliefs.[34]

---

[33] *Ibid.*, p. 87.

[34] Kaplan, *Greater Judaism*, p. 120.

Symptomatically, Kaplan attempted to improve on the philosophical model. While Maimonides formulated thirteen principles of belief, Kaplan introduced a liturgical declaration of "thirteen wants" or desires meant to inspire the worshiper. Kaplan believed, according to Mel Scult, that "it was no longer possible or even desirable to have a set of abstract principles that all Jews should accept." He did however, think that Jews could agree on goals for their lives. These goals focused on personal and social salvation as Kaplan understood that term. His liturgy proclasimed the desire to overcome temptation, to gain a sense of responsibility, to utilize leisure time well, to enhance the Jewish home, to enable Jewish children to accept their Jewish heritage joyously, to reinterpret that heritage in relevant terms, to develop creative forms of Jewish organization, and to enable Judaism "to function as a potent influence for justice, freedom and peace." As Scult points out these thirteen liturgical declarations reflect Kaplan's conviction that "Sincerity and authenticity were indispensable" aspects of prayer. Kaplan felt that the philosophers had sacrificed the practical means of achieving these through a sterile rationalism.[35]

Kaplan's interpretation of Maimonidean Judaism contrasts with the approach of Marvin Fox whose reflections on the practical consequences of Maimonidean thought for the life of piety represent one of the major contributions of his book on Maimonides. Unlike Kaplan, Fox insists that "there is here not a simple opposition between what the philosophers believe and what the masses should be taught to believe, but rather between two kinds of belief both of which are necessary."[36] From this perspective, Kaplan

---

[35] Scult, *Judaism Faces the Twentieth Century*, pp. 291-292.

[36] Fox, *Interpreting Maimonides*, p. 320.

misrepresents both the intention and achievement of Maimonides in creating a viable Judaism for his times. While Kaplan's view of the philosophers is flawed, it shows how, using Sidgwick's categories, he finds a reason to criticize the rationalists.

Democracy and Kaplan's Critique of Irrationalism

If Kaplan rejects the philosophers as naive, why does he advance the rationalist cause? The answer lies in his understanding of democracy. Kaplan embraces American democracy as an ideal which fulfills the utilitarian values of providing the indirect benefit of legitimating Jewish particularism, of balancing an affirmation of tradition with a willingness to change, and of motivating an active commitment to social improvement. Kaplan criticizes irrationalism as inextricably linked to theurgy, to magical techniques designed to coerce supernatural forces to satisfy human needs its very survival. Such an irrationalism, he thinks, aims to control the world in which humanity lives by using occult power. Unlike the powers of science, empirically verifiable to anyone who tests them, mystical powers, Kaplan charges, draw on sources beyond general knowledge which lie in a supernatural realm of spirits, demons, and invisible powers. Kaplan considers this view of reality dangerous for several reasons. Originally, he contends, such a supernaturalist view derived from a widely held conception of reality. As part of a complex pattern of belief this supernaturalism, he admits, indirectly supported Jewish survival. When people turned to theurgy in hopes of satisfying certain immediate needs--for food, health, success--they also, he thinks, affirmed the primacy of Jewish symbols and images. As Kaplan puts it, the specific acts associated with Jewish culture had a more general, universal meaning in a supernatural world view. While they contributed to Jewish survival, they did so according to Kaplan's utilitarian explanation, only as an unintended result of other aims. The modern Jew, according to Kaplan's analysis of modernity, does not share the preconceptions of earlier generations. This Jew, Kaplan asserts, must choose between the modern world view created by science and that associated with traditional Jewish mysticism. A traditional Judaism, he thinks, leaves Jews alienated from their modern context. Kaplan deplores this situation and calls for a reconstitution of the earlier situation in which Judaism was part of an entire system of thought. Yet, he realizes, Jews "cannot go back to a belief in the miraculous and supernatural" that validated Judaism in the past.[37]

Kaplan supports his claim for the impossibility of returning to supernaturalism by suggesting that people automatically reject a faith that conflicts with their basic assumptions. Theurgy, he believes, draws on presuppositions no longer regarded as valid. It arises from what he considers an animistic conception of the world that views the entire universe populated by individual living souls. Mysticism, as Kaplan understands its presuppositions, seeks to control those souls, get in touch with the unseen forces animating reality, and so manipulate the world in which people live. Kaplan condemns this mysticism as a "survival of the prehistoric theurgic approach to reality" that uses such discredited means of controlling the universe as "astrology and Kabbalah."[38] Judaism, therefore in his view, risks being relegated to the irrelevant and untenable if it advances the claims of the

---

[37] Kaplan, *Greater Judaism*, p. 457.

[38] See Kaplan, *Judaism Without Supernaturalism*, p. 41.

mystics. A group, he contends, that espouses beliefs that experience contradicts cannot survive.[39]

Kaplan, in this argument, follows Sidgwick's intuition about indirect utility. He does not argue that Jews must consciously affirm the value of Jewish survival. He believes, on the contrary, that such survival occurs only when Judaism corresponds to those ideals and values which Jews already espouse as members of modernity society. He holds that human experience of the world and themselves depends on the culture in which they live. A belief in the value of Judaism, Kaplan feels, grows out of that experience, and he argues that only a concept of religion related to the civilization and society in which Jews live can ensure such a belief.[40] Since the beliefs on which irrationalism depends explicitly contradict the presuppositions of modern science, Kaplan claims that Jews are forced to choose explicitly between the aims of modernity and those of Judaism. Like Sidgwick, Kaplan prefers an indirect approach. He believes that a Jewish religion derived as a by-product of other, more persuasive goals, has a better chance of survival.

Kaplan rejects irrationalism not only because of its unscientific presuppositions, but also because of its effect on human initiative. He argues that modernity expects human beings to transform the world using their own energies. He views irrationalism as a misguided approach which turns away from the natural resources available to every human beings and suggests that magic alone has the power to improve human life. Whereas reason teaches Jews to help themselves, irrationalism, he thinks, leads to passivity and helplessness. Because modern life focuses on what people can do for

---

[39] See Kaplan, *Questions Jews Ask*, p. 237.

[40] *Ibid.*, p. 88.

themselves, Kaplan urges modern Judaism to reject its mystical foundations. Indeed, he claims religion "should renounce all magic or theurgy and should reinforce man's efforts to better his own nature as well as his social and physical environment."[41]

The Mystics Against the Philosophers

Kaplan contrasted the mystics favorably to the philosophers. In his view mystics succeeded in preserving Judaism precisely where the philosophers failed. Jewish mysticism revitalized the latent national consciousness among Jews in the diaspora. Here, in contrast to the philosophers, Jewish mystics followed the utilitarian technique of indirect accomplishment of their goals. On an explicit level, he notes, Jewish mystics emphasized the transcendent meaning of Jewish tradition. He shows how they explained the laws and rituals of Judaism as a means for attaining personal and social goals. As theurgy, Kaplan admits, the kabbalah claims to aid people in their search for personal success and for a redemption of the world. Yet even in this theurgy, Kaplan sees a more utilitarian purpose. This mystical theology, he contends, created a greater attachment to the symbols and practices of the Jewish people. By teaching that the essential elements of Judaism were means for attaining personal and social redemption, the mystics, he claims, cultivated a loving relation to Judaism itself. Thus, Kaplan construes the mystics as indirect Utilitarians who taught the people, indirectly, to adapt to their exilic condition by strengthening rather than weakening their attachment to their homeland and their national consciousness. An adaption to the diaspora that might have become assimilationist, Kaplan asserts, became instead, through

---

[41] Kaplan, *Religion of Ethical Nationhood*, p. 7.

the medium of the kabbalah, a means of reinforcing every Jew's connection to the people of Israel.[42]

Both explicitly and, even more, implicitly Kaplan argues, Jewish mysticism conveyed the centrality of the Jewish people in more immediate and dramatic ways than did Jewish philosophy. Unlike the philosophers, Kaplan feels, the mystics did not deny the great diversity and often apparently contradicting meanings in Jewish texts. They, however, he suggests, celebrated that variety and excelled in the generation of diversity. The mystics whom Kaplan presents as antithetical to the philosophers, did not, he claims, try to reduce the teachings of Judaism to a unified rational system. Kaplan thinks that they saw their task not as that of reconciling "the teachings of the Torah with those derived from reason, but how to discover the hidden meaning of what the Torah itself taught."[43] That task, he avers, provided the mystics with a greater flexibility when approaching traditional Jewish teachings. While philosophers set themselves against the tradition, forcing it into an alien mold, mystics, according to Kaplan's reconstruction of their agenda, balanced their innovations with a deep reverence for the past. Kaplan portrays the mystics as anticipating his own Reconstructionist approach. They do not embrace superstition but use radical interpretations of traditional images to revitalize a set of beliefs and structions essential for Jewish survival. The mystics on Kaplan's reading look extremely postmodern. He seems to share Umberto Eco's characterization of the medieval kabbalah in contrast to the symbolic, allegorical readings of philosophers.

---

[42] Kaplan, *Future of the American Jew*, pp. 270-271.

[43] *Ibid.*, p. 125.

Kaplan's Celebration of Mystical Realism

Kaplan's argument for the mystics, however, develops through practical evidence. The kabbalah, he feels, served the Jewish people better than did philosophy. Mystics, in Kaplan's view, took a more realistic approach to Jewish practice than did the philosophers. They did not seek to fit all Jewish religion into a predetermined mold. They proceeded pragmatically, selecting what they needed to restore Jewish self-confidence. From that perspective, they "regarded tradition as an inexhaustible mine of truths that might help the Jewish People recover its ancient glory..."[44] Rather than reconcile the teachings of the Torah with teachings derived from rationalism, mystics, Kaplan proclaims, demonstrated the continued relevance of the Torah in the daily life of the Jewish people. Thus, Kaplan declares, that while philosophers failed to influence the masses of Jews, the mystics, through their flexible approach, succeeded in reviving Jewish life. Kaplan uses gustatory images to emphasize this point. The mystics created a palatable food for exilic Jews from the substance of Torah and so received a "hearty welcome" from the mainstream tradition in contrast to the antagonism aroused by philosophy.[45] The mystic, for Kaplan, resembles the modern utilitarian by knowing enough to compromise. Unlike the philosophers, he asserts, the mystics did not place an untenable choice before the Jewish people. They allowed the Jewish community to create a balance between innovation and conservative continuity with the past.

Kaplan also admires the Jewish mystic's commitment to action. He pictures the mystics as actively seeking to end Israel's exile and restore its

---

[44] Kaplan, *Greater Judaism*, p. 130.

[45] *Ibid.*, pp. 124-126.

status as a living nation.[46] Jewish mysticism, he feels, succeeds in mobilizing the Jewish people and motivating creative action. The Jewish philosopher, by contrast, Kaplan thinks, exalted a contemplative ideal. Inspired by Hellenic intellectualism, Jewish philosophers, according to Kaplan, sought the highest good in thought, not in deeds. This lack of concern for the daily problems of Jewish living, he insists, blunted their effectiveness. Jewish mystics, according to Kaplan, attracted a greater following because of their concern for the daily of life of each Jew.[47] Mystics, he argues, were activists, oriented more to how people lived than to the esoteric subtleties of philosophy.

This activism of Jewish mysticism appeals to Kaplan as a source for genuine religious insight. Such genuine religion calls upon human beings to take responsibility for their own lives, to act like members of a democratic society in which all citizens share the duties of government. Kabbalistic activism anticipates the ideal democracy which Kaplan exalts. He declares that "Jewish mysticism caught the true spirit of the kind of religion man needs," and characterizes that as a religion in which humanity and the divine share responsibility. The mystics transmit this spirit through their tales and mythology, a mythology exemplified in the classical text of Jewish mysticism, the Zohar. Kaplan approvingly notes the way in which the Zohar speaks of a "creative power" exercised by human beings, a power Kaplan identifies with the power exercised by pursuing "ethical truth."[48] Kaplan views the supernaturalism of the Zohar like Sidgwick's "religious fiction." He understands it in its own context as ethical rather than theurgic, as

---

[46] Kaplan, *Future of the American Jew*, p. 455.

[47] *Ibid.*, p. 127.

[48] Kaplan, *Meaning of God*, p. 78.

motivational rather than as false science. He interprets the heroes of the Zohar as models of ethical activism who show how human beings can shape their own world. In its ancient form, then, Jewish mysticism, in contrast to Jewish philosophy, resembles Kaplan's ideal democratic religion--by preserving Jewish survival through indirection, balancing tradition and creativity, and affirming the role of human beings in transforming their own lives.

Chapter 13:

Kaplan, Mysticism, and Postmodernism

Jews in a Postmodern Age

Jean-François Lyotard describes the postmodern world as one in which people no longer find the great "metanarratives" of the Enlightenment credible.[1] The modern world espoused a great hope for liberty. As humanity trained itself in knowledge it would liberate each person's potential. This vision of a redeemed humanity, born in the French revolution, no longer seems either reasonable or possible to the postmodern sensibility. Tutored by the social sciences people recognize their fetters more clearly than ever before. A second story on which the modern world pinned its hopes was the accessiblilty of truth. Newton managed to combine the insights of Descartes and Bacon into a new synthesis. Philosophers like Hegel sought to encompass reality in a single comprehensive system. Postmoderns have abandoned that search. Kaplan's modernist view of Judaism might seem at odds with this new temperament and view of reality.

---

[1] See Lyotard, *The Postmodern Condition*, pp. 4-54.

Indeed, Jewish thinkers generally tend to resist the postmodern. They criticize it, even if some of its foremost proponents write out of a Jewish context.[2] Strangely enough, however, Reconstructionists prove an exception to this rule. They have turned from rationalism to Jewish mysticism, from a search for eternal verities to a celebration of the kaleidoscopic possibilities in the Jewish tradition. Arnold Eisen calls them the "wild card" in modern Jewish movements because they have "apparently abandoned the Jewish rationalist tradition in favor of the mystical."[3] Less sanguine observers level a more emotional charge against the Reconstructionists: they have reintroduced paganism into the pure monotheism of Judaism.[4] Thus Samuel Dresner associates modern Reconstructionists with sexual abandon, false messianism, and other irrationalities inimicable to Jewish religion. Such a retreat from reason, he argues, flows directly from Kaplan's naturalistic humanism. The lack of a personal deity and the warmth of involvement implied by such a view of God, he warns, alienates modern Jews. These Jews, he claims, "seek *religious* reasons" for remaining Jewish. Providing such reasons, he argues, has become "increasingly difficult" for religious naturalism.[5] Because Kaplan's naturalism fails them, he contends, Reconstructionists have no recourse but to return to ancient superstition. Trapped by Kaplan's rationalism, Dresner laments, they retreat to the very supernaturalism against which Judaism raised

---

[2] Compare the fascinating study in Finkelstein, *The Ritual of New Creation.*

[3] Eisen, "Changing Patterns," p. 44.

[4] See Samuel H. Dresner, "The Return of Paganism?", *Midstream* (June/July 1988), pp. 32-38.

[5] *Ibid.*, p. 37.

a protest. Kaplan seems disproven by the latest developments in contemporary philosophy and religious thought.

Not only Kaplan but many twentieth century thinkers would find contemporary philosophy disconcerting. Postmoderns have learned to distrust those broad universal categories of reason that so delighted earlier thinkers. The new approach argues that literature may have many meanings, not just one, an idea that Kaplan associated approvingly with the mystics in contrast to the philosophers. The power of association and evocation rather than intellectual categories, the postmodernists argue, may offer the best entry into reality. From this perspective, those who associate the Jewish tradition with rationality may be misreading their past. Like Dresner, for example, Max Weber traced modern rationality back to the Hebrew Bible. He saw the modern world as "disenchanted" and found the roots of that disenchantment in Hebraic religion. Contemporary rationalists contend with the patent failure of the "disenchantment thesis." They must explain a world which has been "re-enchanted" by postmodern thinkers.[6]

Kaplan himself would not have been dismayed by the turn toward a new metaphysics. He eschewed metaphysical language. Questions of ontology, of absolutes, of essences seemed beside the point. He may, indeed, have had an implicit metaphysics. He might have, as William Kaufman suggests, have constructed a metaphysics from his choice of categories and terms.[7] Nevertheless, he did not link his philosophy to any single view of reality. As a utilitarian he adjusted to the dominant paradigm of his society. He could

---

[6] See Germain, *A Discourse on Disenchantment*; compare, over twenty years earlier, Gregory Baum, "Does the World Remain Disenchanted?," *Social Forces* 37 (1970), pp. 153-202.

[7] See William E. Kaufman, "Kaplan's Approach to Metaphysics," in Goldsmith, et. al, eds., *The American Judaism of Mordecai M. Kaplan*, pp. 271-282.

adjust to another paradigm shift, particularly the postmodern paradigm in which change and flexibility are the primary realities. What critics such as Dresner fail to realize is that Kaplan had already anticipated a turn toward Jewish mysticism and had justified finding ever new ways of reviving Jewish tradition.

His utilitarianism taught him to create new beliefs to motivate modern Jews. Belief in democratic religion served him as such a motivating idea. While Kaplan, unlike Sidgwick, never brands this vision of democratic religion as a "fiction," he does use the language of social science in the same way that Sidgwick's religious leaders use their fictions--to transmit a transnatural truth through naturalistic language. Thus when Kaplan turns to functionalism and scientific methodology because "metaphysics has become virtually obsolete," he is applying the same technique as Sidgwick's creators of religious fictions.[8] He might well accept a more mystically tinged language were he to see it as a necessary instrument for the revival and survival of the Jewish people in the contemporary world. Democracy and mysticism are not inherently at odds with one another, and Kaplan recognizes this truth even while believing it untenable in the modern world.

Democracy and Jewish Mysticism

As noted in the previous chapter, Kaplan recognizes the value of the emotional aspects of religion. He may distrust the supernaturalism of Jewish mysticism, but he still hopes that its virtues may be integrated with modern Jewish religion. He sees that integration as a natural occurrence in a democratic society. Kaplan trusts to a democratic constituency to see that its

---

[8] See Kaplan, "Between Two Worlds," p. 139.

own best interests entail the personal development and improvement of its members. Kaplan will not legitimate a society that willfully restricts its member's individual search for self-fulfillment. In that case, a trust in democracy activates personal initiative rather than represses it. Kaplan presents his ideal of democracy not as a realistic portrait of any existing nation but precisely as an exalted value. Since Jewish mysticism advocates a reliance on supernatural values rather than on political ones, it seems at variance from the motivating ideals of democracy. Nevertheless, certain aspects of kabbalah appear to him useful in the modern world. Transposed into a modern key Jewish mysticism may have much to teach a democratic society and its religions. Students of Kaplan's thought recognize this aspect of his philosophy. Although the editors of *Dynamic Judaism* do not specifically mention the Kabbalah in their essays on Kaplan, they show their sensitivity to this aspect of his thought by reproducing a selection from his *A New Zionism* that gives a positive description of Jewish mysticism. Nestled among other passages that extol Jewish peoplehood, this passage recognizes the social dimension of Jewish mysticism and expresses his high regard for the passionate side of religion.[9] Kaplan's approach to modern Judaism seeks to find ways to introduce the positive aspects of the kabbalah into a contemporary Jewish life.

Kaplan, for example, suggests that the Zionist movement represents a modern version of Jewish mysticism that preserves its valuable attributes while eliminating the dysfunctional ones. Mysticism, Kaplan explains, serves a necessary and indispensable function in Jewish life. Mysticism, generally, he contends, brings a person "into rapport" with what is considered "ultimate reality." For the Jew that reality is the Jewish people and the living

---

[9] See Kaplan, *Dynamic Judaism*, pp. 64-65.

connection between that people, its land, and its history. Since he identifies the Jew's ultimate reality with Jewish peoplehood, he accepts as mystical any vehicle for strengthening the Jew's attachment to that reality. Zionism, he suggests, affirms the same truth as the medieval Jewish mystics--the centrality of the Jewish people; Zionism demands that Jews identify with the people of Israel; thus in Zionism, "identification with the Jewish people provides Jewish religion with the indispensable dimension of the mystical."[10] Zionism, in this formulation, is not a new type of messianic activism. Instead, it is a revitalization of the Jews' commitment to the survival of their culture. At first blush Zionism seems a strangely archaic movement for a postmodern. Its nationalism draws on both the enlightenment tradition that assures individuals civil liberties and the romantic theorists who articulated a view of national and cultural rights. It seems to take the metamyths of modernity as its point of departure. Kaplan transposes Zionism into postmodern terms, a transposition not as antithetical to contemporary Zionist thinking as some might imagine.

Zionism and a Positive Jewish Mysticism

Kaplan's positive assessment of Jewish mysticism shows itself in his explication of Zionism. Scholars have long recognized the messianic aspects of Zionism and their connection with Jewish mysticism. This association, of course, raises some difficulties. Zionism may, in some ways, be understood as a realistic and anti-messianic movement. Its messianic language may be merely a rhetorical flourish. The nuanced differences between secular

---

[10] Kaplan, *A New Zionism*, pp. 114-115.

messianism, the messianism of religious Zionism, and the political messianism of some German Jews need special investigation.[11]

Kaplan did not investigate the messianic and mystical aspects of Zionism in any academic fashion. Nevertheless, he did interpret the movement as a whole as a modern incarnation of traditional Jewish mysticism. That interpretation shows how he associated the mystical spirit with a utilitarian purpose. Analyzing Jewish political history, Kaplan traces two "conflicting tendencies" -- one toward isolation and the other imperialistic. He identifies the messianic strand in Jewish thought as imperialistic -- it seeks to transform reality to fit the categories of Jewish thought. Kaplan regards this desire to create a new world as compatible with the highest values of democracy. "Traditional messianism," he comments, "coincided with democracy's aim to eliminate exploitation and oppression from human life." Nevertheless, in its original form, he believes, the messianic ideal expressed a supernaturalism at odds with modern democratic thought. Allied with mysticism, this messianism appealed for a miraculous intervention into natural history which Kaplan rejects as wishful thinking. He rejects such an approach because it encouraged a passive expectancy that God alone, without human effort, would effect the desired change of political life.[12]

Kaplan portrays Theodor Herzl's Zionism as a modernized version of this messianism. Herzl, he claims, introduced three changes in the traditional idea. First, he advocated an active political engagement that replaced the passive anticipation characterizing earlier messianism. Secondly, he rejected

---

[11] See the various essays collected in Jonathan Frankel, ed., *Jews and Messianism In the Modern Era; Metaphor and Meaning.* Studies in Contemporary Jewry VII (New York: Oxford University Press, 1991).

[12] Kaplan, *Future of the American Jew*, p. 360.

the interpretation of the Jewish exile as a divinely decreed fate which Jews must accept without question. Finally, he worked to create a nation state which would function "as a means of securing the maximum welfare and collaboration to all who came within its purview."[13] Each of these innovations parallels the utilitarian goals which Kaplan accepts as Jewish aims.

Zionism's rejection of traditional theology and its advocacy of modern nationalism aims, explicitly, for the creation of an independent political state. Implicitly, however, such a plan presupposes a transformation of Jewish religious values from a supernatural orientation to a naturalistic one. He acknowledges that different Zionists articulated this idea in diverse ways. Cultural Zionists sought a "spiritual center" in the Land of Israel. Even Herzl declared that "Zionism involves a return to Judaism, preceding the return to the Jewish land." Kaplan admits the religious aspects of the Jewish national movement. He acknowledges that Zionist leaders often sought to transpose tradition into a modern key.

Nevertheless, Kaplan charges that Zionist leaders provided only an inadequate articulation of a new, naturalistic Judaism. They focused on the needs of a small, self-contained, group of Jews. They failed, he thinks, to address the needs of the Jewish people as a whole. Their theology of Judaism could only satisfy their most dogmatic of followers, it could not, Kaplan insists, provide a basis for renewing the religious life of every Jew. Zionists, intensely concerned with providing physical security for a vulnerable Jewish people, failed in Kaplan's view to consider the spiritual well being of every Jew. Because of this failure Kaplan concludes that by failing "to reckon with the future of the Jewish People as a whole," Zionism has "augmented the

---

[13] *Ibid.*, p. 361.

spiritual insecurity of all Jews."[14] The problem with regarding Zionism as a response to a crisis, as "an emergency affair" lies in the neglect of long range planning. Yet that long range perspective alone leads to the indirect result of Zionism that Kaplan desires: the transformation of Judaism itself.[15] While regarding past Zionist philosophy inadequate, Kaplan does not despair of the future. He offers his own new conception of Jewish nationhood, of an ethical Zionism. He reconceives Zionism as an instrument for developing, indirectly, a new spiritual status for modern Jews. This Zionism expresses in a political medium what Kaplan calls the "inner drive" of the Jewish people to transpose "its spiritual heritage into the key of naturalistic and this-worldly salvation."[16] Kaplan's critique of contemporary Zionism can be construed as a complaint that it has inadequately appropriated the techniques used by Jewish mysticism to foster loyalty to the Jewish people.

Kaplan salutes Zionism for taking the egalitarian hopes that animate Jewish mysticism and rechanneling them in a democratic way. Zionism represents, according to Kaplan, a triumph of voluntaryism, of individual will as the arbiter of the balance between tradition and innovation. He hails the creation of the State of Israel as an environment within which voluntary religion can flourish.[17] The inevitable voluntaryism of religion in the State of Israel, Kaplan thinks, should provide a paradigm for Jewish religiousness generally. He conceives of an organic community of world Jewry. The hub of the community in the State of Israel provides a focus and spiritual center

---

[14] Kaplan, *Greater Judaism*, pp. 440, 448.

[15] Kaplan, *A New Zionism*, p. 174.

[16] *Ibid.*, p. 71.

[17] *Ibid.*, p. 92.

that legitimates diversity and individualism. The spiritual solidarity provided by that center would allow religious pluralism to flourish. Kaplan claims that such a condition would "mitigate the divisive forces of Jewish denominationalism" which threaten Jewish survival.[18] Just as the Jewish mystics recognized the danger in the intellectual uniformity imposed by Jewish philosophy, so a self-reflective Zionism will, according to Kaplan, respond to the threatened survival of the Jewish people arising from various imperialistic religious claims, whether from the Orthodox, the secularists, or the religious liberals.

By its very nature Zionism transformed the passivity of classical Jewish messianism into an activism. Kaplan stresses the psychological aspect of this activism and suggests that modern Jews have lost their sense of a Jewish task, of a uniquely Jewish contribution to the world. Zionism must revitalize that sense and thereby stimulate Jews to action.[19] Zionism also encourages activism by teaching Jews to think of themselves in a new way. They must identify their own welfare with that of the Jewish people. Once they make that identification they will necessarily act for the good of the Jewish people since that good is also their own. Reinterpreting the idea of salvation "in the modern mental climate," Zionism, in Kaplan's presentation, provides Jews with the needed motivation for action--by serving Zionism and the Jewish people they advance their own self-interests.[20]

Kaplan recognizes the similarities between this Zionist activism and earlier Jewish mysticism. He points to Rabbi Judah Alkalai, an early supporter

---

[18] Kaplan, *Religion of Ethical Nationhood*, p. 11; compare pp. 120-125, 132.

[19] *Ibid.*, p. 120.

[20] Kaplan, *A New Zionism*, pp. 98-99.

of Religious Zionism, as a mystic who did not allow mysticism to sap his strength but directed its hopes into a naturalistic politics.[21] Just as the medieval Jewish mystics addressed the determinism that led to inactivity by stressing the power of humanity to effect change, so too Zionists correct the modern tendencies to inactivity. This contribution to Jewish self-understanding, like the other positive values that Kaplan identifies with Zionism, testifies to the possibility of preserving the best aspects of Jewish mysticism within the context of the modern mentality.

Zionism as Postmodern Metaphysics

Kaplan saw clearly the postmodern undercurrents in modern Zionism. He noted its affinity for the Jewish mystical tradition and its ability to utilize symbols that point beyond mere philosophical rationalism. Ehud Luz intimates a similar recognition when he notes the decisive influence of Nietzsche on Zionist theory. Luz construes the basic struggle within Zionism as that of concretizing the spiritual, of reviving an earthy engagement with the ideals of the Jewish people. Luz traces the roots of this effort to achieve *hagshamah*, or realization of the spirit, back to Nietzsche's call for a revaluation of values, for a healthy-mindedness that would create the "new man."[22] In many cases this ideal took on the nature of an impossible goal, of an exalted value that could only be approximated. Luz himself notes this aspect of the theory, particularly as expressed by the Russian thinker Vladimir Soloviev (1853-

---

[21] Kaplan, *Greater Judaism*, p. 402

[22] Ehud Luz, "Spiritual and Anti-Spiritual Trends in Zionism," in *Jewish Spirituality: From the Bible through the Middle Ages*, ed Arthur Green (New York: Crossroad, 1986), p. 378.

1900).[23] Luz does not comment, however, on the explicit use Soloviev makes of the Jewish mystical tradition. As modern scholars show, Soloviev, drawing on the kabbalah, undergirds his activist positions by the demand that spirit always be translated, if imperfectly, into concrete form.[24] This represents a view close to the postmodernist approach to history. Soloviev by emphasizing the spiritual in the physical and the physical as the necessary form of the spiritual, stands at the same crossroads where mysticism and positivism meet as does Walter Benjamin.[25] This crossroads seems inevitable if, as Luz suggests, there is an enduring and unending tension within Zionism itself, one he characterizes as "the attachment to a "spiritual" tradition and the longing for renewal on an earthly basis."[26]

The background of this struggle is Zionism's clear recognition of another key element in the postmodern consciousness--that human beings reinterpret the heritage they receive from the past. One of the outstanding successes of Zionism was its ability to fashion a new Jewish culture and transmit that culture as the "authentic" Judaica tradition. Zionism used the rhetoric of the Jewish national heritage as it, in fact, "called into existence" a Jewish identity that had never before existed. The symbols and values of this newly constructed Judaism borrowed eclectically from the Jewish past.

---

[23] *Ibid.*, p. 385.

[24] See D. Stremooukhoff, <u>Vladimir Soloviev and His Messianic Work</u>, trans Elizabeth Meyendorff, ed Phillip Guilbeau and Heather Elise MacGregor (Belmont, MA: Nordland, 1980).

[25] This famous critique by T. Adorno of Benjamin's "Arcades Project" is often cited; see Buck-Morss, *The Dialectics of Seeing*, pp. 227-228; Handelman, *Fragments of Redemption*, p. 37 and also Jay , *The Dialectical Imagination*, p. 209.

[26] Luz, "Spiritual and Anti-spiritual Trends," p. 298.

Religious images and allusions were reshaped and attached to secular folk expressions. Political movements were lifted out of the profane into the sacred realm by such maneuvering. Michael Berkowitz notes this self-conscious ability to manipulate symbols and create a Jewish culture. He comments on "the Zionists' ability to integrate their political liturgy with the religious liturgy of traditional Judaism."[27] Kaplan's enthusiasm for the process for transforming traditional symbols so they addressed modern needs found an echo in the activities of the early Zionists.

Finally, the Zionist call for "normalization" of Jewish life actually meant that Jews should have an opportunity to construct their own systems of meaning, their own metaphysical language. Paul Mendes-Flohr makes this point clear in his personal reflections on Zionism and Existentialism. Mendes-Flohr contends that in the diaspora Jews could only create an "uneasy alliance" between themselves, as members of a particular social, cultural, political, and religious group and the great universal ideals, values, and philosophies supposedly common to all people. The search for a universal good or truth among diaspora Jews, he thinks, either leads to a dilution of Jewish identity or is hampered by a natural retreat when investigations look as if they might swallow the particular identity of the Jew in a wider selfhood. In Israel, he contends, the political structure allows personal experimentation with philosophy impossible for Jews in exile. He comments that "through the normalization of the social and cultural context of Jewish life the possibility is established for the renewal of Judaism as a metaphysical

---

[27] Michael Berkowitz, *Zionist Culture and West European Jewry Before the First World War* (Cambrdige: Cambridge University Press; 1993). p. 27.

framework providing a system of symbols and cognitive structures in which ultimate and thus universal questions of existence are addressed."[28]

As Kaplan recognized, systems of meaning are universals; there is no peculiarly "Jewish" way of constructing reality. Zionism, unlike Kaplan, was unwilling to adapt any and every system of meaning to Jewish thought. Instead it makes adherence to the Jewish State, participation in the Zionist society the criteria for the Jewish validity of a metaphysical system. Thus while Kaplan and Zionism disagree about how to respond to the universal and arbitrary aspects of systems that provide meaning or significance, they agree in their diagnosis of the situation. That diagnosis draws on much that has become characteristic of the postmodern mentality.

The Contemporary Relevance of Kaplan's Thought

Kaplan's affinity to the postmodern aspects of Zionism clarifies his general approach to Jewish religion. Kaplan's rationalism does not deny the importance of emotional commitment for Jewish survival. Kaplan, as a realist, uses the variety of tools available for preserving Jews and Judaism. Insofar as Jewish mystics stress experience and the need to transcend a dry rationalization of Judaism, Kaplan learns a valuable lesson about religion from them. Insofar as they give answers to questions that should remain unanswered, he rejects their teachings because they offer a dangerous precedent that destroys religion from within. The Jews of their time could accept the "religious fictions" of the Zohar; modern Jews cannot accept them. If a religious fiction motivates commitment to Jewish life, it is legitimate.

---

[28] Paul R. Mendes-Flohr, *Divided Passions : Jewish Intellectuals and the Experience of Modernity*. Culture of Jewish modernity. (Detroit: Wayne State University Press, 1991), p. 430.

When the fictions of the Zohar perform that function, Kaplan affirms them. Since modern Jews recognize only the fictional character of those claims and not their motivational power, Kaplan rejects them. Thus while Kaplan agrees with the mystics that genuine religion requires acceptance of the limitations of human knowledge, he cannot accept the means they used to express this truth. "No religious experience," he argues, "is possible without an overwhelming awareness of reality as baffling man's power of comprehension."[29] Nevertheless, he feels that Utilitarians such as Sidgwick preserve that sense of mystery better than the traditional mystics. That judgment may no longer be valid. If, so, Kaplan would agree to reinstate the mystics.

Thus Kaplan transposes the mystical into modern terms without negating its spiritual aspects. Kaplan's great opponent in his later years, Abraham Joshua Heschel recognized this aspect of his theology. Celebrating Kaplan's ninetieth birthday, Heschel noted the older thinker's passion for the Jewish people and commented: I have a suspicion that just as the mystics of old used to stay up at midnight worrying about the *Shekhina*, he stays up at midnight doing *Tikkun Hatzos* (midnight prayers of repairing cosmic damage), and worrying about the Jewish people.[30] Both Heschel and Kaplan knew the mystical tradition well and realized that in the Kabbalah another name for *Shekhina* is *Knesset Israel*, the Jewish people. Kaplan's reconstruction of the Jewish people, Heschel was claiming, is identical with the mystical attempt to repair the world.

---

[29] Kaplan, *Future of the American Jew*, p. 198.

[30] Scult, *Judaism Faces the Twentieth Century*, p. 15.

Reading Kaplan carefully leads one to find sentiments that would shock those who, like David Hartman, characterize his thought as pedestrian and dismay those who, like Samuel Dresner, worry about a return to paganism. The basic motivation, however, is utilitarian--that of finding ways to motivate Jews to fulfil their personal potential through the social mechanism of the Jewish people. Jews today can look to Kaplan for guidance and motivation in their lives. Not only Kaplan's view of the kabbalah, but his entire system presenting Jewish thought in its democratic form stimulates a modern commitment to Judaism. Kaplan identifies in every person an "inner drive to outdo himself, not to accept as final and unchangeable the conditions of life." He interprets the existence of this drive as evidence that people move "in a direction toward self-transcendence."[31] Religion as he understands it serves to point in that direction. Judaism in Kaplan's thought earns its right to survive by furthering the goal of transcendence. While rationalism once fulfilled that task, Jewish mysticism served it in the past and may do so in the future. Certainly the decision to reclaim medieval Jewish mysticism as a resource for modern democracy represents such a self-transcendence consistent with Kaplan's thought. He would, on the basis of his own thinking, embrace the new ways that render his earlier system more utilitarian and thus more appropriate for the postmodern Jew.

---

[31] Kaplan, *Questions Jews Ask*, p. 110.

Index

South Florida Studies in the History of Judaism

South Florida Academic Commentary Series

The Talmud of Babylonia, An Academic Commentary

South Florida-Rochester-Saint Louis
Studies on Religion and the Social Order

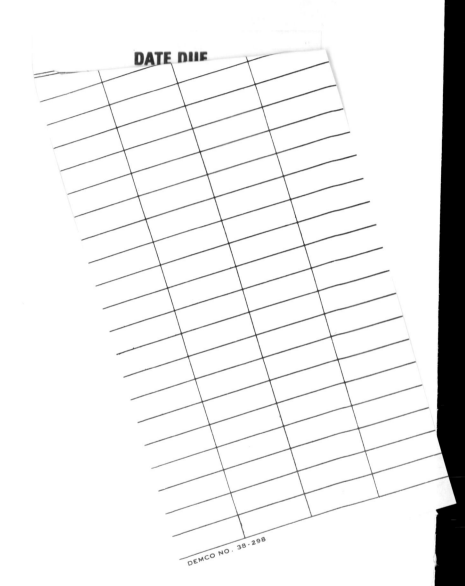

DATE DUE

DEMCO NO. 38-298